KLD

WITHDRAWN

Neighborhood
Politics

Park Avenue, Reservoir Hill. Photograph by Charlotte Crenson.

Neighborhood Politics

Matthew A. Crenson

Harvard University Press
Cambridge, Massachusetts, and London, England   1983

This book is printed on acid-free paper, and its binding materials
  have been chosen for strength and durability.

Library of Congress Cataloging in Publication Data

Crenson, Matthew A., 1943-
  Neighborhood politics.

  Includes bibliographical references and index.
  1. Neighborhood government — Maryland — Baltimore.
2. Baltimore (Md.) — Politics and government.   I. Title.
JS583.C73   1983   352'.007   82-23286
ISBN 0-674-60785-6

Designed by Gwen Frankfeldt

To Alene

Preface

"**W**ho governs?" was the question that preoccupied analysts of urban politics not so long ago. More recently, the question has been whether cities can be governed at all. The first question was worth asking because it called attention to the conditions for democracy in urban politics. The second is worth pursuing because it could contribute to our understanding of urban political order.

Democracy and order are both concerns of this book. It examines the grassroots activities of citizens within their neighborhoods, and it therefore deals with some of the most commonly recognized manifestations of urban democracy. But it considers these civic exertions of neighborhood residents primarily as they contribute to the management of allegedly ungovernable cities. Stated briefly, this book is about the kind of neighborhood political activism that helps to make society civil enough to be governed.

Neighborhoods have probably been best known in urban politics for the organizations that they generate. Most visible are the neighborhood groups that make it their business to fight City Hall. These combative organizations, of course, seldom receive much credit for making cities more governable, but by aggregating and articulating the political sentiments of its constituents, even the most pugnacious community association contributes to the structuring of public opinion, and it may smooth the way for democratic government in the process.

Neighborhood organizations do not exhaust the range of neighborhood politics, although they are probably the most easily noticed tokens of it. Less frequently acknowledged in the political system of the city at large is the unofficial work that neighborhoods perform in the production of public goods and services. The street-level bureaucrats who try to maintain the public order, public safety, and public sanitation of the municipality have their unofficial counterparts in the city's neighborhoods—residents who make the preservation of domestic tranquillity and the promotion of the general welfare a personal concern. What these unofficial public servants add to the governing of the city should be obvious, but their efforts are scarcely ever acknowledged in accounts of urban politics. In fact, these ventures in neighborhood governance are rarely recognized as political activities at all.

But the neighborhood is at least a potentially political enterprise, and its essential political character is defined by the functions that it performs. The production of public goods and services, the aggregation and articulation of public sentiment—these are tasks usually associated with the institutions of government. Neigborhoods are not quite governments, because they lack governmental authority, but when they carry on the business of governing, they qualify as polities or "political societies." The aim of this inquiry is to find out why some neighborhoods function as polities more fully than others.

There is no simple answer to this question. Neighborhood politics is just about as intricate as politics anywhere else. The fact that it occurs within a relatively small compass and close to home may encourage most people to regard themselves as experts on the topic, but it does not make the subject any less complex. The research results discussed in this book naturally reflect some of this complexity. In the first place, they cannot provide an uncomplicated portrait of the neighborhood polity. Political arrangements vary widely from one neighborhood to the next, and it is no more feasible to construct a single profile of the neighborhood polity than it is for students of comparative politics to supply a standard set of blueprints for the political system of a nation. There are, of course, recognizable continuities from one polity to another, and these can sometimes be incorporated into schemes for analyzing politics in nations or in neighborhoods. But even these analytic frameworks are designed not so much to identify uniformities across polities as to chart the main dimensions of variability among them.

Political variability and its explanation are the chief concerns of this study, and the explanation is sometimes as perplexing as the variation. This is a second place in which the complexity of neighborhood politics becomes evident. There is no single-factor theory that accounts for the differing political accomplishments of neighborhoods. Conventional statistical techniques are used here to untangle and describe the relationships between neighborhood political activities and the various factors that seem to promote them. One need not be a statistician in order to make sense of these relationships. They may be complex, but they are certainly no more difficult to understand than one's neighbors.

The diversity of neighborhood politics and the multiplicity of things that help to shape it should not obscure the unity of the phenomenon under examination. In a sense, the investigation is aimed at a substratum of the political system — the civil society on which government depends. Such explorations follow well-established paths of inquiry in American political science. The group theory of politics, for example, attempted to uncover the half-hidden engines that drove the machinery of government. It made sense of formal political institutions by referring to a substructure of organized interests on which laws and policies and constitutions all rested. The study of neigborhood politics scarcely represents a theoretical alternative to the study of group politics. In some respects it simply carries forward the tradition of political analysis formed by Bentley and Truman. But it also seeks to clarify a dimension of the tradition that seems to have received insufficient attention.

The group politics approach has tended to emphasize the process of allocating public benefits between competing interests. The production of these benefits, however, was presumably a technical problem that could be left to specialists in public administration and management. The recent misfortunes of many American cities have demonstrated that this technical problem is also a big one, and my investigation suggests that it is not merely technical. An unknown but certainly significant share of the public services consumed by the society is generated by the consumers themselves. The importance of these unofficially produced benefits probably becomes most evident when citizens stop producing them. It is then that neighborhoods fall into disorder and decay.

When neighborhoods are generating some of their own public services, it means that neighbors have formed political relationships with one another. The residents who argue about the loudness of a radio — or join together to clean a public alley — are not engaged in merely private business. They are shaping and creating public goods, and for that reason they are performing a kind of political work. To understand fully the nature of the enterprise, one must turn back from the modern group theory of politics to the early modern political theories of the seventeenth and eighteenth centuries. Locke and Rousseau recognized that citizens must establish political bonds with one another before they could make covenants with kings or legislatures. The authority of government was supposed to have been preceded by the construction of a political community among those who were going to be governed. This imagined historical sequence in the development of commonwealths expressed a conviction that hierarchical relationships with political authorities somehow depended upon the existence of collegial relationships among citizens. This book attempts no historical account of these relationships. Instead, it recognizes that the efficacy of these bonds may vary from place to place, and it examines these variations in an effort to identify some of the conditions for the functioning of a political community.

This is not what I originally set out to do. The aims of the present study took shape over a dozen years and three research seminars, in which several dozen graduate and undergraduate students at the Johns Hopkins University participated. I am grateful to all of them — and to my colleagues Robert Crain and Peter Rossi, who got me started in this line of research. Hank Becker not only participated in one of those formative seminars, but also played a vital role in designing and executing the current study. His calm expertise, and the good-natured tenacity of the staff at Survey Research Associates, kept this enterprise moving forward in the face of obstacles and complications more exasperating than any I had imagined at the outset.

The enterprise was supported by a grant (MH 31262) from the Center for the Study of Metropolitan Problems, now the Center for Work and Mental Health, of the National Insititute of Mental Health. Elliott Liebow and Maury Lieberman of NIMH both gave early encouragement to the venture, and Dr. Lieberman patiently steered the project clear of administrative troubles from its start to its completion, while offering useful substantive advice along the way. David Jackson, also of NIMH, supplied some helpful advice concerning the analysis of the data presented in Chapter 2.

At Johns Hopkins, Evelyn Scheulen contributed both typing and administrative assistance from her command post in the Department of Political Science. Diane Richey saw to the needs of the project in the Center for Metropolitan Planning and Research, and three undergraduate research assistants — Julie Rindfleisch, Brian Peters, and Cynthia Simon — all did valiant service in maintaining diplomatic relations between me and the university's computer. Ralph Taylor of the Center's staff was also helpful. Among my academic colleagues, William Ascher, Richard Flathman, Michael Grossman,

Robert Hearn, Robert Kargon, Richard Katz, and Francis Rourke all provided comment and advice when it was needed.

The Baltimoreans provided themselves. Almost two thousand of them played parts in this study. Only a handful of them could be acknowledged by name in this book. But the conduct of this inquiry depended upon all of them just as surely as the running of their city does. Having spent most of my life among them, I feel that I owe them more than the obligatory expression of thanks. They have been friends, fellow citizens, and teachers — not just survey respondents.

Several Baltimore institutions gave special kinds of help in the collection of research materials. The staff of the Maryland Department at the Enoch Pratt Free Library guided me to some historical information about Baltimore neighborhoods. The Baltimore Neighborhoods' Institute has given me opportunities to become acquainted with neighborhood leaders and activists, and I am especially grateful to Richard Cook, executive director of the Institute, and to Allen Holmes, its former president, for their asssistance in testing some of the questionaire items that were used in the study. The district planning staff of the Baltimore City Department of Planning and the members of the Division of Planning and Research at the Department of Housing and Community Development supplied essential background information for the research, and Brent Flickinger of the Planning Department took special pains in helping me to identify the neigborhoods that were subsequently included in the study.

Michael Aronson of Harvard University Press expressed an active interest in this project even before the results were in, and he continued to give encouragement and advice until the last word was written. My sister, Charlotte Crenson, took the photographs that illustrate the words.

My wife, Alene, read and commented upon drafts for most of the chapters in this book. She used her skills as a librarian to track down stray facts or elusive sources. But she made her most important contributions to me, not to the book.

Contents

Neighborhood Politics

1.
The Neighborhood as a Polity

Whitelock Street, Reservoir Hill. Photograph by Charlotte Crenson.

O n the last day of the Washington's Birthday weekend in 1979, Baltimore lay muffled in snow. A storm had strengthened suddenly during the night. No more than eight inches' accumulation had been predicted, but by morning the snow stood two feet thick — and twice as deep in drifts — from the curving, tree-lined roads of the semi-suburban fringe to the narrow streets of mid-nineteenth-century rowhouses that edge the wharves, warehouses, and factories near the city's harbor. For the moment at least, the blizzard seemed to have muted the contrasts between these two frontiers of Baltimore.

Almost midway between the industrial waterfront and the prosperous-looking approaches to suburbia, Whitelock Street follows a crooked east-west course no more than ten blocks long. It is the chief commercial thoroughfare of a neighborhood called Reservoir Hill — a community that was once a prosperous suburb itself. Members of Baltimore's early Victorian patriciate laid out their country estates and summer retreats on the long slope of the hillside; a generation or so later, representatives of the late Victorian upper middle class built solid townhouses of brick and brownstone there. But by the close of World War II, many of the surviving mansions and townhouses had been subdivided into sleeping cubicles for defense plant workers. In a sample survey of neighborhood residents that happened to be under way at the time of the great blizzard of 1979, 43 percent of the respondents living in Reservoir Hill reported family incomes of less than $5,000, and 87 percent of the residents interviewed were black.

There had been other changes, too. The onetime summer retreat was now regarded by some Baltimoreans, including many residents of Reservoir Hill itself, as one of the most dangerous places in the city to go strolling after dark. Even the municipal water storage facility from which Reservoir Hill drew its name had disappeared years before, its site now occupied by an expressway interchange. Whitelock Street itself was one of a few survivals from the era of country estates. It had been the first public thoroughfare in the area, cut through a forest by a local landowner of the last century for the convenience of some tenant farmers. The deep snow restored something of its former rustic character, though now the street's long commercial block—known to local residents as "Whitelock City"—was lined with barber and beauty shops, carryout restaurants, and grocery and liquor stores instead of trees.

With the waning of the blizzard, small groups of men began to collect in doorways along Whitelock Street, as they do most mornings, to await the opening of the liquor stores. This morning, however, no one arrived at the customary hour to unlock the doors. Snowbound in their homes outside the neighborhood, owners and managers could not easily reach their places of business. Neither could the police.

It was well after the usual opening time—"about tennish," according to one eyewitness—that looters began to smash in the doors and metal gratings of businesses along Whitelock Street. Stores carrying stocks of liquor seem to have been the principal targets but not the only ones. By early afternoon, four businesses in Whitelock City were empty shells, and a sizable supermarket several blocks away, on the southern frontier of the neighborhood, had been reduced to a shambles.

The same acquisitive impulse that surfaced in Reservoir Hill was simultaneously sweeping through other Baltimore neighborhoods. By the time the police reasserted their control of the snow-clogged streets a day and a half later, they had arrested almost a thousand people all over the city for looting and curfew violations. It was Reservoir Hill, however, that distinguished itself as a locus of mayhem—not because the looting there was especially violent or extensive, but because the hill occupied by the neighborhood is close to another prominence whose topographical advantages have attracted the broadcast and transmission facilities of several local television stations. For camera crews forced to contend with heavy snow and heavy equipment, Whitelock Street was probably the most conveniently located site of civil disorder.

The cameras arrived before the police—even before the locked door of the Brookfield Pharmacy had given way to physical force. By suppertime the happenings on Whitelock Street were an item of national network news. Television images showed young people laughing as they ran heavy-footed through the snow, their arms filled with stolen goods. A middle-aged man, dazed by drink and swaying where he stood, stared blankly into the camera until he became the target for a group of snowball-throwing children. A store owner who had managed to reach his business a bit too late was gamely trying to clear away the layer of broken glass and debris that blanketed the premises.

The city's mayor called it a "disgraceful exhibition" and declared a curfew. He was "very disappointed," he said, "in the people in certain communities that would take advantage of a situation like this in their own neighborhoods and hurt themselves."[1] A local newspaper editorial two days later called the looters "anti-social individuals ready to take advantage of other people's helplessness." They were "virulent indicators of the social and moral decay that new downtown office towers and renovated Victorian townhouses have not changed."[2] For another journalist, the disorders signaled an end to "the rule of the blizzard," an unwritten law that ordained neighborly socializing and mutual help and that had governed the conduct of Baltimoreans in great snowstorms of the past. But a police patrolman spoke more bluntly about "anarchy in the streets," and the local prosecutor announced that he would not take action against business owners who happened to shoot looters.[3]

Rudy Williams never got on television. As the looters struck their first business in Whitelock City, he was standing in the doorway of a building across the street, the storefront headquarters of the Reservoir Hill Community Association. After eleven years in the Army, including several tours in Vietnam, Williams had come home to Reservoir Hill in the early 1970s. Now he was chairman of the Community Association's Committee on Public Safety and Justice. For the time being, he could only watch the disorders. But within a few hours he would be recruiting some of the people who were now looting stores to help him carry emergency supplies of food through the snow to the homes of elderly and disabled people in the neighborhood.

About a block and a half to the east, Bernice Payne was standing on the front porch of her Whitelock Street home when Nancy Lawlor came by on the way to her job as director of a homeownership program at the Community Association's offices. Mrs. Lawlor lived on Park Avenue, about a block further east, in an area where young white families had begun to rehabilitate old townhouses. Mrs. Payne, a member of the association's executive board, invited her inside for a cup of coffee. Not long afterward, two of the Payne children ran into the house with news of the first looting incident in Whitelock City. Mrs. Payne ordered them to stay indoors and then began to telephone other women in the area, urging them to keep their children off the streets.

In an interval between calls, Stephanie Hull, president of the Reservoir Hill Community Association, telephoned to suggest that the group should open its Whitelock Street offices in order to respond to requests for emergency assistance from neighborhood residents. Mrs. Hull, a social worker, was one of the white homeowners who had begun to renovate a house in Reservoir Hill. She had already spent the morning consulting by telephone with officers and board members of the Community Association about measures that might be taken in response to the blizzard, and she had heard about the looting. Now, pulling a sled loaded with a supply of blankets and accompanied by her two children, she set out from her home in the eastern part of the neighborhood just as scores of would-be looters were streaming southward through the streets to exploit a break-in at a supermarket.

When she arrived at the Payne home she was met by Nancy Lawlor. With Mrs. Payne's brother as an escort they walked toward Whitelock City, where they found Rudy Williams still doing sentry duty at the entrance to the Community Association's headquarters. Soon they were joined by Bernice Payne and by Willie Mae Davis, a neighborhood leader of long standing who lived around the corner from Whitelock City on Brookfield Avenue. "She's a well-known person," observed one local resident, "and she could walk out there in the middle of a riot, and everybody in there is going to respect her." A short time later the team of volunteers had expanded to about fifteen members; during some periods over the next two days, it would include as many as thirty or forty people. Some, like Rudy Williams, tried to reason with looters and those who seemed about to join the looters, but other tasks were just as urgent.

In a neighborhood where many families customarily buy no more than a day's groceries at a time, the distribution of food to snowbound residents was probably the volunteers' most pressing piece of business. A priest at a nearby church contributed a generous supply of groceries, which was later supplemented by donations from local merchants and from the kitchens of the volunteers themselves. To locate people who needed food or assistance, radio and television stations had already been asked to announce that neighborhood residents could contact the offices of the Community

Association for emergency help. The broadcast message brought calls, however, not only from Reservoir Hill, but from neighborhoods miles away and even beyond the city limits.

Abandoning its radio and television announcements, the association turned instead to its own block leaders, who were asked to canvass their territories in search of families needing food or assistance. At the northern end of Brookfield Avenue, for example, Mertha Morrison had already established an operations center in her basement, which doubled as the headquarters of her block organization. Her helpers fanned out through the surrounding area to locate families short on food, elderly residents who needed prescriptions filled, mothers who had run out of feeding formula for newborn babies. Their requests for assistance were relayed to the Community Association's offices. Other residents — those who lived in buildings where fuel oil tanks had run dry — were brought to Mrs. Morrison's basement to keep warm. Mrs. Morrison, in the meantime, was upstairs cooking, so that the workers on Whitelock Street would have something to eat themselves.

By afternoon, shipments of food were going out from the headquarters of the Community Association. Some were dragged or sledded to their destinations by children. Others were transported as far as possible in a four-wheel-drive vehicle that had been pressed into service and then carried the remaining distance on foot. Several workers who were not engaged in the packing or distribution of food bundles were shoveling out streets so that oil trucks could make deliveries and residents could get to their jobs. Others were helping a Whitelock Street merchant to clean up the wreckage in his store.

The police were busy on Whitelock Street as well. Represented at first by a lone patrolman who was helpless in the face of widespread looting, they had arrived later in large numbers, riding in borrowed National Guard trucks. Now they were massed in Whitelock City waiting for the seven o'clock curfew to go into effect. When night came, however, it was not only the police who went out to patrol the streets. At about the time when national television audiences were watching videotaped looting in Reservoir Hill, representatives of the Reservoir Hill Community Association were putting on makeshift armbands and paper badges. Then they set out, with the approval of the police, to encourage compliance with the curfew and to calm "some of our rebellious youth" who might be bent on a confrontation with the representatives of law and order.

It appeared to some volunteers that a few of the patrolmen might need calming themselves. Although the police response was gener-

ally restrained, some officers still seemed angry about their im-
potence earlier in the day, and their mood alarmed Community
Association workers. To one local resident, it seemed that "you could
see the blood running out their eyes onto the street." While some
volunteers walked through the neighborhood trying to pacify the
residents, others who remained behind on Whitelock Street took
responsibility for soothing the tempers of fatigued police officers:
"We gave them coffee the whole time — trying to get them
together — gave them some doughnuts, telling them how hard we
knew they were working and wasn't it something, and trying to hold
it together."

It held. Whatever viewers of the evening news might think of the
neighborhood, there were those among the volunteer workers who
believed that it had been Reservoir Hill's finest hour. One young
block leader perceived in the day's events something quite different
from what the television cameras had seen: "The blizzard — that
really opened my eyes . . . because I didn't have any idea that we
had so many strong-willed people in Reservoir Hill that you could
depend on in a time of adversity — unselfish people." "Oh my, it was
a beautiful thing," said Willie Mae Davis, "come together all of a
sudden."

Signs of "Political Society" in Urban Neighborhoods

What appeared so suddenly in Reservoir Hill was a capacity for
mutual assistance and self-government. Against the background of
the snowstorm, it stood out more sharply than it would have under
normal circumstances — but so did the neighborhood's inclination
toward civil disorder. Temporarily cut off from public services and
public authorities, Reservoir Hill was compelled to rely more
heavily than at other times on its internal political resources — the
ability of local residents to maintain order among themselves, to arrive at collective decisions, and to produce public services of their
own. If these capabilities proved unexpectedly impressive in some
respects, it was also apparent that they fell sadly short in others.
Those residents who labored to restore order during the emergency
and those who exploited the opportunity for looting and vandalism
conducted their respective businesses quite literally across the street
from one another. (In fact, eyewitnesses reported that there were at
least a few residents of the neighborhood who managed to work
both sides of the street in succession.) Reservoir Hill's response to the

blizzard provides an unusually vivid example of unofficial governance in an urban neighborhood, but it is a vivid example of an ex-
tremely complex and perhaps even contradictory phenomenon. In
this case at least, the distance that separates order from disorder,
public service from private pillage, is hardly so great as one might
imagine. In other cases, it is not only these conventional distinctions
that may become elusive but the processes of neighborhood governance themselves. Without the drama of an emergency to give them
visibility, the unofficial practices of a neighborhood polity may be
overshadowed by the official operations of a municipal government,
or they may simply disappear among the everyday activities of a
neighborhood, so ordinary and taken for granted that they escape
the attention of casual observers. In Reservoir Hill, after all, even
some of the local residents themselves had not expected their
neighbors to respond with so much public spirit to a crisis; they had
seen little in the everyday life of the neighborhood that bespoke such
a capacity for generating informal public services.

Under ordinary and undramatic circumstances, therefore, the
unofficial processes of self-government in urban neighborhoods may
signal their presence only through their by-products. Most experienced city dwellers, for example, can think of some residential
sections whose forbidding appearances are unaccountably coupled
with solid reputations for safety after dark. Or, in the midst of a city
garbage strike, some observers are almost sure to note that there are
certain neighborhoods whose streets remain mysteriously free of
trash. And occasionally, urban law enforcement officials acknowledge that the maintenance of public order in many neighborhoods results less from the activities of police officers than from the
unselfconscious efforts of local residents who police one another informally.[4]

One is not likely to find anything that deserves to be called a
government along the streets of most residential areas. The outward
signs of governing are plentiful nevertheless, even when municipal
authorities and their official agents have not been at work.[5] These
perceptible residues of unofficial governance lend additional weight
to the contentions of observers who assert, like Milton Kotler, that
"it is an error to define the neighborhood as a social unit. The
neighborhood is in origin and continuity a political unit."[6] What
needs to be added, however, is that some neighborhoods are more
nearly "political units" than others. For every residential area that
polices its own streets or rises like Reservoir Hill to an emergency,
there are others where residents only peek through their curtains at

the public crises and chronic troubles of their neighborhoods. The political status of urban neighborhoods is not simply a matter of definition. Once definitional questions have been settled, the fact is likely to remain that some neighborhoods actually *function* as fully developed political units; others, in a more limited way; and still others, hardly at all. This study attempts to take some initial steps toward an explanation for the political variations among urban neighborhoods. It is an effort to find out why some neighborhoods operate as polities and others do not.

While this task is more than a matter of definition, it is also one for which certain definitions are indispensable. More than most enterprises in political research, the examination of unofficial neighborhood polities draws attention to the outer limits of the political, and therefore to behavior whose political status may be questionable. "Politics" is more difficult to recognize when it occurs on street corners or front porches than it is when practiced in explicitly political institutions like legislatures or public agencies, and it is necessary to be explicit about the elements that can convert ordinary instances of neighborliness—and even some manifestly unneighborly activities—into political events. Alexis de Tocqueville saw these political elements clearly. Discussing the propensity of Americans to form associations, he offered a classic example of unofficial neighborhood governance: "If a stoppage occurs in a thoroughfare and the circulation of vehicles is hindered," he wrote, "the neighbors immediately form themselves into a deliberative body; and this extemporaneous assembly gives rise to an executive power which remedies the inconvenience before anybody has thought of recurring to a pre-existing authority superior to that of the persons immediately concerned."[7]

The terms in which Tocqueville chose to cast his illustration of the American proclivity for self-help reveal something of the meaning that he attached to it. In the management of a neighborhood traffic jam, he saw the makings of a kind of government—an ersatz legislative assembly with the capacity for articulating and aggregating the interests of local residents, and an "executive power" capable of producing public goods or alleviating public harms. The same functional elements—or others very similar to them—reappear in more systematic accounts of political systems and their inputs and outputs. They become easier to recognize when seen not in an urban neighborhood but in the more familiar surroundings of a modern nation-state, where the functions of interest articulation and aggregation are conventionally allocated to pressure groups and political parties; legislatures perform the function of rule making; and the "executive power" of applying rules is usually assigned to public bureaucracies, sometimes in combination with the function of rule adjudication.[8]

Locating these political functions when they are not so conveniently encased in specialized political institutions is a problem with which anthropologists are probably more familiar than political scientists. There is a rough parallel, in fact, between the task of finding the political system in an urban neighborhood and the business of discovering politics in a tribal society that has no distinct government or formally designated rulers. In both settings one is likely to encounter examples of "diffused government": the political authorities may consist of the population at large, and varying political purposes or occasions may activate different "political communities" or subdivisions within the local population.[9] As if to emphasize this similarity of political form, there is also a certain romantic appeal in the seeming affinity of tribal villages and "urban villages," but the kinship does not run very deep. In tribal societies, the diffuseness of government reflects the absence of any institutions specializing in the performance of political functions. In city neighborhoods, however, governing remains a diffuse activity precisely because these specialized institutions are so fully developed that they have reduced both the need and the opportunity for urban subcommunities to create explicit governing bodies of their own. This preemption of neighborhood government by City Hall is seen most plainly in those cases where independent villages have been transformed into urban neighborhoods by annexation to an expanding metropolis.[10] Once the official institutions of local government have been moved downtown, what remains of neighborhood governance is chiefly the informal, dispersed, and intermittent activity of political nonprofessionals.

The polity of the neighborhood, as Tocqueville himself recognized, operates against a background of "pre-existing authority superior to that of the persons immediately concerned." In practice this means that the unofficial government of the neighborhood is almost always dwarfed by the massive bulk of official government and inevitably seems to be something less than the real thing. In fact, it *is* something less than the real thing, and not just because neighborhood political activities are more diffuse or less impressive in scale than the ones that are concentrated at city hall. More critical than the disparity in size or specialization is the fact that neighborhood polities seem to lack the very element that has traditionally been regarded as the single distinguishing feature of all authentic political systems — the exercise of legitimate physical coercion.

For Max Weber the modern state was defined by its monopoly of legitimate force.[11] Although some political anthropologists have correctly pointed out that this conception is too restrictive to encompass the stateless political systems of premodern societies,[12] it is clearly appropriate to the kind of society in which one usually finds urban neighborhoods. On the one hand, the classical Weberian definition identifies the distinctively political character of modern government. On the other, it indicates the main political deficiency of the urban residential subcommunity, for in a society where the state monopolizes the exercise of legitimate force, this essential political instrument must be denied almost entirely to mere neighborhoods.

Physical force is not uncommon in neighborhoods, but only in exceptional instances is it ever endowed with legitimacy. Such things may happen, for example, when a neighborhood gang comes to exercise police powers within its territory,[13] but even then the establishment of a right to employ violence is open to question, and the "political" gang itself does not seem to be a widespread phenomenon in any case. It should be regarded, perhaps, more as a fleeting sign of the political potential that exists in neighborhoods than as proof of a political standing already achieved. So long as there is a "superior authority," at City Hall or elsewhere, that jealously guards the exclusiveness of its right to exercise force, instances of legitimate coercion by unofficial neighborhood authorities are likely to appear only as aberrations, not as regular manifestations of ongoing political systems.

Like the communities that Tocqueville observed, today's urban neighborhoods frequently have their own unofficial arrangements for performing certain essential political functions — a capacity to form and express a collective interest, the executive power to produce collective or public goods. What is usually missing is the distinctively political means for conducting this political business — legitimate physical force. Political systems certainly use many other kinds of instruments to carry on their operations, but this is the one by which anthropologists, sociologists, and political scientists have most frequently distinguished political arrangements from others.[14] Like economic organizations, political systems often rely on material self-interest to coordinate the behavior of their members; like families and clans, they may depend also on bonds of

sentiment. But they are set apart from these and other social formations by their employment of legitimate coercion. "The political
system," as Almond and Powell have pointed out, "is not the only
system that makes rules and enforces them, but its rules and en-
forcements go all the way to compelling obedience or performance."[15]

Considerations of this kind would seem to relegate neighborhood
polities to the twilight zone of "parapolitical systems," along with
private groups like churches, trade associations, or universities
whose functions and structures may be analogous to those of the
larger political system but whose powers and responsibilities are
narrower in scope.[16] Reservoir Hill illustrates some of the most important limitations of the species. It was a neighborhood where at
least a few local figures had achieved recognition as legitimate authorities — leaders who might command respect even in the middle
of a riot — but their authority did not extend to the use of force,
violence, or compulsion. Force and violence, of course, were certainly present in the actions of the looters on Whitelock Street, but
these actions were not regarded as binding or legitimate by local
residents or even, one suspects, by many of the looters themselves.
As they patrolled the streets in the aftermath of the blizzard, in fact,
several representatives of the Reservoir Hill Community Association
were approached by local residents who discreetly inquired how
stolen property might be returned to its rightful owners.

This disjunction between force and legitimacy, in Reservoir Hill
and in all other residential areas, leaves a significant gap in the
political credentials of the urban neighborhood. One further shortcoming that might be cited is the limited jurisdiction of the
neighborhood polity. It does not perform its political functions for
an entire society, as some analysts have required of a true political
system, but only in a diminutive pocket of the wider society.[17] What
we expect to find in a neighborhood, therefore, is only a polity and
not a true political system, governance rather than a government.
But it does not follow from all this that the politics of a
neighborhood, like the internal politics of country clubs, business
corporations, or other parapolitical systems, is only a scaled-down
imitation of real politics. There are several respects in which the
political life of a neighborhood must be regarded as something more
substantial than a mere facsimile of the genuine article.

It is obvious, in the first place, that even parapolitical systems occasionally enter the larger political struggle on the same footing as
the other combatants. Cast as pressure groups or lobbies, they play

politics in earnest, attempting to influence government decisions that will be backed up by government force. Neighborhoods and organizations claiming to represent neighborhoods probably behave like political interest groups more frequently than do most other types of parapolitical systems, and many of the political studies of urban residential communities have concentrated on this aspect of neighborhood political life.[18]

At times, neighborhoods have attained a political status somewhat more elevated than that of pressure groups. Under the Model Cities and Economic Opportunity programs of the 1960s, for example, municipal and federal governments delegated fragments of official decision-making authority to urban neighborhoods and to groups representing these neighborhoods.[19] Residential communities may have little prospect of maturing into governments or political systems on their own, but with the blessing of the established authorities they have frequently become official agents of government, and there have been many advocates of municipal decentralization and community control who favor further enhancement of the neighborhood's role as an urban subgovernment.[20]

Even when they are not acting as pressure groups or officially recognized outposts of government, neighborhoods may still be functioning as extensions of the political system. Though Tocqueville seems to have regarded the processes of neighborhood governance as merely analogous to authentic political processes, he also perceived that those purely "civil" activities might prepare citizens for the larger tasks of political organization and self-government.[21] They served as devices for political socialization, the acquisition of political skills, and sometimes as mechanisms of political recruitment. The urban political bosses of the past were often graduates of such informal training programs — products of a career line that ran through precincts and neighborhoods to the pomp and patronage of City Hall. More recently, candidates for municipal office have emerged in significant numbers from neighborhood associations and community corporations.

Such observations testify to the significance of neighborhoods as direct participants in politics, and not just to their capacity for imitating political processes. But similar observations might conceivably be made about labor unions, fraternal organizations, or "parapolitical" formations of almost all sorts. Neighborhoods may act as pressure groups or agencies of political recruitment more frequently than do stamp clubs or sandlot baseball teams, but there is no reason in principle why almost any private group, formal or informal, might not perform political functions of this kind. The political distinctiveness of the neighborhood becomes more pronounced, however, when one considers the nature of the setting in which residential communities conduct their governmentlike activities.

By definition, the neighborhood is a territorial unit, and the same has often been said of states and political systems.[22] If physical force is regarded as the hidden engine that drives political systems, physical space is seen as the traditional and singular medium in which this energy source achieves tangible expression. There is nothing about territory itself—or about territoriality—that necessarily transforms human groups into political organizations. The political character of a territorial group seems to grow instead out of the kinds of relationships that become possible in organizations that use mere geographic boundaries to define their memberships. Many anthropologists, for example, have regarded the emergence of territorial groups as an essential step toward the development of the state, and what seems to be most essential to political development in this species of organization is the fact that the "territorial link" offers a substitute for kinship and personal relationships in defining and maintaining a group.[23] In the eyes of some anthropologists, this social innovation by itself marks the threshold of politics, for they hold that "the sphere of politics begins where that of kinship ends."[24] But even without defining the political sphere so generously, it should be apparent that territorial organization raises the possibility, and the problem, of maintaining regular and peaceful relationships between people who may be bound together by no tie more deep-seated or compelling than physical proximity. It is the sort of tie that is apt to bind, perhaps, only when it can be reinforced by at least the distant prospect of legitimate physical coercion. And it is clearly the kind of social relationship whose management and regulation tends to become the distinctive business not only of full-grown political systems but also of neighborhood polities.

Because they are both territorial units, neighborhoods and political systems may share to some degree in another distinctly political endowment. Physical space is an encompassing envelope that can contain the entire repertoire of social relationships, activities, and groups, and the political system as the territorial organization of a society therefore becomes the society's most comprehensive institution. This, at least, is one of the properties by which political organization has traditionally been distinguished from other sorts of social institutions.[25] Individual neighborhoods, of course, can hardly lay claim to social inclusiveness of this kind. By definition they are partial and geographically limited segments of a society, and in practice they tend to be predominantly residential segments rather than commercial or industrial. In one sense, however, they are nearly as inescapable and all-embracing as the state itself. This is not to say that there is no escape from one's neighborhood. Economists, in fact, are fond of pointing out that consumers in the housing market can shop for an optimal mix of amenities or public goods by moving freely from one neighborhood to another,[26] and although exit from a neighborhood may be a good deal more sticky than some of the economic theories make it seem, residents can obviously quit their neighborhoods just as surely as they can resign from labor unions, churches, political parties, or the places where they work. The difference is that after divorcing themselves from these other types of groups, citizens have a clear opportunity to become non-union, unchurched, politically independent, or unemployed; but one flees from a neighborhood only to seek asylum in another neighborhood. Because of the simple rule that everyone must be someplace, the neighborhood is probably the society's most compulsory voluntary association.

The neighborhood remains something less than a fully formed political system all the same, since the exercise of legitimate force is scarcely ever one of its capabilities. Yet the neighborhood polity is also something more than a parapolitical system, because it has a distinctive public character that sets it apart from the private groups for which this designation seems intended. Like any parapolitical system, the neighborhood can sometimes be a direct participant in the political process, and it performs internal functions that seem to imitate those of the political system itself. Unlike other groups, however, it is set up on the same terms as the political system itself. Membership comes as an adjunct to geographic location, and although access to some locations may be impeded by restrictive covenants or economic obstacles, the necessary qualifications for being a neighbor are about as indiscriminate and inclusive as the requirements for citizenship. This means that neighborhood relationships may sometimes be little more than spatial relationships, no stronger and no more personal or private than ties among fellow citizens. It also means that although some resolutely nomadic people may conceivably succeed in disconnecting themselves from any neighborhood at all, like the Man Without a Country, there is in fact little more opportunity to escape the neighborhood than to elude membership in a state. It is possible, after all, for large numbers of people in a society to avoid the roles of father, sister, Odd Fellow, or employee, but it takes extraordinary measures to avoid being "one of the neighbors." This inclusive and near-compulsory character differentiates the neighborhood from virtually all other private groups in the society. In fact, the central point is that the residents of a neighborhood do not constitute a private group at all, but a miniature "public"—more like citizens than like members of a private association.

Suspended in mid-typology between political systems and parapolitical systems, the neighborhood's political character defies easy classification. To find something that resembles it, one might resort to John Locke's antique notion of "political society," a condition that he conceived as intermediate between an anarchic state of nature and the existence of a formal, specialized government. Locke endowed it with qualities that sound much like the attributes of a strong and well-ordered neighborhood. Men brought it into being, he said, "by agreeing with other men to join and unite into a community for their comfortable, safe, and peaceable living one amongst another, in a secure enjoyment of their properties and a greater security against any that are not of it."[27] Unfortunately, Locke's vision of this "politic society" that lay beneath the formal institutions of government was highly uncertain, and along with many other elements of his political philosophy it has remained a subject of controversy among commentators. He was nevertheless careful to distinguish it from private groups like the family[28] and to differentiate political society from the government to which it customarily delegated the coercive power of making and enforcing laws.[29] In short, whatever the exact form of Locke's political society, its theoretical position closely resembles that of the neighborhood polity, and there is also some similarity in the functioning of the two bodies. Locke points out, for example, that when "government visibly ceases and the people become a confused multitude, without order or connection,"[30] political society resumes its earlier role as an active guarantor of public order—the informal, "diffused government" of the society. Locke can hardly have had in mind the visible cessation of public services that sometimes occurs in a modern city as the result of a heavy snowstorm, but in the framework of his political thought he has left an easily recognizable place for the kinds of emergency arrangements that arose in Reservoir Hill on just such an occasion.

In Locke's scheme, of course, this underlying political society would rarely rise to the surface all of a sudden, as it seemed to in

Reservoir Hill. It was expected to reemerge gradually from beneath the formal and official institutions of government in response to persistent nonfeasance or "a long train of abuses."[31] For Locke, political society was a historical stage in the development (or disintegration) of a political system, and not merely a theoretical device for distinguishing one of the essential ingredients in a political order that was already fully developed. My investigation provides a view of political societies not as they strengthen or weaken over time but only as they vary from place to place. There is no attempt to match Locke's historical account of political society with a developmental theory of neighborhood polities.

A further difference is that Locke intended his political society to serve primarily as a counterweight for the tyrannical excesses of arbitrary rulers. In today's cities, however, anxiety about municipal tyranny often gives way to a contrary suspicion that the powers of City Hall may in fact amount to much less than meets the eye. The immensity of municipal organization — as measured by public expenditure or employment — has prompted many students of urban affairs to inquire how so much government could produce so little in the way of actual governing.

Critics argue, for example, that enormous public investments in education, law and order, and urban economic development have produced scant returns for their intended beneficiaries. The intractability of urban problems and the vagaries of "implementation" are thought to have frustrated reformist efforts to reduce poverty and unemployment[32] or improve health care.[33] Occasionally they also cast doubt on a city's ability to deliver even the most basic public services. Research results have suggested, for example, that the educational programs of school systems may have remarkably little to do with the academic performance or subsequent occupational success of their pupils.[34] Other investigations indicate that the patrol activities of police departments may make scarcely a dent in the stock of urban crime and disorder.[35]

Observers have argued more generally that the capacity of municipal government to do good is far more limited than we have imagined.[36] Others go further still; they argue not only that City Hall's well-intentioned efforts may be fruitless but that they tend to have evil results in the end.[37] It should not escape notice, however, that the alleged failings of city governments are frequently distinguished from the failings of cities themselves. Indeed, some of the most severe judges of the disabilities in municipal government have also insisted that American cities today are safer, cleaner, healthier, and generally more livable than ever before.[38] For those who remain unpersuaded by these reports of progress, it should at least be evident that some neighborhoods in today's cities seem far richer in civility and in public goods than others, notwithstanding the limited efficacy of government, and these "well-governed" neighborhoods are not necessarily identical with the ones that are well-to-do.

Starting from observations that John Locke would hardly have recognized, the modern critics of public authority have come to the verge of rediscovering Locke's political society—an alternative source of public services, public order, and public goods that lies beyond the limits of official government. But the critics' line of argument usually leads them instead only to an endorsement of political quietism or to an invocation of the "private sector." Modern political theorizing and criticism seem to have lost contact with Locke's vision of the diffuse polity that keeps the institutions of government afloat. In the place once occupied by his political society, contemporary political analysts usually see only a swarm of "special interests" whose function is less to produce public goods than to contend for the private ones.

The modern perception results in a considerable narrowing of the region for political, as opposed to private, action. Oddly enough, Locke himself sometimes bears the blame for obscuring "the political character of civil society," largely because he chose not to derive the social order from the existence of government but to give precedence to civil society instead.[39] Locke may be faulted, perhaps, for failing to allow the possibility that government institutions might reshape, strengthen, or destroy the unofficial arrangements of a political society. But since he distinguished it from private groups, endowed it with obviously political functions, made it the source of political legitimacy, and called it *political* society, he can hardly be accused of ceding public space to the private sector. Locke has clearly labeled his concept a political one, though it may lose this character when Locke is read through the lens of twentieth-century interest-group democracy.

Understanding exactly what Locke meant, of course, is less important for present purposes than attempting to understand the political objects that seem to fall within the general scope of his meaning. Locke's "political society" concept helps to clarify the character of the neighborhood polity. It is neither a government nor a private group but something in between, and it derives its political status both from the functions that it performs and from the public nature of the constituency that it serves. In a sense, the task of this book is to determine whether something like political society may be found in urban neighborhoods, and under what conditions.

It requires no special insight, of course, to recognize that the unofficial governing capacities of neighborhoods do not acquire their significance from John Locke. The operations of the neighborhood polity, though seldom noticed, are likely to have implications more practical than philosophical for the functioning of the larger urban political system and for the civility of civil society. This practical importance is magnified at those times when discussions of urban policy turn morbid, as they have recently. City government, pinched by shrinking financial resources and confronted by problems that were apparently beyond its capacity to solve even in prosperous times, is urged to practice a kind of neighborhood euthanasia. Municipal authorities, it is argued, should devote their life-sustaining efforts to the sick but salvageable neighborhoods, while the healthy communities are left to their own devices and the helpless ones are left to die.[40]

Such proposals lend more than theoretical interest to the ability of neighborhoods to make do on their own. But they also serve to underline the gloomy contemporary answer to the question of whether there is political life after government. The purpose here is to consider an answer of a different kind. Though we may not be able to create political societies by contract, as Locke would have it, we may at least find that the conditions for political existence that he perceived beyond the limits of government can sustain political vitality, not only on the primeval fringes of the state of nature but also in modern cities. Once we know something of the extent and configurations of today's political societies, we may also be able to facilitate their maintenance and formation.

Finding Neighborhood Polities in Baltimore

The purpose of this study is, in a sense, to reconnoiter the "political society" of the city. It examines the signs of political life in urban neighborhoods; it attempts to chart the major dimensions of variability in the political regimes of different neighborhoods; and it seeks to explain why the capacity to support an unofficial polity varies from one neighborhood to the next. These intentions lead naturally to a research design that is comparative, ranging across a variety of neighborhoods in order to establish whether there are any systematic connections between variations in the strength and character of community governance on the one hand, and the varied attributes and activities of neighborhoods and neighborhood residents on the other.

Reservoir Hill and twenty other residential neighborhoods in Baltimore are the subjects of the comparisons to be made here. These twenty-one communities were selected from all the residential areas in Baltimore, as a probability sample of the 120 or so neighborhoods into which the city has been divided by municipal officials. It cannot be assumed, of course, that the officially recognized neighborhoods are Baltimore's "real" neighborhoods; in fact, there may be no such thing as a single true definition of a neighborhood. But the official definition provides an easily accessible starting point for the investigation, and not at all an arbitrary one.

The designation of the city's neighborhoods was the work of the municipal housing and community development agency, the local department responsible for planning and overseeing neighborhood projects of many kinds and for enforcing the city's housing code. The agency's inventory of city neighborhoods was undertaken as an informational service and was not tailored to fit any specific program or administrative purpose. Many of the neighborhoods identified are the ones that agency staff members encountered during the course of their work. Others were discovered by consulting local traditions and local activists. Whatever else may be said about the merits of the inventory, its results are validated by at least one unambiguous criterion of neighborhood definition: the neighborhoods that it designates are the ones whose existence has been recognized by citywide authorities.

The names and locations of these communities supplied a basis for more detailed mapping of neighborhood territories, guided by the principle that every household in Baltimore must be assigned to one and only one neighborhood. The neighborhoods to which residents were assigned were not necessarily the ones that they would have chosen for themselves, and in fact the residential communities conceived by administrators at City Hall do not necessarily bear any resemblance to the ones that local residents have in mind.

Finding out what the residents had in mind was one object of a survey conducted in all twenty-one sample neighborhoods. The people contacted in each neighborhood were adults living in a probability sample of local households. One person was interviewed by telephone in each sample household for which there was a current telephone listing. In a 50 percent subsample of the remaining

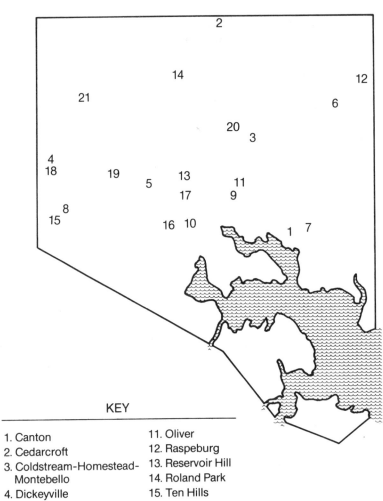

Locations of Sample Neighborhoods in Baltimore

KEY

1. Canton
2. Cedarcroft
3. Coldstream-Homestead-Montebello
4. Dickeyville
5. Easterwood
6. Gardenville
7. Highlandtown
8. Hunting Ridge
9. Johnston Square
10. Little Lithuania
11. Oliver
12. Raspeburg
13. Reservoir Hill
14. Roland Park
15. Ten Hills
16. Union Square
17. Upton
18. Wakefield
19. Walbrook
20. Waverly
21. West Arlington

households—the ones that were unreachable by means of the telephone directory—residents were interviewed in person. To make up for the fact that the final total included only about half of the sample households not appearing in the telephone book, the personal interviews were weighted more heavily than the telephone interviews.

Altogether more than sixteen hundred Baltimoreans were interviewed between October 1978 and March 1979. During these interviews, with an average length of slightly more than half an hour, respondents were asked questions about their perceptions of their neighborhoods, their attitudes toward their neighbors, and their own activities within their neighborhoods. Their answers to these inquiries helped to show, for example, whether the people living in a residential area conceived of their neighborhood in the same way that city officials did. The responses of the residents also provided a series of limited but systematic glimpses into the operations of neighborhood polities. Respondents reported on the efforts that they and their neighbors had made to maintain public order, public safety, and public sanitation within their communities and to relieve public tedium—all manifestations of what Tocqueville saw as the unofficial "executive power" of the neighborhood. Other questions were designed to seek out the proceedings of Tocqueville's extemporaneous "deliberative body" in activities ranging from casual conversations between neighbors to formal meetings of community associations convened to act on specific resolutions or policy proposals. The answers to these inquiries help to disclose the processes by which individual interests may be expressed in a neighborhood polity and aggregated to form a neighborhood interest.

In general, the household survey was an instrument for discovering the character of the citizenry in each of a number of neighborhood polities. A second and more focused survey attempted to disclose the outlines of neighborhood leadership patterns and governing institutions. Beginning in the early fall of 1979, personal interviews were conducted with an average of eleven informants in each of the sample neighborhoods. Instead of selecting residents likely to be representative of the local population, this second survey attempted to reach people who were apt to be especially knowledgeable about neighborhood issues, neighborhood activities, and the neighborhood itself. Each of them held a local position that might be expected to command a superior view of the neighborhood's political operations. The informants themselves were not necessarily the most important leaders and decision makers in their communities, although some of them undoubtedly were; they should be regarded instead as likely eyewitnesses to the conduct of important neighborhood business.

In each of the sample neighborhoods, the first informants to be interviewed were usually the executive officers of all neighborhood improvement, civic, or protective associations. Others interviewed at about the same time were the president of the parent-teacher association at the local elementary school, a city council member who represented the neighborhood, and a full-time staff member of any community corporations whose territory included the neighborhood. When a neighborhood did not fall within the territory of community corporations, interviewers contacted either of two alternative informants — both of them full-time staff members of municipal agencies who had been assigned responsibility for dealing with neighborhood groups in the area and for handling community complaints.

Other informants were found with the assistance of the initial set of informants. Staff members of community corporations, for example, were asked to identify a member of the local clergy who had been especially active in neighborhood projects or programs. The city council representative for each community was asked to name the owner or manager of a neighborhood business who had been notable for participation in the affairs of the community. And the presidents of neighborhood improvement associations were asked to nominate their most active members, four of whom were interviewed in each neighborhood. Finally, presidents and active members of the neighborhood associations were all asked to name a few people outside their organizations who were widely recognized as activists in the community, and in each neighborhood interviews were conducted with one or two of the unaffiliated activists who had been mentioned most frequently.

Some of the questions addressed to this panel of presumably expert witnesses were similar to the ones that had been asked earlier of respondents in the household survey. Both groups, for example, were asked about the names and boundaries of their neighborhoods, in an effort to find out how local residents conceived of their communities. In general, however, the information requested from the panel of neighborhood informants was more detailed than the kind that had been sought in interviews with the larger sample of household respondents, and it often had to do with a somewhat different level of neighborhood political operations. The household respondents, for example, were asked to indicate what kinds of neighborhood issues and problems had been bothering them during the preceding year. But the more select group of informants was asked what kinds of local issues had actually reached the agendas of community organizations and decision-making groups. Household respondents talked about their own personal attitudes, experiences, and perceptions. The informants who were interviewed later discussed the experiences and the character of the neighborhood as a whole and its institutions.

Taken together, the two information sources provide raw material for constructing political profiles of the twenty-one neighborhoods under study. These portraits are not so richly detailed as they might have been if the research effort had been designed to capture the political complexities of just one or a few neighborhood environments. Several outstanding studies in the past have concentrated their attentions in this way, and they have given us coherent and full-bodied accounts that help to make sense of social life in particular subcommunities, sometimes with implications for neighborhood societies in general. But even the best of these studies have necessarily been confined to single neighborhoods or single types of neighborhoods, and were therefore unsuited to encompass or explain the readily apparent variations in community climate from one neighborhood to the next.[41] Other less intensive investigations have studied large samples of residents from the entire population of a city in order to uncover the influence that neighborhood environments of all kinds may have on the attitudes and activities of urbanites.[42] But since the samples of respondents in most of these inquiries have been thinly spread across a large number of communities, the responses do not add up to a social portrait of any particular neighborhood. In most cases these investigations have been designed to explain the behavior of individuals, not the behavior of neighborhoods.

The present enterprise stands midway between the intensive, single-neighborhood studies and the extensive but thinly spread sample surveys. It attempts to explain not only the behavior of detached individuals who happen to live in neighborhoods but also the collective conduct of neighbors who live together in the same communities, where they may have developed their own unofficial political arrangements and their own informal public services. For this reason the study's respondents and informants must be sufficiently concentrated in particular communities so that the information they supply can be aggregated to disclose the social composition and political structure of each neighborhood under study. At the same time, the enterprise cannot be so narrowly concentrated in a few neighborhoods that it forfeits the opportunity to make the comparisons necessary for describing and explaining variations among neighborhood polities.

In one significant respect, of course, the design of the research forecloses comparative analysis. Because all its neighborhoods lie within a single city, the investigation cannot reveal how the capabilities or operations of neighborhood polities might be affected by exposure to differing municipal climates. This restriction of the study's scope undeniably places several important questions about neighborhood governance beyond its reach, but it is a limitation deliberately chosen to sharpen the explanatory and interpretive capabilities of the research — and to keep it manageable. In a study of different neighborhoods in different cities, we might be hard put to say whether the observed contrasts among neighborhood polities could be attributed to variations in neighborhood characteristics or to variations among the cities in which the neighborhoods happen to be located. It is true that city effects and neighborhood effects might be distinguished from one another if the range of cities and the number of neighborhoods studied were large enough. But even if we discount the reception that such a massive enterprise would be likely to encounter in the offices of organizations that dispense research funds, its complexity and its weight would make it unsuited for an exploratory expedition like the present one.

A study that does not wander beyond the city limits of Baltimore can devote all its attention to the analysis of political variations between neighborhoods, and leave for later investigations the complications that are introduced by political differences between cities. Apart from the virtue of relative simplicity, Baltimore also offered several more positive advantages as a location for neighborhood research. One advantage is convenience: the city was chosen in part because it happened to be close at hand, and because it was familiar to me — it was not only an object of research but also my home or workplace for more than thirty years. Another more substantial virtue of Baltimore is that the city includes neighborhoods with characteristics so pronounced and so improbably diverse that many of the local residents, without prompting from the social sciences, habitually improvise their own homemade comparative analyses of generally recognized cultural variations between neighborhoods. The city seems to invite comparative studies of its residential communities. Even among the sample of twenty-one drawn for the present investigation, the variety of locally well-known neighborhood subcultures is striking. In the northern part of the city, the long-established Anglo-Saxon gentility of Roland Park has supplied the model for several novels about life in the respectable classes.[43] West of the city's geographic center is the black community of Upton — even longer established — where Cab Calloway, Eubie Blake, and Thurgood Marshall grew up and where Billie Holliday played the local clubs. Still further south, along the eastern edge of the harbor, the residents of Canton still work the wharves and factories as they have through several waves of European immigration, since before the men of the neighborhood forged the iron plates for the U.S.S. *Monitor.*

Almost any large city can equal Baltimore's social diversity, and some of the larger ones undoubtedly surpass it. What strikes observers as distinctive, perhaps, is the extent to which the city's internal variety seems to be organized into distinct neighborhood communities. Other large cities are alleged to provide a less congenial environment for them. "But for some reason," writes an urban geographer, "neighborhoods seem to be a real and universal phenomenon in the Baltimore region. I would attribute this to a remarkable correspondence of scale among physiography, the organization of the construction industry, pedestrian range, and the social units within which children play and grown-ups gossip and keep up with the Joneses. The elaborate and nearly indestructible differentiation of the physical landscape was the basis for gradual historical variation."[44]

The fact that Baltimore's neighborhood units have achieved such prominence in the eyes of the city's observers does not signify that local residential areas are uniformly well defined and well organized. It means that the local assortment of neighborhoods includes a full range of variations, from the strongly defined communities to the barely perceptible, and that the city does not run short of neighborhoods toward the upper end of this range. In other cities, apparently, the higher registers of the scale may contain only a handful of exceptional cases, and the opportunities for productive comparisons among neighborhoods are limited accordingly. For cities at large, says Suzanne Keller, the evidence suggests that "people do not generally identify the subareas they live in by name or distinct boundaries unless such areas are either geographically or socially insulated or have a definite class or historic identity."[45] In Baltimore, however, the general run of indistinct neighborhoods can be contrasted with a reasonably plentiful supply of residential communities that seem to be sharply defined and widely known. These more conspicuous neighborhoods, of course, are the ones that usually capture the attentions of journalists, visiting federal commissions, and urban spectators of other sorts. The result, as one urban historian notes, is that "Baltimore has achieved, almost alone among the ten largest cities of the United States, a unique reputation for strong neighborhoods and remarkably smooth cooperation between local neighborhood organizations and city hall."[46]

Because there is no standard strength-of-neighborhood index for Baltimore and comparable American cities, this unique reputation rests on scarcely visible foundations. Only a few rough fragments of evidence suggest that there may be some solid grounding for the prevailing impressions about Baltimore's neighborhoods. A mail questionnaire study of city officials and citizen groups in twenty-two cities, for example, found that Baltimore's local authorities were more responsive to citizen and neighborhood groups than were municipal governments in any of the other cities surveyed. Unfortunately, the exact definition of "responsiveness" in this case seems to have been left to the relatively small numbers of citizen group representatives who served as informants in each city, and the notion was used broadly to include attentiveness to citizen groups in general, not just to neighborhood groups.[47]

A more elementary indication of neighborhood vigor is the extent to which local residents have distinctive names for the areas where they live. Applying a particular name to one's home territory is an essential step toward the development of a sense of neighborhood identity, and several studies have attempted to find out how likely it is that the step will be taken. A study in West Philadelphia, for instance, discovered that the community names employed by social workers and neighborhood associations were not used by most of the local residents, seven-tenths of whom offered no neighborhood designation more specific than West Philadelphia. The results were similar in a British new town, where only three-tenths of the residents knew the extensively publicized "proper" names for their neighborhoods.[48] But in Baltimore almost half of the household respondents in the present investigation volunteered the "official" designation when asked whether their neighborhood had any particular name. While these results imply a more widespread sense of neighborhood identity than was found in the British or West Philadelphia studies, they are less impressive than the findings of a survey conducted in one Boston residential area, where 68 percent of a sample of respondents gave the traditional name for their neighborhood.[49] The neighborhood in question, however, was

Beacon Hill — an old, established, prestigious, and well-known community that hardly represents the middling multitude of urban residential areas. When such a distinguished neighborhood is the standard of comparison, perhaps the most striking fact to be noted about its Baltimore counterparts is that residents in one-third of the sample neighborhoods equaled or surpassed the inhabitants of Beacon Hill in the likelihood that they would use the standard names for their home territories. A less exotic comparison is provided by Albert Hunter's valuable study of residential communities in Chicago, where 42.3 percent of a citywide sample of respondents used the "official" names that Ernest Burgess had assigned to their neighborhoods almost fifty years earlier.[50] The figure is not appreciably lower than the 48.8 percent of Baltimoreans who referred to their home territories by their standard names.

Even when joined together, the available scraps of evidence do not create a solid ground for beliefs about the strength of Baltimore's neighborhoods, especially since neighborhood strength itself is so elusive a notion that it is difficult to say just what is believed. The fragmentary evidence at hand hints at the complexity of the phenomenon. Although Baltimore and Chicago residents give roughly similar proofs of a sense of neighborhood identity, for example, the same study of municipal responsiveness that awarded first place to Baltimore for its attentiveness to citizen and neighborhood groups gave Chicago last place.[51] Neighborhood strength appears to come in several different varieties that are not necessarily associated with one another, and the evidence at its best offers only shaky testimony for certain varieties of strength in Baltimore's neighborhoods. It suggests that the city's reputation for neighborhood vitality is not entirely groundless, though perhaps not entirely justified either. Baltimoreans may use traditional neighborhood names more extensively than Chicagoans, but they do not surpass the Midwesterners by very much. The city's larger than average supply of well-defined residential communities creates greater than usual opportunities for the comparative study of neighborhoods, but the indications of neighborhood vigor are not so exceptional that they mark Baltimore as an urban eccentric.

Baltimore, of course, is no more typical or representative an American metropolis than Boston or Cleveland. The very characteristics that make it a congenial setting for comparative neighborhood research may also reflect a special local environment whose peculiarities need to be taken into account when we consider neighborhood polities that operate in the social or political climate of Baltimore. A city that is known for its vigorous neighborhoods, after all, probably has other distinctive traits as well; those traits may explain why the neighborhoods became so vigorous in the first place. In Baltimore, as Sherry Olson suggests, "the elaborate and nearly indestructible differentiation of the physical landscape" may have been the original stimulus for the emergence of community subdivisions. To the southeast, where the city rests on the coastal plain, inlets and tributaries of the Chesapeake's Patapsco estuary help to divide the town into neighborhood-sized parcels; to the northwest, where the city climbs into the piedmont, stream valleys serve as neighborhood partitions.[52] These natural features have undoubtedly been important in shaping Baltimore's development, but today they lie beneath a stratum of urban history — nearly as indestructible as the landscape itself — that has been responsible for translating streams and inlets into neighborhood boundaries and for generating the atmosphere that surrounds today's neighborhood polities.

The polities themselves seem to have made an early appearance in the city's history, long before Baltimore's boundaries were stretched to their present extent through successive annexations. Distinct traces of neighborhood governance extend at least as far back as the generation before the Civil War, when residents in many of the city's twenty wards appear to have been making their own unofficial arrangements for self-government. The arrangements were hardly democratic. According to Joseph Arnold, in fact, their existence depended on the presence of confidently assertive local notables whose townhouses were scattered throughout the city rather than confined to a single silk-stocking district. In neighborhoods that exhibited more racial and social integration than today's, the members of the urban elite occupied fine houses along the main thoroughfares; tradesmen and shopkeepers lived on the side streets; and the alleys were reserved for the unskilled black laborers and domestics.[53] In each ward, some of the local aristocrats usually appointed themselves to speak for the neighborhood's interests at City Hall. They also deliberated among themselves about the management of neighborhood problems and distributed charity to their less fortunate neighbors in times of need. The local physician might serve as unofficial public health officer, and a volunteer fire company could be called upon in emergencies. Taken together these various products of voluntarism and improvisation suggest a fairly comprehensive and impressive apparatus for preserving domestic tranquillity and promoting general welfare. But the system, says

Arnold, began to disintegrate soon after improvements in mass transportation made it possible for Baltimoreans of the more respectable classes to separate themselves more completely from their less prestigious fellow citizens. The ward system itself was formally abolished by reformers after the turn of the century.[54]

Although the territories claimed by a few contemporary neighborhood associations bear an almost eerie resemblance to some old wards of pre–Civil War Baltimore, today's neighborhood communities cannot be regarded as mere ghosts of yesterday's urban villages. In the first place, some of the modern city's most notable residential communities were still undeveloped tracts outside the municipal limits when the ward system began to fade from law and custom. More important, the official and unofficial features of the ward system seem to have been common to many eastern cities, not just Baltimore.[55] Yet neighborhoods appear to be a more pronounced feature of contemporary life in Baltimore than in many other cities, and the political decentralization that was embodied in the ward system is obviously not sufficient to explain their distinctive vitality. Other developments must have distinguished Baltimore from other cities where the ward system was just as important.

In fact, the distinctive developments in Baltimore's history may have been less important for local neighborhoods than the city's lack of development. From its beginnings Baltimore has exhibited symptoms of urban retardation. Compared to other cities in the Northeast, it was a late arrival. Its original boundaries were not laid down until 1730, and for a long time afterward nothing much happened. While Boston and Philadelphia were making their reputations as hometowns for founding fathers and revolutionary patriots, Baltimore was scarcely more than a village. The place did not attract much serious attention until the western limit of settlement had moved up the near side of the Alleghenies and into the valleys beyond. It was then that merchants and shippers discovered how close Baltimore's port was to the western farmers and western markets — closer, in fact, than Boston, Philadelphia, or New York. Processions of heavy freight wagons loaded with grain rumbled into the city from western Maryland and Pennsylvania. Flour milling soon became an important local business, then shipbuilding, and by 1850 one thing had led to another with such astonishing success and rapidity that Baltimore was the third largest city in the country — first station of the nation's railroad lines, first American city to employ commercial gaslighting, financial center for the American South.

In retrospect, it is easy to see where the city's timing went wrong. In the middle of the nineteenth century, a city that staked its financial future on the continued prosperity of the South was bound to encounter some serious dissappointments before long. The ten years of sectional conflict that preceded the Civil War were a period of violence and political confusion for an ambivalent border metropolis,[56] and the war itself brought drastic economic dislocations to Baltimore — although it did not mean complete ruin for the city as a whole. With an amiable adaptability that was probably appropriate for the residents of a border town, some Baltimore merchants redesigned their business arrangements to extract profits from the Union army — or the Confederate army. And, after a brief recession in 1861, the business of the city and the port began to grow once again. But the local business community was not the same. James Crooks suggests that the long-term effects may have been chiefly psychological. Imposed political conformity, financial reverses, military occupation, and the polarization of the city by civil war had "sapped the vitality of a generation . . . Economically, Baltimoreans became more conservative; politically, they became apathetic; and psychologically, they became less daring and willing to take a chance."[57]

It is difficult, of course, to confirm changes in anything so elusive as civic temperament, but the signs of Baltimore's declining vigor soon became more tangible. Beginning in the 1880s the city's standing as a national manufacturing center began to slip, gradually at first and then more rapidly. Between 1880 and 1914 "Baltimore maintained a position among the leading industrial cities, but with increasing difficulty." The value of the city's manufactured products, ranked eighth among American cities in 1880, had dropped to eleventh by 1910.[58] The loss of rank may not seem serious in itself, but it reflected specific infirmities that could have damaging consequences. At the turn of the century, for example, the average amount of capital invested in Baltimore firms was well below the average for companies in the nation's ten largest cities, and the average number of employees in local establishments was also somewhat smaller. Perhaps the most serious indication of the sluggish pace of industrial progress was the fact that Baltimore's investment in machinery lagged behind that for other large cities.[59] In a period when aggressive national trusts were devouring smaller, less efficient, and less progressive firms, Baltimore's locally owned companies were vulnerable. The first of them fell in the mid-1870s, when John D. Rockefeller consolidated some of Baltimore's independent oil refineries into a single company and later attached them to Standard Oil. During the next twenty-five years, out-of-town industrial titans absorbed Baltimore's major manufacturing concerns in a number of fields — sugar refining, tobacco products, fertilizer, canning and tinware, iron and steel, and crackers and biscuits, among others. These raids on local industry left lasting effects. By the late 1970s only four corporations listed in the *Fortune 500* still had their headquarters in the Baltimore metropolitan area, and two of these had joined the ranks of the fortunate five hundred only after 1975.

The city was never a major command post for the moguls of commerce. Even in the palmy days before the Civil War, when Baltimore was the nation's third largest city, not a single millionaire made his home there, and only four local residents had individual assets valued at more than half a million dollars.[60] The business of Baltimore was carried on through relatively small and diverse enterprises that, especially after 1890, were owned and controlled increasingly by people who lived elsewhere. The concentration of capital, the emergence of industrial giants, and the new "technology" of large-scale organization were for places like Chicago, Pittsburgh, or New York — not Baltimore.[61] The city stood somewhat apart from the mainstream of urban development. In most of the nation's large cities, according to Samuel P. Hays, the coming of the industrial age meant that tendencies toward institutional centralization and integration became dominant.[62] But in Baltimore, where the industrial order arrived haltingly, with reduced force and an out-of-town base, there is at least reason to suspect that the attendant progression toward political and institutional centralization may have been somewhat retarded as well. For example, though we can only guess at the processes that linked economic and industrial retardation with other developments in Baltimore, it may be significant that the local Democratic political machine — always beleaguered by centrifugal impulses — suffered a decisive electoral defeat in 1895, subsequently fractured into a hopeless miscellany of district "machinelets," and never again recovered its unity.[63] For our present purposes, an even more important sign of Baltimore's loose-jointed approach to the twentieth century was the proliferation of neighborhood protective and improvement associations. They began to appear in the 1880s, just as the competitive performance of Baltimore industry was starting to sag, and by 1900 there were more than thirty of these community associations. Their aggregated jurisdictions covered the entire city and several of its suburbs.[64]

Mere coincidence does not establish a connection, but it seems plausible to hypothesize that the apparent vitality of today's neighborhood communities in Baltimore may be related to the city's lack of industrial and organizational vitality during a critical period in its political development. The tenacity of neighborhoods may reflect not so much the innate and original strength of the neighborhood communities themselves as the relative weakness of the local forces that were likely to undermine the vigor and autonomy of such parochial institutions as the neighborhood. Pressures for political and organizational consolidation may have been more easily resisted in a city where the pace of industrial and economic expansion was relatively sluggish and where giant corporations were represented only by their branches and subsidiaries.[65] Stated briefly, Baltimore may have remained more attached than other large cities to some vestige of nineteenth-century dispersion and decentralization because it experienced the great changes of the early twentieth century less intensely and directly than many other cities.

Though greatly simplified, the hypothesis suggests one plausible line of explanation for the distinctive social and political condition of many neighborhoods in contemporary Baltimore. It also helps to make sense of some common impressions that observers have had about the "atmosphere" or the climate of the city. Civic diffidence, for example, was an understandable attitude in a city whose surge of success came late and faded early—at just about the time when other cities were celebrating their great industrial adventures with outbursts of chest-thumping civic boosterism. Baltimore seemed outclassed by the competition. In the Northeast corridor, between fast-paced New York and stately Washington, the city was like a slow learner assigned by mistake to the advanced class. "We don't have as much history," explains a local newspaperman, "we don't have as many ancestors, we don't have as much money. We are an innocent city. We never surrendered to the success dream. We are a city where people don't think they are very bright."[66]

Perhaps an unnoticed by-product of this tendency toward self-deprecation was that in a city where almost no one felt very professional, few strong objections were likely to be raised when amateurs took matters into their own hands, as they frequently did in Baltimore's neighborhood communities. There was also a more truculent side to the city's sense of its backwardness—a parochial inclination to fume about "wasteful" large enterprises and to trumpet the virtues of small ones. In the 1930s, for example, local journalist

H. L. Mencken grumbled characteristically about an expensive municipal construction project: "Wasting millions on such follies is simply not Baltimorish. Every enterprise of the sort is a kind of confession that Baltimore is inferior to New York and should hump itself to catch up. No true Baltimorean believes that. He accepts the difference between a provincial capital and a national metropolis as natural and inevitable, and he sees no reason why any effort should be made to conceal it. He lives in Baltimore because he prefers Baltimore. One of its greatest charms, in his eyes, is that it is not New York."[67]

Like Mencken, many Baltimoreans seem to have judged their city by standards that did not originate in the gospel of twentieth-century civic progress. They did not expect great things from the city, and they professed not to want great things. Elements of the same attitude may also have shaped Baltimoreans' judgments of one another's conduct. According to Russell Baker, another journalist with Baltimore roots, "permissiveness" has been a local tradition. Baltimoreans recognize the difference between moral principles and moral conventions, but they seem disinclined to complain about the disparity. "The pleasures of the flesh, the table, the bottle and the purse," says Baker,

> are tolerated with a civilized understanding of the subtleties of moral questions that would have been perfectly comprehensible to Edwardian Londoners . . . That any politician with a drop of Baltimore in his blood might conceivably cast his fortune with the forces of uplift — blue noses, temperance ladies, Comstocks, parsons, the Watch and Ward Society, Y.M.C.A. secretaries and similar tilters against permissiveness of the sage's time — would doubtless have struck Mencken as a notion tenable only to persons far gone into imbecility.
>
> Any politician who had done so would probably have been regarded as a civic disgrace to Baltimoreans of a generation or two ago. To such Baltimoreans, moral salvation of the Republic seemed slightly comic work to be left to gloomy clods from Boston, deepest Appalachia and kerosene-lit backwaters of the prairie.[68]

A generation or so later, when federal prosecutors with little appreciation for local ways began to uncover the shoddy practices of local politicians, the mores of the city might become an embarrassment for Baltimoreans. But moral particularism and flexibility may have had other correlates besides corruption. If Baltimoreans were improbable recruits for great reformist crusades, perhaps they felt more comfortable with the less dramatic and abstract issues of their own neighborhoods, and perhaps they would be content to let other neighborhoods go their separate ways.

In short, there are several different kinds of indications — all more or less uncertain — that the ingredients of neighborhood vitality may have been present in Baltimore for some time. The evidence is sufficiently sharp in a few instances to suggest that these contributing factors may have been more pronounced in Baltimore than in other cities. But to clarify the processes by which these factors produced their results within the city's neighborhoods would require a much more detailed examination than can be conducted here. What can be said with reasonable certainty is that it makes a difference that the neighborhoods under study are located in Baltimore rather than in, say, Nashville or Salt Lake City. In Baltimore the political and social environment has probably been more congenial to neighborhood-based activities than it has been elsewhere, and in some respects this local peculiarity may redound to the advantage of the present investigation. Not all Baltimore neighborhoods are tightly knit, clearly defined, and vigorously active, but the local setting has permitted the development of considerable variability among neighborhoods, and such variation may have considerable value in a comparative study. To the extent that Baltimore's neighborhoods exist in peculiar circumstances, we can at least have some confidence that the peculiarities are not simply the short-term products of recent municipal policies.

Recent policies, however, may have contributed something to the vitality of the city's neighborhoods. During the 1970s Baltimore embarked on an effort at urban revival that combined downtown development with neighborhood rehabilitation, and brought Baltimoreans more out-of-town attention than they had been accustomed to receiving in the past. The chief engineer of the city's revitalization was its single-minded mayor, William Donald Schaefer, who presided over a municipal government that was almost certainly more centralized than it had been during the era of the ward system. In place of the neighborhood-sized wards, there are now six large districts, each of which elects three representatives to the City Council. The council itself is only a modest counterweight to mayoral control. Under Baltimore's charter, for example, it may only reduce, never raise, the mayor's proposed budget allocations.

A similar consolidation of authority is also evident in other governmental arrangements of the city. Baltimore probably controls a wider range of its public services, for instance, than do most American municipalities. Functions that are elsewhere assigned to county authorities — like welfare or waste disposal — are administered in Baltimore by the city government. This is because the city does not lie within the boundaries of any county but operates as a freestanding subdivision directly subordinate to the Maryland state government. Although it depends heavily on financial support from both state and federal governments, Baltimore is functionally self-contained to a far greater degree than the majority of cities in the United States.

These and other elements of municipal centralism have no doubt strengthened mayoral leadership of Baltimore's energetically advertised renaissance, but they do not appear to have stifled the parochial political lives of neighborhoods. If City Council members exercise limited influence in the shaping of city budgets and programs, for example, the political standing of the residential communities that they represent is not necessarily diminished. It may even help to explain why some council representatives have chosen to devote most of their political energies to neighborhood and constituency service efforts. The mayor himself, through a variety of city programs, has attempted to encourage not only the reconstruction of many neighborhoods but also the mobilization of their residents in advisory councils and committees — significant islands of organized support in a city where political party forces add up to something much less than a cohesive machine. Neighborhoods that were scarcely thought to exist before the beginning of the Schaefer administration have since acquired sharper definition and wider recognition as residential communities.

In some cases at least, the recent interplay of City Hall and neighborhoods seems only to have reinforced the long-term conditions that permitted neighborhood institutions to flourish in Baltimore. The result has been not to impose a single kind of political character on the city's residential communities but to allow many of them to develop their own distinctive political capabilities.

What Makes a Neighborhood

The range of neighborhood variability is sufficiently wide in Baltimore that one may wonder whether the concept of neighborhood itself is broad enough to cover all of the local variants.

Some analysts may conceivably object, for example, when the term is applied to residential areas that are simply nameless lumps of urban territory for a majority of the local residents, where next-door neighbors may frequently be strangers to one another and where most of the local inhabitants go elsewhere to find friendship, shopping facilities, and religious worship. All these conditions can be found among the sample of twenty-one neighborhoods in Baltimore, and their presence may be taken as evidence that some of these places do not deserve to be regarded as "real" neighborhoods.

It should at least be evident that these places, whether they are authentic neighborhoods or not, cannot be omitted from an investigation of neighborhood polities. One need only consider what kinds of biases would be likely to result if we began an inquiry into the political capabilities of urban neighborhoods by first deciding to ignore all residential areas where people lacked a sense of neighborhood identity or rarely fraternized with their neighbors. By systematically excluding areas where social conditions could be expected to discourage collective action, such a study would probably arrive at misleading conclusions about the political attainments of city neighborhoods. More important, it could seriously restrict the opportunities for comparison that are essential for explaining how and why some neighborhoods develop into unofficial polities. We cannot find out what makes the politically vigorous neighborhoods distinctive, after all, if we do not have the chance to contrast them with the residential areas that fail to exhibit signs of vigor.

The conception of a neighborhood as something immanent in the activities and attitudes of local residents is simply impractical for the purposes at hand. In general, the problem with definitions drawn in this way is that the process of becoming a neighborhood may be merged with the process of becoming a polity — which is also a matter of the residents' attitudes and activities. To qualify as a neighborhood for the purposes of our investigation, a residential area might also have to be functioning as a political unit. If such a conception of a neighborhood were to serve as the starting point for our inquiry, we would run the risk of defining away at the outset the very thing that we seek to explain — the fact that some neighborhoods become political units and others do not.

To adopt this approach to the investigation might be more than just impractical. It rests on ideas about neighborhoods that are confusing and possibly even mistaken. One major source of the confusion, according to Suzanne Keller, is the failure to distinguish the phenomena that are likely to be found within a neighborhood from the neighborhood itself. Among the neighborhood's social contents, for example, is the role of neighbor, "implying a particular kind of social attitude toward others." Associated with this role, but distinct from it, are "various activities . . . ranging from highly formalized and regular neighborly rituals to sporadic, informal, and casual contacts." Finally, there is "the area itself—the neighborhood— where neighbors reside and in which neighboring takes place ."[69] Keller suggests, in other words, that we should conceive of a neighborhood as something distinct from the occurrence of neighborly attitudes and activities. It may serve as a social container for these things, but "neighborhood" itself is not defined by them.

The distinction between the neighborhood and the manifestations of neighborliness has been drawn even more sharply by Gerald Suttles, who has used it as one element in a persuasive account of community formation in cities. His view represents an alternative to the conception of urban neighborhoods as immanent "natural communities." Suttles criticizes a line of thinking and research in which neighborhood identities seem to emerge spontaneously from the ties of loyalty and sentiment that exist among the residents of an area. "The emphasis on sentimental ties," says Suttles, "also tended to focus research on interactional networks, shopping practices, and local usage patterns as a way of accounting for the progressive development of a localized web of interpersonal relations and intimacy. The local community, then, could be seen as a sort of gradual aggregate by-product of individual action. This has never struck me as a very likely line of argument, for there seems no reason for such unbounded networks to eventuate in a corporate identity and any sharp sense of neighborhood boundaries."[70]

Individual acts of neighborliness, in other words, are not sufficient to explain the appearance of distinct neighborhood identities. There is also considerable evidence that clearly defined neighborhoods may emerge even if local residents do not exhibit any notable tendencies toward neighborly activities or sentiments.[71] These are some of the indications that community identities "do not emerge solely from the crescive internal development of relations among co-residents." Instead, says Suttles, the neighborhood usually develops a corporate identity through its "foreign relations" with outside groups and institutions, for whom a simplified, collective representation of the area and its population may be a convenience or a necessity. In Suttles's view, neighborhoods tend to receive their identities as distinct urban units "through an ongoing commentary between themselves and outsiders." A neighborhood acquires definition not so much because its residents gradually become conscious of their common ties, but because residents and nonresidents arrive at a conception of what it is that makes the area and its inhabitants different from other areas and other groups in the city. Government officials, realtors, developers, boosters, and members of nearby residential groups may all participate along with the local inhabitants in a "broad dialogue that gravitates toward collective representations which have credence to both residents and nonresidents alike." Neighborly relations among residents are not essential to the formation of a neighborhood because some of the most important participants in the process of neighborhood definition may not be residents at all but outsiders.[72]

The procedures used here to identify sample neighborhoods in Baltimore parallel the processes of community formation that Gerald Suttles has described. As in Suttles's account, each neighborhood area was defined by two elementary features—a recognized name and territorial boundaries.[73] A citywide neighborhood map drawn up by the local Department of Housing and Community Development provided a preliminary list of community names. This official inventory of Baltimore's neighborhoods, discussed above, was itself the product of "a broad dialogue" between local residents and city officials. As partial corroboration for these neighborhood designations, the community names of the official map were checked against the area names used in classified newspaper advertisements for houses and apartments. The purpose was to find out whether local realtors had "discovered" any neighborhood identities that had been omitted from the official inventory. There were hardly any disparities in neighborhood nomenclature, and the differences that occurred were chiefly instances in which the real estate advertisements added refinements to the official neighborhood names—"North" or "Upper" Hamilton, for example, instead of Hamilton. Since the advertisements were themselves inconsistent in their use of these refinements, the list of official neighborhood names was retained as a basis for the next step in neighborhood definition.

Although the official neighborhood map gave names to residential areas and indicated their approximate locations, it did not chart exact boundaries for neighborhoods. Another document prepared by a city agency supplied initial guidance in making up for this deficiency. A comprehensive directory of neighborhood improvement, civic, and protective associations compiled annually by the municipal planning department lists geographic boundaries for the area that each organization claims to represent. The territorial borders for each of these organizations—almost four hundred of them in all—were plotted on a map of the city, and the resulting atlas of community organizations was compared with the official map of city neighborhoods. In many instances the correspondences between organization names and neighborhood names and between organizational territories and neighborhood locations were so obvious that it required hardly any exercise of discretion to specify tentative boundaries for a sample neighborhood. In other cases the inconsistent territorial claims of community organizations or the absence of any organizations at all made it necessary to resort to other clues concerning the location of neighborhood frontiers—most frequently, physical features such as railroad tracks, parks, cemeteries, or major thoroughfares. By one means or the other, tentative boundaries were fixed for each of the twenty-one sample neighborhoods.

Each set of provisional boundaries was then submitted to a member of the local planning department's district planning staff who was responsible for the area of the city where the neighborhood in question was located. When boundary changes were suggested by a city planner, the revised set of community frontiers would next be discussed with at least one formal group leader in the area under consideration. Usually, these leaders were presidents of neighborhood improvement or civic associations, but in the absence of these organizations, inquiries were sometimes made with staff members of community corporations or areawide umbrella organizations. In the few cases in which the neighborhood boundaries suggested by city planners differed from the ones specified by community leaders, successive rounds of consultation were held with both parties until their boundary recommendations were substantially the same. The process was a greatly simplified version of the ongoing commentary between residents and outsiders that Suttles describes as the medium for community definition.

In one respect, however, this simulated dialogue may have differed significantly from the more extensive and informal colloquy on which it was modeled. When community leaders or district planners excluded any piece of residential territory from a neighborhood whose boundaries were under review, they were asked to designate some adjacent neighborhood to which the discarded territory could reasonably be assigned. The object of this procedure was to ensure that every residential area was included in some neighborhood, so that the sampling process could avoid the biases that would almost certainly result if socially incoherent or anonymous parts of the city were systematically excluded from consideration. But the effort to avoid these biases means, in principle, that an area that has no identity as a neighborhood may be incorporated into the territory of a more clearly defined community adjacent to it. Another possible effect of the procedure is to replace the vaguely defined borderlands or transition zones that people sometimes perceive between neighborhoods with sharp, unambiguous, and perhaps unrealistic boundaries.

In practice, neither of these problems appears to have been especially serious. Among the twenty neighborhoods originally sampled, only two presented difficulties of this kind. In one of these the recent construction of a large apartment complex within the traditional boundaries of an older neighborhood had apparently created disagreement about the correct definition of the community. Representatives of the older residents insisted that the apartments were not to be included in their neighborhood and that the apartment dwellers did not enjoy local citizenship, but they were unable to suggest any other neighborhood to which the apartments might be assigned. The City Council added its authority to the territorial disclaimers of the older residents when it declared their neighborhood a historic preservation district whose boundaries did not include the new apartments. It was therefore decided to regard the apartment complex as a separate neighborhood in its own right, and the original sample of twenty neighborhoods became a sample of twenty-one. Results of the household survey later supported this territorial partition. Among residents of the apartments, a majority of those interviewed called their neighborhood by the name of the apartment complex, not the more traditional name of the older neighborhood. In the apartment complex, 98 percent of the people interviewed were black; in the older portion of the area, 99 percent of the residents interviewed were white.

In a second case, the problem presented by unclaimed territory did not require such drastic action as the partition of an officially designated neighborhood. The difficulty was encountered along one boundary of a large residential area where the neighborhood verged on a deteriorating commercial strip. The leader of the only community association in the area and a district planner assigned to the area both agreed that the commercial strip and the residential blocks adjoining it should not be regarded as part of the sample neighborhood. The questionable corridor might easily have been regarded as a narrow zone of transition that did not belong to any neighborhood. But after additional discussions it became apparent that, although the area's identity was uncertain, most of it belonged less clearly to the sample neighborhood than to another community nearby. The borders of the sample neighborhood were adjusted accordingly. The entire region whose identity had been in question amounted to no more than a small fraction of the sample neighborhood's total area.

The method used for mapping neighborhoods created no sizable problems in practice, but it undoubtedly produced sharper geographic images of Baltimore's neighborhoods than most Baltimoreans have formed in their own minds. In fact, local residents do not envision their city's territory as a mosaic of spatially exhaustive and mutually exclusive neighborhoods. To some extent, therefore, the map of any sample neighborhood is an artifice created for the purposes of research, an unnaturally refined construct based largely on local public authorities' perception that a particular piece of territory may be regarded as a unit and its residents considered as a group. The artifice is necessary in order to ensure that every household in the city has some chance of being included within the scope of the investigation. It is also necessary in order to detach the definition of neighborhoods from the attitudes and activities of neighborhood residents, so that the task of examining neighborhood polities may be at least partly independent of the job of identifying the neighborhoods themselves. The two tasks cannot be entirely independent of each other, however. The political arrangements and activities that occur within a residential area must certainly have some influence on the likelihood that public authorities will perceive it as a distinct neighborhood. Moreover, neighborhood identity itself may legitimately be regarded as a political phenomenon, comparable to the sense of national identity in more conventional political systems.[74]

These conceptual impurities are unavoidable, but the practical harm that they do can at least be estimated by appealing to corroborative evidence about neighborhood identities. An initial test was to search the Baltimore telephone directory for business firms and public facilities like schools, libraries, and churches that bore the names of sample neighborhoods and then to see whether these firms and facilities fell within the boundaries of the neighborhoods after which they had been named. All of them did. Whether the neighborhoods that have been defined correspond to "real" neighborhoods of Baltimore is a question that will be raised at several points in this study. The chief test of their reality, of course, is the extent to which the existence of these unnaturally defined units is actually reflected in the conduct and attitudes of local residents.

Chapter 2 examines this question. It attempts to determine whether neighborhood environment has an impact on residents that can be distinguished from the influence of the residents' own personal characteristics — their ages, incomes, and levels of education, for example. The statistical technique used to separate the influence of the neighborhood from the effects of individual attributes may seem mysterious to nonspecialists. But the results it produces and their implications should be accessible to attentive readers who have never taken introductory statistics courses.

The remaining chapters employ more elementary techniques to examine particular components of the neighborhood polity. Chapter 3 is about the sense of neighborhood identity, the extent to which residents perceive that they live in an identifiable urban territory with its own name and boundaries. Such perceptions are fundamental to the emergence of political community. They designate a public space that residents occupy in common with their neighbors, and they help to define an arena for public action. Chapter 4 deals with two politically vital kinds of action. The first of these is the occurrence of informal deliberations about neighborhood issues among fellow residents; the second, unofficial efforts to handle these issues without "recurring to a pre-existing authority superior to that of the persons immediately concerned." The two sorts of behavior resemble the ones in which Tocqueville saw mirrored the legislative and executive powers of government.

More formal expressions of these powers — especially the "legislative" one — will be considered in Chapters 5 and 6. First to be examined is the participation of neighborhood residents in formal organizations that aggregate and articulate local public opinion and therefore attempt to provide the neighborhood with a collective voice. Finally, in Chapter 6, we will consider the efforts of such neighborhood institutions and their leaders to conduct diplomatic relations with the city and the state, bringing the "political society" of the neighborhood into direct contact with the official authority of legally constituted governments.

2.
Local Political Climates

O'Donnell Street, Canton. Photograph by Charlotte Crenson.

The force of memory is probably stronger in Canton than in most other neighborhoods of Baltimore. Local reliance on recollection began almost two hundred years ago when the area received its name. According to local tradition, a successful sea captain nearing the end of his career afloat settled on a large estate near the entrance to Baltimore's harbor and named the place after the Chinese port where he had taken on some of his most profitable cargoes.[1] Neighborhood reminiscences today are seldom so exotic as the captain's, but they are more widely shared — so widely, in fact, that some of the most tenacious carriers of neighborhood recollection live miles beyond the limits of Canton. They are people who grew up in the neighborhood but were scattered to the suburbs by postwar economic prosperity; now they maintain their local loyalties from a distance. Many of them come back to Canton each weekend to attend the churches in which they were confirmed as children. "The congregations used to live in Canton," explains one community activist, "but no longer live in Canton. They drive in on Sunday. And that's all they want their church to be — what it *used* to be . . . A lot of our problems are people with memories. They'll keep their parents' house vacant for thirty years because that's where they were born. They couldn't dare sell it. And we have an eyesore." Less mobile residents, left behind in Canton to cope with such problems, are sometimes just as firmly bound to their recollections as the emigrés: "They feel that the neighborhood has changed, and they feel that there's nothing they can do . . . It's gone. And they probably feel insecure or inferior in being able to solve the problems, so rather than attempt and failing at it, they just don't bother . . . Memories are killing us."

Before World War II the relative stability of Canton's population helped to create the circumstances in which a neighborhood might begin to store up its past. Between 1880 and 1930, when the decennial turnover rates for adult males in American cities ranged from 40 percent to 60 percent, the average rate of turnover for Canton was only 25 percent. Approximately three-quarters of the men who were living in Canton at the time of a national census could still be found there ten years later when the census-takers came again. The residents' tendency to remain rooted in their neighborhood almost certainly contributed to the development of neighborhood memory, and the tendency to stay put may have been encouraged in turn by industrial firms whose paternalistic policies helped to restrict the mobility of a skilled labor force.

Until the 1920s, in fact, the neighborhood bore some resemblance to a company town, though the sponsoring company was in real estate rather than in manufacturing.[2] An heir of the founding sea captain had joined several other businessmen in 1828 to organize the Canton Company, a partnership formed to develop his father's estate and some adjacent waterfront lands. Over several generations the company gradually sold off parcels of shoreline property for such enterprises as copper smelters, fertilizer plants, oil refineries, coal yards, and canneries. Meanwhile, the firm was also building houses a few blocks from the waterfront for the families of factory workers employed in these concerns, and it was acting jointly with the factory owners to provide community facilities like churches and a recreation center. But by the 1920s, says Randall Beirne, the regime of industrial paternalism had run its course. Canton's largest industries, along with many others in Baltimore, had passed to out-of-town owners, and leadership in matters of community welfare passed from local management to local trade unions.[3]

Later still, battered by the depression and uprooted by World War II, second- and third-generation Canton residents began to drift away from the neighborhood, and in 1960 the Canton Company itself became a subsidiary of a New York–based conglomerate. One local resident, the third generation of her family to occupy the same Canton rowhouse, was struck by the magnitude and suddenness of the neighborhood's postwar transformation when, in 1962, she helped to organize the twentieth reunion of her high school graduating class: "We wrote invitations to people in Guam, in Hong Kong, in Alaska, in Ethiopia, in Saudi Arabia . . . Those kids that had grown up in this blue-collar neighborhood would all have been somewhere in the Baltimore metropolitan area if we hadn't had a war . . . They would have been superintendents at Bethlehem Steel and Western Electric because they would have followed their fathers in the factory . . . But because of the War, all of those bright young men could go to college on the G.I. Bill, and they wound up all over the world." Such jarring contrasts between the former stability of Canton's population and its postwar mobility have left many local residents acutely sensitive to signs of social change in their community — more sensitive, perhaps, than the residents of neighborhoods where population change has actually been more pronounced but also more constant. Yet the wholesale exodus of longtime neighbors and the arrival of newcomers from Appalachia, the Midwest, and the Pennsylvania coalfields may also have obscured some impressive continuities in neighborhood life. In Canton even some of the most trivial and casual neighborhood customs have exhibited a remarkable persistence in the face of population change.

In 1899, for example, a neighborhood drifter planted six mulberry trees in a vacant lot on Clinton Street. The public-spirited vagrant moved on shortly after his act of philanthropy, and no one seems to have caught his name. But Canton residents called him Charlie-Got-Your-Shoes-On-Wrong.[4] Similar nicknames were still being used in Canton as much as seventy years after the departure of the tree-planting stranger. In 1971 a Baltimore newspaper reporter working on a story about the decline of neighborhood business on O'Donnell Street happened to interview a shop owner whose specialty was making and repairing venetian blinds. The proprietor was a Polish immigrant named Albert Nasdor, but Canton residents ignored his given name and called him Little Charlie. "When I came here," he explained, "if people didn't know your name, they called you 'Charlie.' Because of my size, I became 'Little Charlie,' and it stuck."[5]

Although no one can have had any particular interest in maintaining a standard system of nicknames for strangers to the neighborhood, a formula that seems to have originated sometime before the turn of the century was still being applied well into the 1970s. The customary practice for naming strangers may also have been adapted to some new uses. One community leader recalls that when she was growing up in the neighborhood during the 1950s, a local organization recruited Canton children each summer for campaigns to remove litter and trash from the blocks where they lived. They were called "Clean-Up Charlies."

Evidence of durability in neighborhood customs is not limited to such incidental matters as nicknames. A neighborhood's own name, for example, is likely to be more important to local residents than the names they bestow on strangers, and neighborhood names commonly outlast neighborhood populations. Canton's name has remained unchanged since the eighteenth century, although its population has been dominated successively by Welsh, Irish, and German immigrants and eventually came to include a large concentration of Poles. In Chicago a more comprehensive study of the persistence of neighborhood identities found that major population shifts had left most neighborhood names similarly unaffected over a stretch of almost fifty years.[6] The existence of such continuities in the social usages of urban neighborhoods lends at least some substance to the more general and uncertain impression that different neighborhoods tend to develop their own distinctive social climates or cultures — more lasting than any single group of residents — and that the social atmosphere of a neighborhood may tinge the attitudes and the behavior of its inhabitants.

Although it often seems merely a concession to local color, the recognition of distinct neighborhood cultures may also carry implications for the political status of an urban subcommunity. It calls attention not simply to the residual quaintness that has been accidentally preserved by cultural inertia but also to the broader possibility that the habits and customs of a neighborhood may amount to something more than we can explain by merely aggregating the individual social characteristics of its current residents. When the content of these collective habits and customs happens to be political, their presence suggests that "neighborhood" has ceased to be a politically neutral container for the civic pursuits of individual citizens. It is on its way to becoming a polity itself with its own distinct norms and practices. Once exposed to its influence, local residents no longer exhibit the political attitudes or behavior that might have been expected otherwise. They have become members of an emergent political society and not merely disconnected elements in a political aggregation.

Two Ideas of Political Culture in Neighborhoods

When neighborhoods have crossed the invisible boundary that separates political aggregations from "emergent political societies," we should be able to detect the influences of distinct community political climates or cultures among local residents. These influences are shadowy, of course, because the idea of neighborhood culture itself is so elusive and imprecise. In fact, it is two different ideas, either of which might conceivably tell us how to recognize the effects of neighborhood cultures when we see them. The first conception requires simply that we find differences in the political attitudes or behavior of people who live in different neighborhoods, even when the people in question are similar in their personal characteristics — their ages, incomes, educational levels, and so on. The implication here is that the political variations that cannot be attributed to differences between individuals must be due instead to the neighborhoods where they live. They are products of neighborhood political atmosphere or culture.

A second and more restrictive set of specifications for evidence about neighborhood culture requires, like the first, that similar kinds of people differ politically when they come from different neighborhoods. But it demands in addition that the neighborhoods themselves should be similar in social composition. The result of this added requirement is to exclude from the sphere of neighborhood political culture not only the political effects of one's own personal characteristics but also the political influences that are due to the aggregated personal attributes of one's neighbors. The political attitudes of two high-income persons may differ, for example, because one lives in a neighborhood where most of the residents have low incomes while the other lives surrounded by fellow rich people. Under the first and less restrictive set of specifications, this case would qualify as evidence for the political impact of neighborhood atmosphere or culture: similar types of people have diverged from one another politically because they live in different neighborhoods. Under the second and more demanding set of specifications, however, the example would be counted as evidence not for the impact of neighborhood culture but for the effects of neighborhood social composition.

When distinctive political beliefs or activities originate in the neighborhood's demographic composition, they may be said to reflect the collective impact of class or race or ethnicity rather than the influence of neighborhood itself. The political results that arise from the social constitution of the community might conceivably be altered by mere changes in the makeup of a neighborhood's population — unlike such enduring features of local culture as Canton's nicknames or its identity as Canton, which survived in spite of ethnic succession and postwar migrations. To avoid mistaking demographic effects for cultural effects, therefore, political disparities between the residents of different communities can be regarded as "cultural" variations only when the individual residents *and the neighborhoods as well* are demographically similar. Barred from consideration are both the political effects of each resident's individual attributes and the so-called compositional effects of the neighborhood's aggregate population makeup.[7]

There remains room to argue with this formulation. A neighborhood's social composition, after all, may be regarded as a neighborhood characteristic itself, and compositional effects might therefore deserve to be included among the distinctive results of neighborhood atmosphere. They are not simply the manifestations of societywide formations like class, race, and ethnicity but reflect the particular mixtures of classes, races, and ethnic groups in specific neighborhoods. Moreover, the occurrence of compositional effects in a neighborhood indicates that the social constitution of the community has left its mark on the individual residents. These effects represent the inhabitants' responses or reactions to the neighborhood environment and suggest that the neighborhood itself is not merely an aggregation of residents; rather, it is an operating subsociety whose members have begun to interact or adapt to one another. To set aside the political impact of neighborhood social composition as a mere by-product of class, race, or ethnicity may also place beyond our consideration some important signs of neighborhood political development — indications that a functioning political society has begun to emerge from a territorial assemblage of individual citizens.

The two sets of specifications for evidence about neighborhood political culture are clearly different from one another, yet neither is clearly implausible, and there seems no obvious way to reconcile them. The difficulty of combining the two positions may arise in part from the fact that they rest on two fundamentally different conceptions of neighborhood phenomena. The more restrictive view sees the neighborhood as a residual phenomenon that does not stand on the same footing as other social formations like class or race or family. Instead, it is simply the geographic playing field on which these other social elements meet and interact with one another. The shape, location, and internal life of the neighborhood are all consequences of this process of interaction, but the process itself is not a neighborhood phenomenon; it is only a specific manifestation of some more general process that operates in the society at large. The nature of this general social process has been variously described. In some formulations, the blending of classes, races, and ethnic groups within neighborhoods is simply a secondary consequence of the urban land market as it allocates the geographic zones of the city to their most profitable uses;[8] in other versions, the dynamic of "increasing scale" that accompanies urbanization and industrialization also helps to explain the spatial differentiation of the population;[9] and in still other accounts, it is the process of capitalist exploitation and accumulation that distributes groups and classes among residential areas.[10] However conceived, this larger social process is seen as providing the chief motive force that creates, sustains, and destroys neighborhoods. It is responsible for generating the mixtures of social classes, housing types, races, and family structures that occur in different neighborhoods. The "compositional effects" that result from these varying social mixtures should therefore be attributed to the operation of the larger social process and not to the influence of neighborhood atmosphere or culture.

In fact, once the operation of society's "macroforces" has been taken into account, very little remains to be included within the ambit of neighborhood culture. When neighborhood phenomena are seen as end-products of societywide processes, observes Albert Hunter, neighborhoods themselves appear merely as "residues and repositories" — social dependencies without lives of their own. This perspective yields the dismal view that "the mills of the modern city, driven either by the 'natural' winds of the ecologists, or by the engines and machinery of industrial capitalism, will continue to grind to dust the whims and wishes of local neighborhood residents." Hunter adds, however, that a "more complete dialectic . . . would entertain the possibility that these forces would produce a dust out of which would rise new neighborhood forms and countervailing local forces."[11]

In a sense, Hunter has reintroduced neighborhood social composition as a possible source of neighborhood political atmosphere or culture. Though outside forces may create and recreate the social mixture of a community, the mixture itself may occasion mutual adaptations among local residents, which in turn give rise to modifications in political outlook or conduct and signal that the neighborhood has come to life as a functioning subsociety whose distinctive political tendencies can react on the very "macroforces" that brought it into being. Hunter's description of the process as a dialectic is an appropriate one, and it recalls Gerald Suttles's account of the "ongoing commentary" between neighborhood residents and external institutions through which urban communities tend to develop their distinctive identities. In both cases there is the same pattern of reciprocal influence between the internal life of the neighborhood and the life of the society beyond its boundaries, and the pattern appears again in the two sets of specifications for evidence about neighborhood political culture.

One set — the more restrictive — reflects an effort to assimilate neighborhood phenomena to a more general framework in which the entire society or the entire city serves as the primary unit of analysis, the focal organism from which description and explanation both take their bearings. This is a view that naturally tends to regard the residential community not as a living creature but as an ordered assortment of social objects grouped together by the neighborhood-shaping forces of a larger society. By contrast, the second set of requirements for evidence about neighborhood culture reflects the adoption of a vantage point that lies within the neighborhood itself. These specifications attempt to capture the distinctive mutual adjustments and adaptations among the various elements in a neighborhood's social assortment. It is a view that emphasizes the "horizontal" connections among local residents rather than the vertical relations linking the neighborhood to the more inclusive institutions of a wider society. It considers the neighborhood as a functioning social unit and not as an inventory of social ingredients assembled according to a recipe drawn up by the society's "macroforces."

Identifying the Influence of Neighborhood Environment

The two types of specifications reflect different but essentially complementary perspectives on neighborhood phenomena. Instead of discarding one view and embracing the other, it will be useful to retain both of them as counterpoised devices for putting the notion of neighborhood political culture to the test. The test itself requires that we should find political variations between people from different neighborhoods, and that these variations should persist even when the people themselves are similar in their own personal characteristics — or when the neighborhoods as well are similar in social composition.

Neither version of the proposed test specifies just what kinds of social similarities must be established before we can isolate the political effects of neighborhood atmosphere or culture. But the nature of these resemblances is implicit in the purpose of the test itself. In general, we should require similarity in those family and personal characteristics that seem to explain why people have distributed themselves in different neighborhoods in the first place.

The factors that lead people to live in different neighborhoods may also lead them toward different kinds of political attitudes or activities. We cannot regard these political variations as consequences of the diversity in neighborhood culture because these are the differences that would probably distinguish people from one another no matter where they happened to live. High-income people, for example, tend to live in different neighborhoods from low-income people, but this does not mean that all of the political variations between rich people and poor people arise from their exposure to different neighborhood environments. The political differences that are associated with variations in income are likely to distinguish a rich family from a poor one even before their furniture is unloaded from the moving van. As a rule, after all, people are not rich because they live in certain neighborhoods; rather, they live in certain neighborhoods because they are rich. And the political predispositions that result from being rich are therefore unlikely to have arisen from the distinctive atmosphere of the neighborhood.

Income, of course, is not the only social characteristic that must be taken into account. As we look for the impact of neighborhood political culture, we should attempt in general to control for the political effects of all the demographic attributes that help to explain the differentiation of the city's population into neighborhood or subarea populations. After discounting the effects of the factors that govern the distribution of people among their current neighborhoods, we can be reasonably certain that whatever variations remain are the results of neighborhood environment itself — not the reflections of the family and individual attributes that regulate the creation of neighborhood environments.

The unwieldy task of controlling for all these attributes is made more manageable by the fact that a coherent course of social research, pursued for more than thirty years, has already attempted to identify the underlying elements that account for the differentiation of cities into distinct "social areas." In the early formulation of Shevky and Bell, based on an analysis of census tract data, there were three of these differentiating factors, each of which was a composite of two or more census measures. Shevky and Bell designated these factors "social rank," "segregation," and "urbanization." In other words, their statistical analysis indicated that urban census tracts tended to differ from one another along three dimensions that reflected the social status of their populations, their racial and ethnic composition, and a combination of family and life-cycle characteristics that Shevky and Bell chose to characterize as "urbanization." When considered together, the three basic types of social differentiation were said to account almost entirely for all the variations in census characteristics between subarea populations.[12] Shevky and Bell also suggested that the explanatory implications of their three factors might extend as well to variations in local subcultures. Their claim was that "the social area generally contains persons having the same level of living, the same way of life, and the same ethnic background; and we hypothesize that persons living in a particular type of social area would systematically differ with respect to characteristic attitudes and behaviors from persons living in another type of social area."[13]

Though some questions have been raised concerning the internal homogeneity of social areas, the most controversial aspect of the three-factor classification system proposed by Shevky and Bell has been the theory of social change in which it was packaged. Each of the three dimensions of neighborhood differentiation was related to an axis of movement in the larger society. The differentiation of residential areas according to social status, for example, was said to reflect a shift in the occupational structure toward clerical and managerial jobs, which led in turn to increased diversity in social rank. Ethnic and racial segregation reflected the mobility of the modern population, which brought "alien" groups into the midst of a native population, where those people with similar origins tended to be spatially isolated from other social groups. Finally, neighborhood variations in family structure were related to a general movement from primary industries to secondary and tertiary production, which had drawn increased numbers of people into cities. In cities they developed characteristically "urban" styles of family life, distinguished, for example, by relatively high proportions of women who were childless and who participated in the work force.[14]

What Shevky and Bell have provided, in short, is an account of the neighborhood-shaping forces that operate in the society at large—one example of the theoretical perspective that views the neighborhood as a by-product of intersecting macroforces. What the account lacks, according to its critics, is a satisfactory explanation of the logical step by which a group of interrelated social trends can be translated into three independent dimensions of neighborhood differentiation.[15] The theory's logical shortcomings, however, appear not to have done any serious damage to the empirical findings around which it was woven. Although the advent of high-speed computers has helped to replace the methods of social area analysis with the more sophisticated techniques of "factorial ecology," the results of most recent research continue to point toward the same underlying dimensions of social differentiation among urban residential areas.[16]

These neighborhood-defining factors are the elements that need to be taken into account before we can distinguish the impact of neighborhood environments from the effects of other things. To identify the impact of neighborhood political culture, we must be able to show that political variations between the residents of different neighborhoods cannot be explained away as reflections of the personal characteristics that put them into different neighborhoods to begin with. To some extent, we must demonstrate that they have become different sorts of people because they live in different neighborhoods, and not that they live in different neighborhoods because they are people of different sorts. Shevky and Bell, along with their many successors, have identified the key attributes that seem to account for the fact that people live in different neighborhoods. By controlling statistically for the effects of these characteristics, we should be able to observe the difference that exposure to "neighborhood" itself has made for the political activities and attitudes of local residents.

The personal attributes to be taken into account here were selected to approximate as closely as possible the census characteristics identified by Shevky and Bell. As a measure of social rank, an index was employed that combined information about a respondent's family income, education, and occupational status.[17] As indicators of the "segregation" factor defined by social area analysis, the current investigation relied on the respondent's race and self-reported ethnic identification.[18] Corresponding to the family and life-cycle characteristics that Shevky and Bell included under the heading of "urbanization" were several other items: type of dwelling unit, presence of children in the respondent's household, and presence of women who participated in the work force. Although it was not included in the scheme proposed by Shevky and Bell, age of respondent was also taken into account.[19] When we control for all of these characteristics, it is as though we were comparing the attitudes and activities of people who come from different neighborhoods but are similar in age, race, and ethnic identification and live in households similar in socioeconomic status, dwelling type, childcare responsibilities, and female participation in the work force.

Controlled statistical comparisons of this sort will be made among the respondents in a probability sample of 1,637 residents from the twenty-one neighborhoods of Baltimore that were chosen for the current investigation. In effect, these statistical comparisons will be used to find out how much of the variation in the respondents' attitudes and activities can be attributed to the fact that they live in different neighborhoods and how much of this variation can be explained away by the fact that they differ from one another in their personal characteristics. The type of analysis used here is nearly identical to the kind employed by Schuman and Gruenberg in a study that attempted to identify the impact of city (rather than neighborhood) on people's racial attitudes while controlling for the effects of personal attributes.[20] The approach treats the neighborhood in which a person lives as a variable like any other — in this case, a variable that can assume twenty-one different values. When this variable is entered into a multiple regression equation following all the other social attributes that have been enumerated, the results indicate what proportion of the variance in a particular kind of attitude or activity can be explained by neighborhood itself — once the effects of people's personal characteristics have already been taken into account. Later, we can also consider how much of the variance in the behavior and opinions of Baltimoreans must be attributed to the social composition of their neighborhoods rather than to neighborhood itself.

Several different sorts of attitudes, activities, and perceptions are examined here. Some of them are not necessarily endowed with political content at all; they refer to private exchanges or merely social interaction among neighbors. Others are actions or opinions whose political character is acknowledged as a matter of convention. They have to do with such things as voting in elections or contacting government officials. Finally, there are types of conduct or beliefs that would probably qualify as political only by the standards of the present study. They have to do with local residents' efforts to carry on the deliberative or executive business of a neighborhood polity. Items of all three kinds have been considered together so that it would be possible to see whether the explanatory importance of "neighborhood" is concentrated in any particular area of activity.

The actions, attitudes, and perceptions to be explained are ranked and listed along the left edge of Table 2.1. The percentage figure in column 1 is the total proportion of the variance in each item that was explained by neighborhood, before controlling for the social characteristics of the respondents. In column 2 is the percentage of the variance accounted for collectively by the seven personal and household characteristics discussed above — age, race, socioeconomic status, ethnic identification, dwelling type, childcare responsibility, and the presence of female labor-force participants in the respondent's household. The percentage figure in column 3 indicates the total variance explained by neighborhood and the personal attributes put together, and the entry in column 4 — perhaps the most important for our purposes — shows how much of the variance can be attributed to the influence of neighborhood *after* the effects of the seven personal characteristics have been removed.

A comparable figure for the personal attributes appears in column 5 — the percentage of variance accounted for by these individual characteristics after the effects of neighborhood have been removed. A comparison of this proportion with the percentage of variance uniquely attributable to neighborhood (column 4) indicates something about the balance of explanatory forces operating for each item in the table — whether a particular attitude or activity is more a reflection of the respondents' individual characteristics or of the neighborhood environments to which they have been exposed. The relative weights of the two factors have been taken into account in ordering the items that are listed in Table 2.1. The variables were first ranked according to the explanatory importance of neighborhood effects alone, indicated by the percentage figure in column 4. But if two or more variables proved to be equally sensitive to the influence of neighborhood environment, then the ranking took account of the balance between the effects of neighborhood and the impact of personal attributes. In such cases, variables were ordered according to the size of the ratio between "neighborhood" variance and variance attributed to social characteristics, so that items for which neighborhood was a relatively important factor take precedence, with the explanatory balance shifting toward personal attributes for the variables that follow. In general, a variable's position in the table is an indication of its susceptibility to neighborhood effects, the influence of neighborhood environment being more prominent for items at the beginning of the table than for those toward the end.

The last column of the table introduces an additional factor to be considered in gauging the impact of neighborhood culture. The entry here indicates how much of the variance in each item was explained jointly by both neighborhood and the seven individual attributes. In effect, the size of this figure shows how much explanatory overlap there is between the two types of factors. It

Table 2.1. Comparison of neighborhood and individual attribute effects on attitudes and activities

Var. rank	Variable description	(1) % variance explained by neighborhood	(2) % variance explained by personal attributes	(3) % total variance explained by neighborhood and personal attributes	(4) % net variance explained by neighborhood after removing personal attributes	(5) % net variance explained by personal attributes after removing neighborhood	(6) % variance explained jointly
1.	Gives "standard" name of neighborhood.	20.2	8.8	21.6	12.8	1.4	7.4
2.	Thinks neighborhood streets are safe at night.	13.4	4.0	16.0	12.0	2.6	1.4
3.	Thinks neighborhood is one of more interesting places to live in city.	15.8	8.7	18.9	10.2	3.1	5.6
4.	Thinks neighborhood has name.	28.6	23.5	33.3	9.8	4.7	18.8
5.	Is satisfied with city garbage collection.	12.0	4.9	14.4	9.5	2.4	3.0
6.	Thinks parents can depend on neighbors to keep children from getting into trouble.	11.1	4.4	12.4	8.0	1.3	3.1
7.	Thinks a lot of people in neighborhood clean up trash, even when not on their own property.	8.0	1.6	8.8	7.2	0.8	0.8

8.	Belongs to organization that works on neighborhood problems.	21.8	25.9	33.1	7.2	11.3	14.6
9.	Thinks neighbors spend too much time minding other people's business.	12.7	8.1	15.2	7.1	2.5	5.6
10.	Thinks ethnic groups are important in neighborhood.	11.1	5.4	12.2	6.8	1.1	4.3
11.	Thinks there are some real leaders in neighborhood.	7.3	3.1	9.8	6.7	2.5	0.6
12.	Thinks a lot of neighbors don't get along.	10.6	5.5	11.9	6.4	1.3	4.2
13.	Thinks a lot of people in neighborhood visit elderly residents to see if they need anything.	9.8	3.7	10.0	6.3	0.2	3.5
14.	Thinks neighbors would get together to solve neighborhood problems among themselves.	6.8	3.4	9.6	6.2	2.8	0.6
15.	Thinks neighbors would put pressure on resident whose house or yard became run-down.	8.9	3.8	9.9	6.1	1.0	2.8
16.	Thinks noisy neighbors would quiet down if asked.	7.5	3.6	9.1	5.5	1.6	2.0

Table 2.1, *continued*

Var. Rank	Variable description	(1) % variance explained by neighborhood	(2) % variance explained by personal attributes	(3) % total variance explained by neighborhood and personal attributes	(4) % net variance explained by neighborhood after removing personal attributes	(5) % net variance explained by personal attributes after removing neighborhood	(6) % variance explained jointly
17.	Knows of local organization that works on neighborhood problems.	11.0	16.9	22.4	5.5	11.4	5.5
18.	Has tried to stop neighborhood children from doing something they shouldn't.	8.3	5.2	10.5	5.3	2.2	3.0
19.	Thinks most people who live in neighborhood are good neighbors.	10.1	7.1	12.0	4.9	1.9	5.2
20.	Thinks more friends live inside neighborhood than outside.	9.4	10.0	14.9	4.9	5.5	4.5
21.	Thinks people in neighborhood are very friendly.	5.4	3.5	7.6	4.1	2.2	1.3
22.	Has talked about neighborhood needs or problems with other residents.	5.4	8.5	12.6	4.1	7.2	1.3

23.	Thinks churches and church groups are important in neighborhood.	6.4	11.5	4.0	15.5	9.1	2.4
24.	Thinks a lot of people in neighborhood try to prevent crime by keeping an eye on strangers.	8.4	6.4	3.9	10.3	1.9	4.5
25.	Names one specific boundary of neighborhood.	8.0	7.6	3.9	11.5	3.5	4.1
26.	Is satisfied with police protection in neighborhood.	4.6	2.8	3.8	6.6	7.0	0.8
27.	Has contacted formal community organization about a neighborhood problem.	6.0	9.3	3.8	13.1	7.1	2.2
28.	Thinks people who run local businesses are important in neighborhood.	5.2	3.5	3.4	6.9	1.7	1.8
29.	Has been annoyed at something that neighbors did.	3.0	5.0	3.4	8.4	5.4	-0.4
30.	Took direct action with neighbors to solve local problem on their own.	2.7	4.0	3.3	7.3	4.7	-0.9

Table 2.1, *continued*

Var. Rank	Variable description	(1) % variance explained by neighborhood	(2) % variance explained by personal attributes	(3) % total variance explained by neighborhood and personal attributes	(4) % net variance explained by neighborhood after removing personal attributes	(5) % net variance explained by personal attributes after removing neighborhood	(6) % variance explained jointly
31.	Thinks a lot of residents try to keep neighborhood children from getting into trouble.	4.8	3.1	6.3	3.2	1.5	1.6
32.	Has argued with a neighbor.	4.2	4.7	7.9	3.2	3.7	1.0
33.	Has contacted city official about problem in neighborhood.	6.1	13.3	16.5	3.2	10.4	2.9
34.	Thinks politicians and political organizations are important in neighborhood.	3.0	0.9	4.0	3.1	1.0	-0.1
35.	Has worked with neighbors to improve appearance of street.	4.4	7.2	9.9	2.7	5.5	1.7
36.	Has kept an eye on neighbors' homes when they were away.	5.0	8.8	11.3	2.5	6.3	2.5
37.	Has visited inside a neighbor's home.	6.3	8.0	9.6	1.6	3.3	4.7

38.	Usually votes in state and local elections.	12.6	23.0	25.4	2.4	12.8	8.2
39.	Has talked to others about voting for particular candidates or party.	5.1	6.8	9.0	2.2	3.9	2.9
40.	Thinks most people on block are personal friends.	4.6	6.0	2.0	3.4	2.6	
41.	Has borrowed tools or household items from neighbors.	5.8	14.3	16.3	2.0	10.5	3.8
42.	Is satisfied with public schools that serve neighborhood.	6.0	15.1	17.1	2.0	11.1	4.0
43.	Has run shopping errand for neighbor.	2.6	2.6	4.4	1.8	1.8	0.8
44.	Has tried to settle disagreement between two neighbors.	2.2	3.0	4.6	1.6	2.4	0.6
45.	Has discussed personal problems with a neighbor.	2.3	2.6	2.9	1.3	0.6	-1.0
46.	Thinks people like self have lots of influence in local government decisions.	3.6	5.6	6.8	1.2	3.2	2.4
47.	Voted in presidential election of 1976.	7.6	17.7	18.6	0.9	11.0	4.7

reflects situations in which individual characteristics and neighborhood characteristics are so closely associated that their respective effects cannot be separated from one another. Baltimore's neighborhoods, for example, differ sharply in racial composition, and the race of the individual respondents also turns out to be associated with sharp variations in attitudes and perceptions. Black residents were much less likely than whites to think that their neighborhoods had names, for instance. But since racial segregation helps to assure that most black Baltimoreans live in predominantly black residential areas, it is difficult to know whether they were disinclined to assign names to their home territories because they were black or because they lived in black neighborhoods. Perhaps it was a combination of both factors. That is, the effects of both neighborhood composition and individual characteristics may operate together to leave black residential areas unnamed. Subsequent analysis of compositional effects in neighborhoods may help to clarify situations such as these. In the meantime, it is worth noting that the variance jointly explained by neighborhood and individual characteristics tends to be relatively small, usually less than the variance explained by neighborhood alone. But whenever this jointly explained variance becomes substantial by comparison with the variance attributed to neighborhood alone, our assessment of neighborhood effects should naturally take it into account.

Two sorts of issues are at stake in this assessment. First, the evidence carries implications for the explanatory importance of neighborhood culture or climate. It can indicate the extent to which people's conduct or opinions are accounted for not by their own personal characteristics but by the characteristics of the neighborhood environment to which they have been exposed. Second, apart from revealing the explanatory importance of these neighborhood effects, the statistical evidence can also suggest what kinds of effects they are, what sorts of attitudes and activities seem most sensitive to the influence of the neighborhood.

Concerning the importance of neighborhood effects, the assessment clearly depends on the standard used. If the criterion is merely statistical significance, then the variance attributed to neighborhood alone (column 4) is important for every one of the forty-seven items listed in Table 2.1. The large size of the sample ensures that even very small fragments of explained variance can be endowed with significance of a technical sort. Another possible criterion is supplied by Schuman and Gruenberg's study of "city effects" in people's racial attitudes. On the whole, the variance explained as an effect of city in their research is smaller than the variance explained as an effect of neighborhood in the present investigation. The fact that the two studies are concerned with variables of very different kinds, however, introduces a serious complication into any attempt to weigh neighborhood effects against city effects.

A more straightforward evaluation of neighborhood effects might begin with the observation that for a dozen of the variables considered—more than one-fourth of all those listed—the total variance explained by neighborhood (column 1) is greater than 10 percent, a large proportion of variance by almost any standard. In three of these cases, the variance explained by neighborhood continues to exceed 10 percent even after the effects of the respondents' personal attributes have been taken into account (items 1, 2, and 3), and in two other instances (items 4 and 5) the figure falls just shy of 10 percent. By this rough rule of thumb, it appears, at least a handful of the items considered would deserve to be regarded as illustrations of the substantial impact that neighborhood environment can have upon local residents.

Perhaps more useful and discriminating than an arbitrary rule of thumb is a comparison between the variance attributed to neighborhood alone (column 4) and the net variance explained by the seven personal attributes (column 5). The results indicate that for more than half of the variables listed (twenty-five of forty-seven), neighborhood by itself accounts for a higher proportion of the variance than all seven social characteristics put together. In fact, when the variance attributed to personal characteristics is added to the jointly explained variance, the sum is still surpassed in eighteen cases by the variance attributed to neighborhood alone. As an explanatory factor, in other words, neighborhood environment seems more than able to hold its own against the collective weight of such variables as individual age, race, ethnicity, and socioeconomic status—explanatory factors that have been the stock-in-trade for social and political analysis.

Its impressive impact may have something to do, of course, with the kinds of factors being explained. The influence of neighborhood environment is readily understandable for items that reflect the residents' evaluations or impressions of the areas where they live. These are precisely the cases, after all, in which they have been asked to reveal the impact of their surroundings. The ranking of variables in Table 2.1 shows that items of this kind generally stood toward the top of the list, indicating that the respondents' perceptions of their neighborhoods were usually more sensitive to the influence of community environment than were their reports of their own conduct, which are concentrated disproportionately in the second half of the table. In this respect, the results parallel those of Schuman and Gruenberg, who found that city effects become most evident when respondents were asked to evaluate city officials and city services, and less evident when they were asked questions about themselves. The pattern is underlined, in the present case, by a comparison of "neighborhood" variance (column 4) and variance attributable to personal characteristics (column 5). The evidence indicates that neighborhood effects were always more prominent than the effects of individual attributes when the respondents were expressing their opinions of neighbors and neighborhood. But when they were reporting their own conduct the reverse was true. People's personal attributes, not surprisingly, seem to be reflected to a greater extent in their own personal activities than in their impressions of the neighborhood surrounding them.

Within the framework of this overall pattern a few other regularities emerge. Some of these general tendencies become evident if we temporarily put aside the items in which the respondents reported on their own activities and consider instead the instances in which they expressed their opinions and beliefs about their fellow residents or communities. With a few exceptions these "perceptual" items are confined to the first half of Table 2.1, and the ranking of the variables here suggests that the perception of a community's name was more susceptible to neighborhood effects than other kinds of perceptions. The impact of the neighborhood environment was most prominent in determining whether or not respondents used the official name for their community (item 1), and it became only a little less important when they were asked whether their residential area had any name at all (item 4).[21] In short, the sense of neighborhood identity seems to reflect local culture or atmosphere more than it does the social attributes of the individual residents. The evidence in this case recalls the staying power of community identity in Canton through successive waves of foreign immigration, and it is consistent also with the previous findings about the durability of neighborhood names in Chicago. To the extent that neighborhood phenomena are not simply products of the local residents' personal characteristics, we can expect them to be relatively invulnerable to changes in the residential population.

Apart from its importance in explaining whether residents knew the name of their community, neighborhood environment also had a distinctive kind of influence on their images of the places where they lived. In general, neighborhood effects were more important in people's perceptions of their community's political order than they were in the residents' views about its status as a fellowship of private solidarity. Among the items ranked in Table 2.1, for example, the impression that people in the neighborhood were very friendly stood in twenty-first place. Only one rank higher than this was the respondents' impression that more of their friends lived inside the neighborhood than outside, and far behind this in the rankings was their declaration that they regarded most of the people who lived on the same block as personal friends (item 40). Neighborhood effects are less substantial in all of these questions of private friendship than they are for most of the respondents' opinions about their communities' unofficial public services and politics—the perception, for example, that the neighbors voluntarily handled matters of public sanitation (item 7), or the expectation that they would keep neighborhood children under surveillance (item 6), or the belief that the community had its own leaders (item 11). In fact, there were only two instances in which people's perceptions of neighborhood public services were outranked by any of their reports of private friendship (items 24 and 31). Even in these two cases, the residents' opinions about unofficial public services were more sensitive to the influence of the neighborhood environment than to the effects of the respondents' personal attributes, and in both instances neighborhood effects weighed more heavily in the explanatory balance than they did for any of the items having to do with personal friendship.

Though the pattern is only roughly defined in the evidence, its general outline should be apparent. When viewing their neighbors' efforts to provide informally for the public welfare, public health, and public order of the community, people are relatively sensitive to the influence of the neighborhood environment. When people are evaluating the private friendliness or general sociability of their neighbors, on the other hand, the balance of explanatory importance shifts toward the personal characteristics of the individual respondents themselves, and neighborhood effects, though not always negligible, become less notable by comparison. Occupying an intermediate position between the highest-ranking reports of public service and the lower-ranking impressions of private friendship are a few broadly drawn items that may embrace both sorts of phenomena—the belief, for example, that most people in the area are "good neighbors" (item 19) and the opinion that there is friction or conflict in the community (item 12). Taken altogether, the evidence implies that neighborhood culture or climate may have a particular impact on people's conceptions about the political status of their community — its informal executive power to produce its own public goods and services. Somewhat less affected by the local atmosphere are people's views of the neighborhood as a network of private social relations or friendships.

The distinctively political impact of neighborhood atmosphere becomes evident again when respondents' reports of their own activities are considered. Most of the items having to do with the respondents' own conduct appear in the second half of Table 2.1, reflecting the fact that neighborhood environment tends to be less important for explaining the personal activities of Baltimoreans than for understanding their beliefs and opinions about the conduct or character of their fellow residents. Two things are worth noting about these reports of personal activity. First, conventional political behavior aimed at institutions outside the neighborhood seems relatively immune to the influence of community climate or culture. Voting in local elections (item 38) or in national elections (item 47) or contacting city officials about neighborhood problems (item 33) — these forms of political conduct can be explained far more effectively by referring to the personal attributes of the respondents than by looking at the character of the neighborhoods where they lived. More susceptible to the influence of the neighborhood environment are a number of unofficial actions designed to keep the neighborhood clean or safe or orderly — trying to police the conduct of neighborhood children (item 18), for example, and talking with neighbors about community problems (item 22). Neighborhood is also a relatively important explanatory factor in membership in a community organization (item 8), but here its effects, though substantial, are outweighed by the impact of the respondents' personal attributes (compare columns 4 and 5).

While the two types of political activity do not stand at clearly separate levels in the ranking of behavioral items, the importance of neighborhood as an explanatory factor was generally somewhat greater when respondents were conducting the internal political business of their communities than it was when they engaged in more "official" political actions directed at external government institutions. Consistent with this admittedly uncertain pattern of neighborhood effects is the fact that the respondents' own impressions of their influence in government decisions (item 46) were much more a product of individual characteristics than of neighborhood environment.

There may also be a second and more definite inference that we can draw from the ordering of the behavioral items in Table 2.1. Like the respondents' perceptions of their neighbors' conduct, their reports of their own activities indicate that the explanatory impact of community environment may be greater for unofficial efforts at public service than for merely private exchanges with friends or personal socializing with neighbors. In fact, neighborhood effects were more notable for almost all reports of public service activities than for the respondents' accounts of such private interchanges as neighborly borrowing (item 41), social visits in the homes of fellow residents (item 37), and discussions of personal problems with neighbors (item 45).

Along with other regularities in the evidence, this pattern of neighborhood influence in the respondents' activities suggests that neighborhood culture has a distinctly political flavor. In people's perceptions, the explanatory impact of neighborhood itself was more pronounced for views about the public service activities of fellow residents than for opinions about their private sociability or friendliness. The same pattern is echoed in the respondents' accounts of their own activities. They were more susceptible to neighborhood effects in their political behavior — especially their unofficial efforts to provide public services for their communities — than they were in exchanges of private favors with fellow residents or acts of personal friendship toward neighbors.

As with the awareness of a community's name, the attitudes and activities that reflect a neighborhood's political status are manifestations of local culture or atmosphere. They cannot be explained away be referring to the personal attributes of individual residents because they are the results of living in a particular neighborhood and not just the effects of being a particular sort of person. Some neighborhoods, it appears, simply have more fully developed identities than others, and residents of these areas are more likely than people elsewhere to know the names of their respective communities, no matter what their personal characteristics may be. Similarly, some neighborhoods are more fully developed as unofficial polities than others, and the political vitality of these communities is evident in the behavior and perceptions of their residents, no matter what sorts of people they are. This is one respect in which the signs of neighborhood political life are different from the indications of private solidarity among neighbors. Personal friendship and sociability are less the result of living in a certain neighborhood than of having certain individual characteristics. On the whole, neighborhood effects are more clearly responsible for variations in the political status of communities than for differences in personal relationships among residents. The evidence, in other words, helps to reveal not only the substantial influence of neighborhood itself on individual attitudes and activities but also the character of neighborhoods as public associations — political societies whose participants are more like fellow citizens than like members of a private social group. Once the personal characteristics of city residents have been taken into account, the difference that it makes to live in one neighborhood rather than another is a difference of a distinctly political kind. It has to do with the varying abilities of neighborhoods to establish themselves as domains of public endeavor.

The Experience of Place and Its Political Impact

Even when they are similar in their personal characteristics, residents of different neighborhoods exhibit different political attitudes and engage in different sorts of political activities. Yet these political variations may still reflect differences in people's class or demographic characteristics. They cannot be explained away by referring to the attributes of the individual residents themselves, perhaps, but they could certainly be related to the aggregated characteristics of the neighbors who surround these residents. People of all sorts may be more likely to police the activities of neighborhood children, for example, if they happen to live in a community where children are relatively plentiful. This propensity to defend neighborhood tranquillity and order against juvenile barbarism or high spirits may have nothing at all to do with the individual characteristics of the defenders or their households. Instead, it might have to be explained by referring to the social composition of the neighborhood as a whole — in particular, the proportion of the local population that consists of children.

From one perspective, such effects of the neighborhood's social composition deserve to be considered as aspects of a distinctive community culture: they represent the adaptations that individual residents have made to the character of the neighborhood itself. From another perspective, of course, they are not really neighborhood phenomena at all but merely artifacts of its demographic makeup. The distinctive conduct and temperament of the neighborhood disciplinarian who keeps local children under surveillance cannot be regarded as a mark of community culture because these habits may not be internalized or transmitted to other carriers of local tradition. After all, if the guardians of community decorum were to move to another neighborhood—one with fewer children—they might immediately abandon the supposed cultural traits.

Whether they are regarded as cultural traits or temporary adjustments to the social circumstances, the effects of neighborhood social composition can help to clarify the nature of the influence that neighborhoods have on the attitudes and activities of their residents. They suggest one possible line of explanation for the neighborhood effects that we have already observed: the residents of different communities have different impressions of their fellow residents simply because they have been observing people with different sorts of social characteristics. And they vary in their behavioral responses to the neighborhood environment because they are responding to different sorts of populations.

The evidence presented in Table 2.2 indicates how far this line of explanation can be carried in accounting for the impact of the neighborhood itself. In effect, the analysis of the data in Table 2.1 has been taken a step further. In Table 2.2 we can see what impact may be attributed to the influence of the neighborhood environment after removing not only the effects of the respondents' own personal characteristics but also the compositional effects that arise from the social makeup of the neighborhoods where they live. Besides controlling for the age of each respondent, for example, we have taken into account the median age of the people living in each respondent's neighborhood. The racial composition of the neighborhood, in addition to the respondent's own race, has been considered. In short, the evidence in Table 2.2 shows what remains of neighborhood effects after we have eliminated the influence of the same seven individual attributes that we considered earlier along with the effects of a comparable set of neighborhood attributes—median age of the local residents, racial composition, median socioeconomic status, ethnic composition, percentage of single-family dwellings, proportion of households with children, and percentage of households that include women who have paying jobs.

The variables listed on the left side of Table 2.2 are the same ones that were considered in Table 2.1, and the items are presented in the same rank order. The percentage figure in column 1 shows how much of the variance in each of the variables listed could be accounted for by the personal attributes of the individual respondents together with the aggregated attributes of the neighbors who surrounded them. The entry in column 2 shows what proportion of

Table 2.2. Comparison of neighborhood and social composition effects on attitudes and activities

Var. rank	Variable description	(1) % variance explained by individual attributes and social composition	(2) % net variance explained by social composition after removing individual attributes	(3) % net variance explained by neighborhood after removing individual attributes and social composition
1.	Gives "standard" name of neighborhood.	14.5	5.7	7.1
2.	Thinks neighborhood streets are safe at night.	10.8	6.9	5.3
3.	Thinks neighborhood is one of more interesting places to live in city.	13.1	4.4	5.8
4.	Thinks neighborhood has name.	29.0	5.5	4.3
5.	Is satisfied with city garbage collection.	9.7	4.8	4.6
6.	Thinks parents can depend on neighbors to keep children from getting into trouble.	9.1	4.7	3.3
7.	Thinks a lot of people in neighborhood clean up trash, even when not on their own property.	5.7	4.1	3.1
8.	Belongs to organization that works on neighborhood problems.	29.1	3.2	4.0
9.	Thinks neighbors spend too much time minding other people's business.	11.8	3.7	3.4
10.	Thinks ethnic groups are important in neighborhood.	8.7	3.3	3.4
11.	Thinks there are some real leaders in neighborhood.	4.8	1.7	4.9

Table 2.2, *continued*

Var. rank	Variable description	(1) % variance explained by individual attributes and social composition	(2) % net variance explained by social composition after removing individual attributes	(3) % net variance explained by neighborhood after removing individual attributes and social composition
12.	Thinks a lot of neighbors don't get along.	9.0	3.5	2.9
13.	Thinks a lot of people in neighborhood visit elderly residents to see if they need anything.	6.5	2.7	3.5
14.	Thinks neighbors would get together to solve neighborhood problem among themselves.	8.0	4.6	1.6
15.	Thinks neighbors would put pressure on resident whose house or yard became run-down.	7.1	3.2	2.9
16.	Thinks noisy neighbors would quiet down if asked.	7.1	3.5	2.0
17.	Knows of local organization that works on neighborhood problems.	17.6	0.6	4.8
18.	Has tried to stop neighborhood children from doing something they shouldn't.	6.3	1.1	4.2
19.	Thinks most people who live in neighborhood are good neighbors.	10.9	3.8	1.0
20.	Thinks more friends live inside neighborhood than outside.	12.0	2.0	2.9
21.	Thinks people in neighborhood are very friendly.	5.4	2.0	2.1

Table 2.2, *continued*

Var. rank	Variable description	(1) % variance explained by individual attributes and social composition	(2) % net variance explained by social composition after removing individual attributes	(3) % net variance explained by neighborhood after removing individual attributes and social composition
22.	Has talked about neighborhood needs or problems with other residents.	10.0	1.5	2.7
23.	Thinks churches and church groups are important in neighborhood.	12.2	0.6	3.9
24.	Thinks a lot of people in neighborhood try to prevent crime by keeping an eye on strangers.	8.2	1.8	2.0
25.	Names one specific boundary of neighborhood.	8.4	0.8	3.1
26.	Is satisfied with police protection in neighborhood.	5.0	2.3	1.5
27.	Has contacted formal community organization about a neighborhood problem.	10.5	1.2	2.5
28.	Thinks people who run local businesses are important in neighborhood.	5.3	1.8	1.6
29.	Has been annoyed at something that neighbors did.	6.6	1.5	1.8
30.	Took direct action with neighbors to solve local problem on their own.	4.9	1.0	2.3
31.	Thinks a lot of residents try to keep neighborhood children from getting into trouble.	5.1	2.0	1.1

Table 2.2, *continued*

Var. rank	Variable description	(1) % variance explained by individual attributes and social composition	(2) % net variance explained by social composition after removing individual attributes	(3) % net variance explained by neighborhood after removing individual attributes and social composition
32.	Has argued with neighbor.	5.6	0.8	2.2
33.	Has contacted city official about problem in neighborhood.	14.4	1.1	2.1
34.	Thinks politicians and political orgainzations are important in neighborhood.	1.7	0.7	2.3
35.	Has worked with neighbors to improve appearance of street.	7.8	0.5	2.1
36.	Has kept an eye on neighbors' homes when they were away.	10.6	1.9	0.6
37.	Has visited inside a neighbor's home.	8.0	1.1	1.5
38.	Usually votes in state and local elections.	24.0	1.0	1.4
39.	Has talked to others about voting for particular candidate or party.	7.2	0.3	1.8
40.	Thinks most people on block are personal friends.	6.9	0.9	1.1
41.	Has borrowed tools or household items from neighbors.	14.8	0.5	1.6
42.	Is satisfied with public schools that serve neighborhood.	15.2	0.1	1.9
43.	Has run shopping errand for neighbor.	3.0	0.4	1.3
44.	Has tried to settle disagreement between two neighbors.	3.3	0.3	1.3

Table 2.2, *continued*

Var. rank	Variable description	(1) % variance explained by individual attributes and social composition	(2) % net variance explained by social composition after removing individual attributes	(3) % net variance explained by neighborhood after removing individual attributes and social composition
45.	Has discussed personal problems with a neighbor.	2.1	0.5	0.8
46.	Thinks people like self have lots of influence in local government decisions.	5.7	0.1	1.1
47.	Voted in presidential election of 1976.	18.1	0.4	0.4

the variance in each item could be explained by the social composition of neighborhood alone, after the effects of the respondents' individual attributes had been removed. In other words, the figures here indicate the effect that variations in the social makeup of neighborhoods would have on individual residents who were similar in their personal characteristics. Finally, the percentage figures in column 3 show what proportion of the variance in each item was still explained by neighborhood itself, even after the personal attributes of the respondents and the social composition of their neighborhoods had all been taken into account.

In every case, the proportion of variance explained by neighborhood is now smaller than it was when only the personal attributes of individual respondents were taken into account. The results could hardly have been otherwise. By controlling for the effects of neighborhood social composition, we have excluded from the scope of community culture some of the most obvious and important aspects of the neighborhood environment — its social class character, for example, and its racial makeup. In the process the neighborhood effects that we examined earlier have been divided into two portions. The first of these, represented by the entries in column 2, is the part that can be attributed to neighborhood social composition. The other fragment, in the last column, is the remainder that continues to reflect the explanatory impact of the neighborhood itself. In fact, some of these fragments are still rather substantial. Although there is only one case (item 11) in which the remaining effects of community culture surpass the combined impact of individual attributes and neighborhood composition, there are numerous instances in which even these diminished neighborhood effects still outweigh the collective influence of all seven aspects of neighborhood social makeup. In fact, a comparison of compositional effects and neighborhood effects, columns 2 and 3. shows that this is what happened in a majority of the cases listed in Table 2.2 (thirty-one of forty-seven).

The effects of living in a particular neighborhood remain noticeable even if we disregard the impact of the residents' individual attributes and the influences arising from the aggregated characteristics of the neighbors who surround them. The individual attributes and the aggregated characteristics, it should be noted, are the same ones identified by previous research as the essential factors underlying social differences between residential areas and as the formative elements in community subcultures. The evidence shows that such societywide elements as class and race and ethnicity do in fact have an important influence on neighborhood life. But it also shows that neighborhood itself — the mere experience of place — is a factor of at least comparable standing in many instances.

The impact of place is more evident for some items than for others. The use of a neighborhood's standard name, for example, continues to reflect the influence of neighborhood environment more than any other kind of attitude or activity that was considered. To a considerable extent, it appears, neighborhood identity is something that becomes attached to the place itself and not merely to the social aggregate that happens to occupy it. In some other respects, however, the results reported in Table 2.2 no longer follow the patterns that were evident in Table 2.1. Neighborhood effects, for instance, were previously found to outweigh the impact of personal characteristics in almost all cases where respondents were reporting their perceptions of their neighborhoods and neighbors. When they told of their own activities, however, the relative importance of neighborhood effects decreased, and personal attributes became more important by comparison. Now that the influence of neighborhood social composition has been taken into account, the pattern of results is virtually reversed. Compositional effects outweigh neighborhood effects for most items having to do with the respondents' perceptions of their neighbors' conduct and character. But the balance generally shifts to the neighborhood itself when the respondents report on their own conduct.

Though the patterns are rather complex, the probable explanation is not. Compositional effects weigh heavily in the respondents' impressions of their neighbors because these impressions are precisely the sorts of things that are most likely to reflect the aggregated social characteristics of their fellow residents. When respondents are recounting their own activities, on the other hand, the social characteristics of the other people who live in the neighborhood are less directly relevant to the subject at hand, and the relative importance of community social composition understandably declines.

The explanation generally fits the evidence, but it leaves some matters unexplained. In particular, among the perceptual items concentrated in the first half of the table, the dominance of compositional effects is less complete than the proposed explanation would anticipate. The most striking exceptions to be found here all share a common character: they refer to the respondents' impressions of neighborhood elites and organizations. Most notable among these exceptional cases is the perception that there are "real leaders" in the neighborhood "who can bring the neighbors together to get things done" (item 11). This is the only instance among those reported in Table 2.2 in which the variance that is attributed to neighborhood alone outweighs the variance that is explained by individual attributes and compositional factors put together. Neighborhood effects are less weighty in other instances, but they exercise a notable influence on people's awareness of local community organizations (item 17), where the variance explained by neighborhood alone clearly surpasses the variance attributable to compositional effects. The explanatory impact of the neighborhood is almost as prominent in people's perceptions of the local importance of ethnic groups (item 10), churches (item 23), and politicians or political organizations (item 34). All these cases represent departures from the prevailing tendency among the perceptual items in Table 2.2, the tendency for compositional effects to outweigh neighborhood effects. And all these exceptions have to do with the respondents' impressions of their community's governing apparatus — its important groups and institutions, its organizational structure, and its leadership cadre.

The reason for these exceptions, perhaps, is that community leadership and organization are usually the business of a small minority among the local residents. The composition of the neighborhood population as a whole may therefore be relatively unimportant for explaining the occurrence of these activities. Even if the active minority were marked by distinctive social characteristics, its presence might go undetected in the social makeup of the community at large. As a result, the social composition of the entire neighborhood would be less useful for explaining the residents' impressions of local leadership and organization than in accounting for other sorts of perceptions. To understand these beliefs about local political order, one might have to refer to the varying organizational or institutional regimes of the neighborhoods themselves rather than the composition of their populations. Once again, the local political arrangements seem, in particular, to bear the imprint of the neighborhood's environment. Even when neighborhood effects are defined narrowly to exclude the impact of social composition, the evidence generally suggests that the experience of living in a particular neighborhood is a distinctly political one. When people consider the patterns of governance that prevail in their communities, their impressions are not simply reflections of personal attributes that are likely to have brought them to the neighborhood in the first place, or even products of the larger social elements that have given the community as a whole its social constitution. In part at least, their images of the neighborhood polity must be regarded as consequences of their exposure to a local political culture that is associated with the neighborhood itself; those images cannot be explained away by the social characteristics of the current inhabitants. More than most other kinds of perceptions, the sense of neighborhood leadership and organization can be identified as a neighborhood phenomenon, not merely a by-product of social forces that happen to be operating in a neighborhood. The residents' impressions of the local political regime reflect the distinctive influence of the place itself.

In practice, of course, the impact of the place itself may be more difficult to recognize than the influence of its population makeup. The effect of living in a particular neighborhood, after all, is relatively comprehensible when it can be explained as a person's reaction to the social characteristics of fellow residents. This is the explanation that seems to operate most clearly for people's perceptions of their neighbors' public service activities. So long as community social composition is included as an essential part of the neighborhood environment, these impressions of unofficial governance seem especially susceptible to the influence of the local atmosphere. But when compositional effects are considered separately, as they have been in Table 2.2, neighborhood effects no longer seem to operate with such special force on people's views of the informal public service activities of their communities. In other words, variations in the social makeup of neighborhood populations seem to account for much of the variation in people's views about their neighbors' unofficial efforts to insure domestic tranquillity and promote the general welfare.

The same explanation is much less effective for other manifestations of the neighborhood polity. Even after community social composition has been taken into account, the singularly political effects of living in a neighborhood remain prominent — not only in the perceptions of local leadership and organization already considered, but in several other expressions of public life (for example, items 8 and 18). These are marks left by the place itself, and while they apparently cannot be traced to the personal attributes of the current occupants, their origins need be no more ghostly or obscure than those of compositional effects. Several factors more tangible than the diffuse mystique of the neighborhood may help to account for the impact that a community may have on its inhabitants.

In the first place, there is a local geography. The physical layout of a community may facilitate residents' identification of their neighborhood. Marked off by a stream valley, harbor frontage, or railroad tracks, one neighborhood may stand apart from the surrounding territory more clearly than other parts of the city, and its inhabitants may therefore be more likely than residents of other places to develop a sense of neighborhood identity, no matter what kinds of people they are. Such physical attributes of the neighborhood may increase the likelihood that residents will use a commonly accepted name for their community (item 1), and they are even more likely to have an effect on the respondents' ability to identify a specific neighborhood boundary (item 25). The results in Table 2.2 indicate that both aspects of neighborhood identity are more sensitive to the influence of place itself than to the social makeup of its population.

Geographically and socially, the neighborhood is usually a territory of limited extent. Within its narrow compass, even a single person of unusual energy, ability, or character might conceivably change the nature and conduct of community business or reshape the mood of the local residents. Considered in relation to the neighborhood's demographic composition, the presence of these exceptional activists may seem to be an inexplicable accident, but some such accident probably plays a significant part in explaining the residents' perceptions of local leadership and organization.

These things are not merely reflections of the community's demo-graphic mixture but also ingredients of the distinctive atmosphere of the place itself.

The current atmosphere, of course, may not always be a simple reflection of current conditions. Organizations and institutions created by exceptional leaders of the past may continue to structure the community's public life long after the founders have ceased to be active. In fact, entire neighborhood populations of the past may contribute to the current customs, institutions, and attitudes of a community. The present mood of the residents in a neighborhood like Canton, for example, may not be fully comprehensible unless one takes account of what local inhabitants were like more than a generation ago. Perhaps current attitudes about neighborhood change and the ability to control it are related to the sudden onset of residential mobility in Canton after half a century of unusual stabil-ity. Actually, the rate of residential turnover in Canton today is no greater than for most other neighborhoods in Baltimore — and much lower than in some of them — but population change assumes larger-than-life dimensions for many Canton residents perhaps because they see it against the background of their neighborhood's former changelessness.

What we have identified as the effect of the neighborhood itself — the mere experience of place — may in fact be the combined effect of geography, personality, and history. The three factors can rein-force one another. The historic identity of a neighborhood may en-dure because the community is geographically isolated, or a casual social arrangement may be preserved as local custom because a revered local leader makes it part of an organizational tradition. These are the kinds of things that help to explain why similar kinds of residents from socially similar neighborhoods may nevertheless have different outlooks on their communities and different ways of behaving within their neighborhoods. They are the probable sources of variations in community culture that do not seem to be explained away by differences in social class, race, or family structure.

Of course they may not be explained by the findings of a sample survey either. A study like the present one cannot reach far into a neighborhood's past in order to identify the critical events that have shaped the present mood of a community or established the current patterns of conduct, but the reported attitudes and activities of the survey respondents do reflect the neighborhood regimes that have arisen from past experience; the survey results can also show that these community customs and habits are indeed neighborhood phenomena and not merely the artifacts of personal attributes or current population characteristics; and finally, they suggest that these neighborhood phenomena tend to be decidedly political in character. Once the demographic features of inhabitants have been taken into account, the remaining differences among neighborhoods are primarily differences in local political life. The sense of neighborhood leadership and organization, together with the sense of neighborhood identity itself, varies from place to place even though the social characteristics of the local inhabitants may not. In fact, people's responses to the attributes of their fellow residents are themselves reactions of a predominantly political sort. The evidence shows that the social climate of the neighborhood has an especially notable effect on people's views about the public welfare and public order of their communities, and a less notable effect in matters of personal friendliness and private sociability.

Taken as a whole, the evidence implies that neighborhoods have lives of their own, and that the neighborhood polity may provide the principal framework in which communities carry on their parochial endeavors. To a significant degree, the political regime of a residential area can be identified as a neighborhood phenomenon — and not just because the political events and attitudes that compose it happen to occur within a neighborhood. People are born, educated, employed, and married in neighborhoods as well, but there is no special reason to regard these events as neighborhood phenomena. They occur in neighborhoods only because they must happen someplace. But the political attitudes and activities that we have considered are different. They are neighborhood phenomena not just because they can be located within particular neighborhoods but because it is the neighborhood itself, in a sense, that explains their occurrence. No matter what people's personal attributes may be, the residents of a community will tend to have certain political attitudes and patterns of conduct in common simply because they live together in the same place. The fact that they are neighbors is the thing that seems to account for their common political adjustments and adaptations, and in the course of these accommodations a spatial aggregation of individual city residents may be converted into a political society.

The fact that people live together in the same place, of course, may be regarded not as the property of neighborhood itself but as a product of those external forces that govern the formation of neighborhoods, sifting rich from poor people or white residents from black. These determinants of community social constitution explain why certain types of people become neighbors in the first place. In turn, it might be argued that the ingredients of the community's social makeup—not the neighborhood itself—are the factors that explain why its unofficial political arrangements differ from those elsewhere.

But in fact they do not explain these political variations. Noticeable political differences remain between neighborhoods even after the effects of social composition have been taken into account. They reflect the existence of an intractable substratum in neighborhood polities that is resistant to the explanatory impact of factors like class, race, and family status. This does not mean that the internal life of the neighborhood can be considered apart from the social forces that operate in the society at large. In fact, some portion of the indissoluble residue of community culture may represent the local consequences of social forces that operated in the past. In Canton, for example, the impact of Baltimore's industrialization, the depression, and a world war have all contributed to the character of the neighborhood, and their impact is clearly recognized by the local residents themselves. At the same time, however, the inhabitants and many of the former inhabitants reflect the durable influence of Canton itself. Their perspectives on the neighborhood are conditioned by its distinctive history; and they exhibit a continuity of custom and memory in the face of social change; and they can still point to a single mulberry tree that struggles up through the pavement on Clinton Street, a lone survivor of the half-dozen planted by Charlie-Got-Your-Shoes-On-Wrong.

3.
Neighborhood
Identity

Part of Coldstream-Homestead-Montebello.
Photograph by Charlotte Crenson.

In 1960 Coldstream, Homestead, and Montebello were three distinct neighborhoods that shared the same ridge of high ground in Northeast Baltimore. By 1976 these separate communities had been drawn together into a single confederation, and a new local identity had been superimposed on the old neighborhoods. Residents have continued to use the traditional names for the various sections of their tripartite community, but the recent union is recognized in a composite name that has been precariously spliced together with hyphens: Coldstream-Homestead-Montebello. As a neighborhood designation, the new name suffers from obvious disadvantages. It sounds like one of the freight trains that roll along the area's southern boundary, and it seems almost as long. Yet as a way of identifying the neighborhood it has been gaining acceptance among local residents. For the sake of convenience they frequently refer to their segmented community by the initials of its three components, and in informal conversation the place has come to be known as "Chum."

Whether it will continue to be known in this way remains an open question. In time, the hyphenated confederation of neighborhoods could give way to a more perfect union under a single name without hyphens. Community improvement associations representing each of the three subareas have already ceased to operate, and some of their most active members have joined the executive board of the new Coldstream-Homestead-Montebello Community Corporation. At the same time, there are at least a few pockets of resistance to the new order; their presence suggests that the possibility of secessionist movements cannot be dismissed entirely. Such uncertainties in the local political situation are signs that the residents may not yet have arrived at a fixed conception of their community. In other subcommunities of Baltimore, neighborhood creation has been rooted in the activities of eighteenth-century landholders or nineteenth-century real estate promoters, and neighborhood identities have endured essentially unchanged through successive generations of residents. But Coldstream-Homestead-Montebello is one place where it may be possible to observe a neighborhood identity still in the process of development.

Similar developments have been occurring elsewhere. In Baltimore and in other cities, observers have noted a recent tendency toward federation among urban neighborhoods. Handfuls of relatively small community groups have taken to constructing formal coalitions, usually for the purpose of reducing the mismatch between the large-scale operations of public bureaucracies and their own neighborhood-sized concerns.[1] In many cases, these new federations seem to formalize an implicit hierarchy of community attachments which had already become evident in metropolitan areas. Scott Greer has pointed out that in the contemporary city a resident may belong not to a single encapsulated community but to a concentric series of progressively larger communities. Such communities range in scope from a few households on a single block, to the neighborhood area that contains the block, to the larger residential sector of the city in which a cluster of neighborhoods may federate for the advancement of regional interests.[2] Each of these nested communities can represent a distinct field of social action with its own functional niche in the social order of the metropolis. Movements toward neighborhood combination might therefore be interpreted as symptoms of an emerging federalism of community attachments.[3] Old neighborhoods may continue to be acknowledged by their inhabitants — but as provinces or cantons of larger communities. This is another of the possibilities inherent in such redefinitions of community as the one that seems to be occurring in Coldstream-Homestead-Montebello.

For residents of the area there is more at stake in the reformulation of the neighborhood than simply deciding on a new name for the place where they live. There may also be, for example, considerations of social prestige. Among outsiders, a neighborhood designation sometimes serves as a coded signal of social status, ethnicity, or social attitudes.[4] Adopting one neighborhood identity rather than another can therefore make a difference for one's standing in the eyes of strangers and passing acquaintances. It can also make a political difference. Following Scott Greer, a number of analysts have recognized that the shape and definition of urban subcommunities acquire special importance because they help to structure citizen access to the institutions of urban government. Community identity can be regarded as a social platform for democratic participation and representation in the official business of the larger political systems.

In the unofficial business of the smaller neighborhood polity, it has an even more elementary kind of political importance. The awareness of a community identity may be as fundamental to the polity of the neighborhood as the sense of national identity is to the nation-state.[5] It delimits the scope of community concern and defines the public with whom the responsibility for these concerns should be shared. The development of a neighborhood identity is one of those critical transformations that can help to convert the individual occupants of an urban territory into fellow citizens with a shared political life—that is, into a political society. The evidence has already indicated that such developments tend to be rooted in the neighborhood itself. Residents acquire an awareness of their community's identity not simply because their personal characteristics lead them in that direction but because there is something about the neighborhood itself that encourages this awareness. Coldstream-Homestead-Montebello helps to illustrate the sorts of local conditions in which this encouragement may originate, and its recent experience is one example of the process by which neighborhood identities may arise.

In one respect, of course, the experience may have been distinctive. The new neighborhood came into being on ground that was already occupied by old neighborhoods, well-established communities endowed with a certain pride of place. Montebello, in the northeast corner of the present neighborhood, had originally been the estate of General Samuel Smith, not merely a hero of the Revolution but the military commander who organized the city's defenses against the British attack during the War of 1812. Grateful Baltimoreans later elected him to Congress.[6] To the west and south of the general's land was the farm of the Gorsuch family—"Homestead"—which they had settled in the 1730s and continued to occupy until a mid-nineteenth-century Gorsuch decided that the family seat could produce more wealth as a real estate venture than as an agricultural enterprise. He was wrong. His creation of a real estate syndicate in 1851 to build a residential community on his land has been marked as the first authentic suburban development in the Baltimore area,[7] but it was not one of the more successful efforts. Financial difficulties soon forced him to abandon both the project and the family estate.[8] He left behind only a small handful of proto-suburbanites. A later generation of real estate developers would finish what he had begun. But even this small, preliminary settlement generated enough community spirit so that it had its own neighborhood improvement association as early as 1892, just a few years after the area was annexed to the City of Baltimore.[9]

At the time of annexation, Coldstream — the westernmost part of the present neighborhood — was still the country estate of the Patterson family. Its most notable claim on local memory was Elizabeth Patterson, whose romance with Jerome Bonaparte, youngest brother of Napoleon, became one of the city's proudest scandals. The couple lived at Coldstream after their marriage in 1803 but sailed for France less than two years later. Napoleon, who seems to have had other marital plans for his brother, refused to allow Elizabeth to land. Jerome was persuaded to give up the woman he loved for a throne: he abandoned his wife to become king of Westphalia. Elizabeth returned to Baltimore with an infant son. Years later, her story would provide the grist for several historical novels, and Hollywood exploited the soap opera possibilities of her life almost immediately after talking pictures were invented. The first film in 1928, with Conrad Nagle and Delores Costello, was quickly superseded in 1936 by a second, with Dick Powell and Marion Davies.

A local builder leveled the Patterson family mansion at just about the time that Elizabeth was being immortalized in celluloid. Other developers had already demolished the Smith and Gorsuch homes. But the new subdivisions retained the names of the former family estates, and since each of them was developed separately, slight differences of housing type preserved the divisions between the older landholdings. The dominant style in all three areas is a variant of the brick rowhouse that was especially popular in Baltimore from approximately 1910 to the 1930s — a two-story version with a square porch that takes up nearly the entire width of each dwelling unit. The design lends itself to variations in size, and the largest of the new houses were concentrated in Montebello. Somewhat smaller models were built in Homestead, and smaller still in Coldstream. Completed at different times, the various kinds of homes seem to have been occupied by people with slightly different income levels. Traditional place names and distinctive family histories associated with them could now serve to accent variations in social status, and distinct community improvement associations arose as expressions of the residents' sense of separateness.

The territorial divisions among the three segments of the area were rooted in social differences that were probably significant to the local residents, and by 1960 a further distinction had arisen to differentiate the neighborhoods. Racial migration on a national scale had helped to trigger movements on a neighborhood scale within the limits of Baltimore. By 1960 roughly one-third of Coldstream's population was composed of black residents recently arrived in the neighborhood, and the proportion was growing. But inhabitants of Homestead and Montebello still had almost no black neighbors, and they were nervous. The common anxiety eventually drew these two neighborhoods together in joint efforts to resist real estate speculators, block-busting, and panic selling. The cooperative venture was probably the first step taken toward the consolidation of the three subareas, but it proved to be a flimsy obstacle to racial change, and it seems to have given way completely after the race riot that followed the assassination of Martin Luther King in 1968. The transfer of the neighborhood from one population to another was complete and rapid. Of the residents interviewed for the present study, 97 percent were black, and more than a quarter of the respondents in Coldstream-Homestead-Montebello reported that they had moved into the neighborhood in either 1968 or 1969.

The change nearly erased racial variations among the three subareas, and it filled them with residents who had no long-standing attachments to their neighbors or to the existing neighborhood identities. Another source of social differentiation also seems to have lost some of its importance. Many houses in all three areas were subdivided so that each floor could be rented to a different tenant. The use of basements sometimes made it possible for three families to occupy what had once been a single-family home. Such arrangements also meant that many of the larger houses in Homestead and Montebello were no longer occupied by people who had larger incomes than those of Coldstream residents. Variations of social status continued to be recognized in the area, but they were differences within neighborhoods and not between them. In particular, black residents who had arrived relatively early in the process of racial transition tended to distinguish themselves from neighbors who had come late. A man who had moved to Coldstream in 1960, for example, later claimed that "when the neighborhood became mostly black, the real estate guys stopped selling houses and began renting." The renters, he suggested, were not always good neighbors: "Just by looking at the houses, you can tell who is renting and who is buying."[10] His views were echoed by another of the early arrivals, a Homestead community activist who was a renter herself:

"When I first moved here sixteen years ago, this was a very beautiful neighborhood . . . I just can't explain to you how beautiful it was. And then the landlords started making apartment houses . . . And when the apartment houses started coming in, and the slum landlords started coming in, the place really started to go down. That's what made me more interested in keeping it up, because I knew what it was before this had begun to happen."

No longer divided by noticeable differences in race or social class, the three neighborhoods now had something in common — each neighborhood had a group of early arrivals who shared an interest in restoring the community to "what it was before this had begun to happen." But instead of leading immediately to unification, the social homogenization of the three neighborhoods was followed by political polarization. Coldstream-Homestead-Montebello was an area with an almost entirely new population, politically unclaimed and unorganized. For local party leaders and factions and ambitious would-be leaders, it represented a political free-fire zone.

In 1969 two separate community organizations became visible in the area, one in Homestead-Montebello and the other in Coldstream. The Coldstream Park Improvement Association was built on the foundations of an earlier organization that existed before the racial transformation of the neighborhood. The group was revived in the late 1960s by a vigorous local leader, a politically active steelworker named Robert Dalton who had run unsuccessfully for the State Senate in 1966. Dalton was a member of the Democratic Central Committee in 1969 when he and the members of his association induced the mayor's office to sponsor a concentrated campaign of housing inspections, street cleaning, and rat eradication in the area. Although the program was to cover both Homestead and Montebello as well as Coldstream, it was known only as the "Coldstream Project."[11] Less than a year after its initiation, the leader of the Coldstream Park Improvement Association ran again for the State Senate, this time successfully. In the process, Dalton seems to have drawn his community association into an alliance with the powerful Eastside Democratic Organization, whose operations had previously been concentrated in the black neighborhoods lying to the south of Coldstream.

Representatives of Homestead and Montebello had meanwhile turned their attentions to the area lying north of their territory, where a new regional alliance of Northeast Baltimore communities was then forming. The chief spokesman for Homestead and Montebello was Walter Brooks, a former civil rights worker who had come from New Haven several years earlier. Brooks was soon elected president of the entire northeastern coalition of neighborhoods, which subsequently sponsored organizing efforts in Homestead and Montebello. But by 1972 the partnership between these two communities and their northeastern allies had come apart, a casualty of disputes about the misappropriation of funds, factional conflict within the coalition, and charges that the two black neighborhoods had been "used" by the predominantly white coalition in order to qualify for federal grants. Brooks resigned as president of the alliance and transferred his activities to the Homestead-Montebello Churches and Community Organizations, a loosely knit group that was incorporated in 1969 but had its antecedents in the cooperative efforts at racial stabilization that had previously drawn the two neighborhoods together. The organization had participated in the northeastern alliance of community groups, and now, with the encouragement of the alliance's ambitious ex-president, it was addressing itself to a variety of local issues that had arisen in the wake of neighborhood change — housing, health, sanitation, recreation, and youth unemployment. Brooks also persuaded the group to break its ties with the alliance, and he offered his own services as "executive director" in a campaign to broaden the organization, so that what was essentially a small collection of local clergymen and church members might mature into a fully formed community council with grants, programs, and an expanded membership. Though the projected council claimed Coldstream as part of its territory, it was to be known only as the Homestead-Montebello Community Council. The most visible product of this organizing effort was probably a summer youth employment and recreation program in 1973. But perhaps even more noticeable was the emergence of Walter Brooks as a rival candidate for Robert Dalton's seat in the State Senate.[12]

Brooks mounted his campaign, in 1974, with some support from the local New Era Democratic Club. Dalton had in the meantime feuded with his allies in the Eastside Democratic Organization, and they had transferred their support to a third Senate candidate who did not live in Coldstream-Homestead-Montebello. The presence of this additional opponent seems not to have deflected much of the animosity that Brooks and Dalton directed at one another. In a primary election contest that was punctuated by televised charges of serious criminal activity, the two local leaders mobilized their forces in Coldstream and in Homestead-Montebello for a neighborhood showdown. Their personal rivalry was so absorbing, says one community activist, that it overshadowed the sense of neighborhood identity itself: "You had those for and those against Walter Brooks. You had those for and those against Bob Dalton. I don't think that people perceived themselves as residents of Homestead-Montebello or Coldstream Park as much as they saw themselves as members of this or that or the other clan. There weren't any programs, and what could have happened in the area got swallowed up in personalities or the political sides that people took."

The Brooks and Dalton campaigns were both swallowed up in the victory of their opponent from the Eastside Democratic Organization. Suddenly united by defeat and cut off from their former allies outside the neighborhood, the two enemies found that they could discard their earlier differences quickly enough to run on the same ticket for the City Council, less than a year after campaigning against one another for the State Senate. For Walter Brooks, the new neighborhood political alliance seems to have supplied an occasion for reviving the proposal for a community council that would embrace all three neighborhoods and the organizations that represented them. This time he presented the plan to officials of the local Department of Housing and Community Development, and suggested that the new council, once created, might serve as the vehicle for distributing community development block grant funds to the neighborhood. According to staff members of the agency, municipal administrators abstained from any commitments — partly because of uncertainty about the strength of Brooks's following or the stability of his leadership.

Brooks and Dalton again faced opposition from the Eastside Democratic Organization in the Democratic primary, and again they were both defeated. Brooks left Baltimore; Dalton withdrew from local politics; and in Coldstream-Homestead-Montebello factional politics suffered at least a temporary loss of energy. Almost immediately an astute community leader used the opportunity afforded by the lull in neighborhood political life to engineer the neighborhood unification that Walter Brooks had only been able to propose. Mrs. Doris Johnson, a Coldstream resident for almost fifteen years, was a professional community worker whose activities made her well known outside of her own neighborhood. She had previously been a youth counselor and community organizer for a neighborhood corporation in another part of Baltimore. Later she had worked as office manager for a nonprofit corporation that provided architectural advice to neighborhood groups all over the city.

Her job had brought her into frequent contact with municipal agencies and administrators. In fact, she had participated in the design of the city's community development block grant program.

In her own neighborhood, Mrs. Johnson had served as president of the executive board of a community health corporation. The area's health practitioners had been swept away in the same wave of change that converted the area from a white neighborhood to a black one. With an estimated population of more than thirteen thousand, Coldstream-Homestead-Montebello had no physician and no pharmacist. The health corporation, established in 1970 with the backing of clergymen from Homestead-Montebello, was designed to make up for this deficiency in local services. In time, it was also able to claim another achievement: its board was the only organization in the area that included representatives from both the Coldstream Park Improvement Association and the Homestead-Montebello Churches and Community Organizations. Mrs. Johnson, one of the corporation's founders, continued to preside over the board until her resignation in 1975, not long after hostilities between the area's two major political factions had reached their peak.

In 1976, less than six months after the leadership of Brooks and Dalton had suffered its electoral collapse. Mrs. Johnson was once again active in her community. This time she appeared as the convenor of a community "charette" for Coldstream, Homestead, and Montebello — a three-day marathon meeting at which local residents could consult with city officials and outside experts about neighborhood problems and recommend solutions. The meeting — promoted, like a political campaign, with television announcements, bullhorns, and posters — had been planned by Mrs. Johnson together with staff members of several city agencies, and it coincided with the development of official plans for the the physical and educational restoration of a large public high school in the northwestern corner of the area. The school had once enjoyed a reputation as an elite, citywide academic institution and many influential Baltimoreans, including the mayor, claimed it as an alma mater. A committee of alumni dissatisfied with the state of the school had secured a pledge from municipal authorities to upgrade its programs and facilities. And now Mrs. Johnson had linked the improvement of the high school to the rehabilitation of Coldstream-Homestead-Montebello.

The charette was held at the school in mid-1976, and it drew a sizable contingent of local politicians and public officials in addition to area residents. But there was little evidence of the political factionalism that had so recently divided the local inhabitants. It was an occasion designed, says Mrs. Johnson, for people who welcomed the respite from partisan infighting as an opportunity to discuss issues that had been overshadowed by the struggle for control of the neighborhood. They were the residents who "could look at the depreciation and blighting of the community while all that other stuff was going on . . . They felt that with all that over now, people could come together and just talk about nothing more than sanitation, cleaning up the alleys, those things that might seem minute but that weren't that power kind of thing—who's going to be in charge of the program and all that. Maybe that's one way to get them together."

In part, disputes about "who's going to be in charge of the program" may have been made unnecessary by the fact that there was so little doubt about who was in charge. Mrs. Johnson herself did not preside over the charette. That duty was delegated to a pair of cochairmen—one an officer of the Coldstream Park Improvement Association and the other a leader of the Homestead-Montebello Churches and Community Organizations. But it was Mrs. Johnson who had not only chaired the steering committee that arranged the meeting but also led the effort to carry out one of the most important resolutions produced by the charette—a proposal for a "strong community council to follow through on charette recommendations and help organize the CHM community."[13] The result was the Coldstream-Homestead-Montebello Community Corporation, with Mrs. Johnson as its executive director and a range of government and foundation grants for the support of neighborhood housing, employment, and recreation programs.

The new corporation was also the organizational embodiment of a new definition of the neighborhood—a conception of the community that seems to have been adopted only three years later by a substantial proportion of the residents. The fact that people have different ways of abbreviating the lengthy name of the three-part neighborhood makes it difficult to determine exactly how many of the local inhabitants now recognize the unification of the formerly separate residential areas. But results of the 1979 survey suggest that at least one-third of the people who live in Coldstream-Homestead-Montebello now regard themselves as residents of a consolidated community, and the actual figure could conceivably be as much as twice that.

Communal Solidarity and the Sense of Neighborhood

In a remarkably short time the residents of three separate neighborhoods began to conceive of themselves as members of a single community. In fact, so hastily formed was this new sense of neighborhood identity that one might easily perceive something artificial about it. A residential area that had so recently exchanged an old population for a new one was a place where most people could hardly have had the time to put down roots or become attached to their neighbors. Many of the local institutions and facilities likely to support a sense of community identity would probably have been undermined or destroyed in the course of residential migration. During the process of racial transition, for example, entire church congregations evacuated Coldstream-Homestead-Montebello, and although many church members moved in to replace them, it appears that most of these new arrivals attend worship services outside the neighborhood.

In the absence of such local ties, there may be reason to ask whether Coldstream-Homestead-Montebello is an authentic residential community or whether it is merely a hothouse variety forced into existence by city bureaucrats, politicians, and community organizers. The rapid development of a new community definition here stands in sharp contrast to the changelessness of neighborhood identity in places like Canton. The dissimilarity of the cases suggests that Coldstream-Homestead-Montebello may represent not an illustration of the process by which neighborhoods identities develop but an aberrant example tainted by federal funds and the political interference of municipal authorities who help Mrs. Johnson to maintain her organization.

In fact, however, the conditions of community identity in Coldstream-Homestead-Montebello may not be at all unusual. It is true that residents here have not yet become strongly attached to their neighbors. Only 10 percent of the Coldstream-Homestead-Montebello residents who were interviewed for the present study reported that they had more friends inside the neighborhood than outside. But neighborly attachments of this kind do not seem to be a prerequisite for the sense of community identity in any of the neighborhoods studied.

This is the conclusion that emerges from the survey evidence collected in all twenty-one sample communities. The findings reported in Table 3.1, for example, show how friendship with neighbors was related to one aspect of the sense of neighborhood identity — the respondents' belief that the parts of the city where they lived had distinctive names. The naming of one's home territory signifies that it has acquired at least a personally recognized identity. "To be able to name an area," as Albert Hunter points out, "is in no small way to know it. A name distinguishes an area as unique. It is a symbol, a shorthand abstraction, for denoting some mutually perceived and mutually shared communality."[14] When local residents can assign a name to the place where they live, they implicitly acknowledge that they perceive their homes to be parts of a larger entity, a common territory that stretches beyond the personal territory represented by one's own yard or living room. A name distinguishes this shared territory from the surrounding real estate, and it suggests that the inhabitants belong to a single social aggregate.

The survey results indicate, however, that this aspect of community identity has almost nothing to do with neighborly intimacy. Section A of the table shows that among people who said that most of their friends lived inside the neighborhood, 71.9 percent assigned names to their residential areas. But among people who reported that most of their friends lived outside the neighborhood, the figure was just about the same — 71.4 percent. Whether or not one's

Table 3.1. Friendship with neighbors and the sense of neighborhood identity (Percentage of respondents in each category who said that the neighborhood had a particular name)

A.	Location of friends		
	More inside neighborhood	71.9	(634)[a]
	More outside neighborhood	71.4	(1,358)
B.	Location of "really good friends"		
	Most on same block	68.7	(242)
	Most in same neighborhood, but not on same block	78.4	(251)
	Most outside neighborhood	70.9	(1,464)
C.	Acquaintanceship with residents of block		
	Most are personal friends	74.4	(699)
	Most are just acquaintances	73.8	(896)
	Most are strangers	61.8	(411)

a. Throughout the tables, the number in parentheses is the weighted number of cases on which the percentage is based.

friendship ties are concentrated within the neighborhood does not seem to make much difference for a person's sense of neighborhood identity.

Nor does the intensity of people's attachments to their neighbors have much to do with their ability to assign names to the places where they live. Those who reported that most of their "really good friends" lived outside the neighborhood were no less likely to assign names to their communities than those who reported that they lived on the same block as their really good friends. Residents who said that they lived in the same neighborhood as their intimate friends but not on the same block were more likely than any of the others to believe that their communities had names. Even among these respondents, however, the sense of neighborhood identity is only a little more widespread than it is for those people whose best friends were mostly outsiders to the neighborhood.

Finally, section C of Table 3.1 indicates that the warmth of relationships with the people on one's block made almost no difference for the likelihood that a respondent would assign a name to the residential area. Those who regarded most of their fellow block residents as strangers were, it is true, somewhat less likely to be aware of community names than other respondents who were better acquainted with their near neighbors. But those who regarded the residents of their blocks as mere acquaintances were just about as likely to assign particular names to their neighborhoods as those who thought of block residents as personal friends.

The personal bonds that sometimes link neighbors to one another do not seem to be responsible for engendering a sense of neighborhood identity. This does not mean that communities can come into being and survive where personal solidarity is absent. It signifies instead that urban neighborhoods should probably be distinguished from the more traditional communities for which personal solidarity may be an essential condition of existence. This distinction between neighborhoods and folk communities has often been obscured by an influential point of view that holds that neighborhoods have their roots in just such communalism. The division of the city into distinct residential areas has been seen as an expression of the urban population's division into communal subgroups, each bound together by ties of tradition or sentiment. When neighborhood residents have failed, on occasion, to exhibit the requisite intensity of fellow feeling or social interaction, it has been concluded that their neighborhood was not a "real" one, or that it was a weak neighborhood, or that contemporary neighborhoods in general were in decline—fallen from a state of communal solidarity that once prevailed in the villagelike neighborhoods of the past.[15]

Exactly what conditions prevailed in the urban neighborhoods of the past may be difficult to determine, although some historical studies have suggested that communal solidarity was hardly the rule.[16] As for the neighborhoods of the present, it is at least apparent that the absence of such solidarity does not diminish the likelihood that city dwellers will conceive of their residential areas as places with names—not anonymous pieces of real estate indistinguishable from the surrounding territory but identifiable neighborhoods. The ability to name one's residential area presupposes a mental image of the locality as a distinct unit, and it reflects a sense that the people who live in this area somehow belong together, even though they may not be especially friendly with one another. If neighborhood identities did depend on personal friendship, they could hardly be expected to survive as long as they do in areas like Canton. The population changes that inevitably occur over a century or two would almost certainly have disturbed the personal ties among residents and eroded the sense of neighborhood identity that is presumed to rest on these ties. The very durability of neighborhood identity in these cases suggests that its foundations may be more impersonal than personal. It suggests, for example, that neighborhood identities tend to originate in conditions very much like the "artificial" ones that gave rise to a redefinition of the neighborhood Coldstream-Homestead-Montebello, and that their continuity is not contingent on the persistence of neighborly intimacy among local residents. Coldstream-Homestead-Montebello may have been an invention of politicians, bureaucrats, and community organizers, but its unspontaneous generation does not represent an exceptional case. Canton, after all, had its beginnings in a business proposition—the neighborhood was a fabrication of real estate operators pursuing profit in the field of industrial development.

Such instances hint that relatively impersonal and utilitarian considerations may be responsible for sharpening the sense of neighborhood identity. One frequently suggested possibility is that a neighborhood acquires definition for its residents simply because the inhabitants use common facilities.[17] People who shop, work, worship, or relax in the same places may soon begin to think of themselves as members of a single neighborhood—not because they feel personally close to one another but because they share a practical interest in the same stores, parks, schools, or churches. If the sense of neighborhood identity does rest on factors such as these, then we can expect to find that it is more strongly developed among those residents who actually do use local facilities than among those who go elsewhere to meet their needs. But the findings reported in Table 3.2 show that this expectation is not borne out by the evidence. The survey results indicate that those who shop, worship, or work inside their neighborhoods are only a little more likely to assign names to the places where they live than those who shop, worship, or work outside the neighborhood. The use patterns connected with the local facilities may serve urban planners as data for defining neighborhoods,[18] but local residents do not seem to pay any special attention to such cues. Like friendship ties with local residents, the use of local facilities does not greatly enhance the respondents' ability to conceive of their residential areas as identifiable territories with distinct names, and the basis for such neighborhood conceptions therefore remains problematic.

A further problem, of course, is that different people may have different opinions about which facilities lie inside or outside the neighborhood, or how near a friend must live in order to qualify as fellow resident of the neighborhood. When the respondents answered questions about the location of their friends or places of worship, they were free to use their own conceptions of the

Table 3.2. Use of local facilities and the sense of neighborhood identity (Percentage of respondents in each category who said that the neighborhood had a particular name)

A. Location of respondents' grocery shopping		
Mostly inside neighborhood	73.3	(860)
Mostly outside neighborhood	68.7	(1,134)
B. Location of respondents' religious services		
Usually attend inside neighborhood	71.4	(597)
Usually attend outside neighborhood	65.2	(808)
Usually don't attend services	78.0	(591)
C. Location of respondents' work places		
Inside neighborhood	83.3	(93)
Outside neighborhood, but less than five miles away	71.5	(433)
More than five miles away	76.5	(819)

neighborhood and their own estimates of its extent. This means that some friends and facilities may have been reported as inside the neighborhood not because they were actually close at hand but simply because the respondent's conception of the neighborhood covered a lot of territory. Another respondent, with a more restrictive notion of the neighborhood's extent, might have reported that the same companions, churches, or shopping places were outside the neighborhood. An additional complication is that when the respondents in a given residential area were asked whether their neighborhood had any particular name, they may have had sharply different "neighborhoods" in mind.

But complications of this sort do not significantly change the meaning of the survey results. No matter how a respondent may have visualized the neighborhood, the fact that this image included friends, shopping places, church, or work place did not make much difference for the likelihood that the image itself would become sufficiently distinct or salient to acquire a specific name. Friendship ties and the use of local facilities do not seem to play an especially important part in people's ability to give definition to their neighborhoods, whatever the definition may be.

The evidence also indicates that the importance of these factors did not increase even when shared definitions of the neighborhood were being considered. Respondents who thought that their neighborhood had a name were subsequently asked what that name was. Over two-thirds of those responding volunteered the "standard" name of their neighborhood—the name that was generally recognized by city agencies and the one that was used in selecting and defining neighborhoods for the present study. A similar consensus about neighborhood names was found not only among the respondents at large but within most of the sample neighborhoods under investigation. In all but five of the twenty-one residential areas, a majority of the people who thought that the neighborhood had any name at all agreed that the name was the "standard" one.[19] Use of a common name, of course, does not guarantee a common definition of the neighborhood, but it is likely to reflect the fact that residents are using roughly similar frames of reference for determining whether friends and facilities are inside or outside the neighborhood. And it is significant that the ability of local residents to provide the standard name for their neighborhood has just as little to do with the reported location of friends and the use of local facilities as the ability to offer any name at all. Local friendships and facility use have scarcely any influence on the chance that respondents would arrive at either the shared public conceptions of their neighborhood or their own private ones.[20]

Finally, there is one more manifestation of the sense of neighborhood identity that also turns out to be independent of local friendship ties and use of local facilities. The residents' ability to specify territorial boundaries for their residential area was similarly unrelated to these factors. Each resident was asked to name a single neighborhood boundary, the one that was percieved to be closest to the place where a person lived. Many people who were unaware that their neighborhood might have a name at all could nevertheless designate a particular street or landmark as the frontier of their residential area; this ability is another reflection of an inclination to conceive of one's home as part of an identifiable neighborhood, distinct from its surroundings. But this inclination has little more to do with neighborhood friendship ties or the use of local facilities than the other signs of neighborhood identity that we have already considered.

City planners and social scientists have proposed a variety of criteria for defining neighborhoods—so many and so various, in fact, that some critics have doubted whether it is actually possible to identify neighborhoods at all.[21] But demonstrating that there is conceptual confusion about neighborhoods is not the same thing as proving their nonexistence or triviality. Large numbers of city residents are confidently convinced that neighborhoods do exist; they readily supply names and boundaries for their own residential territories; and, as we shall see, these working definitions of the neighborhood sometimes provide a framework for people's social and political conduct. But the mental images that people have of their neighborhood are largely unrelated to some of the very social attributes that have been commonly regarded as the defining characteristics of a neighborhood community. Residents' definitions of their neighborhood do not seem to correspond to the geographic area in which they perform such basic functions as grocery shopping or religious worship. Nor do community conceptions grow naturally out of friendship networks.

Some observers have anticipated this estrangement between the neighborhood and its presumed social foundations. The dynamic of urbanization itself was expected to replace local, decentralized patterns of facility use with more centralized ones; it was supposed to supplant the parochialism of neighborhood friendship ties with more cosmopolitan and impersonal attachments.[22] But as the social substance of the neighborhood dissolved, the sense of neighborhood identity was expected to evaporate as well—one further casualty to be counted in a more general loss of community. A few recent investigations, however, have begun to suggest that there is unexpected vitality in the sense of neighborhood identity. Some evidence indicates that the predicted deterioration of neighborhood social relationships may not have been so drastic as once anticipated. Other evidence, like the research results presented here, has shown that the presumed social functions of neighborhoods may not have much to do with the survival of a sense of neighborhood identity.[23]

Observers who look to these social functions for criteria to define neighborhoods are not necessarily misguided. For some purposes it may be useful to define the local areas of a city by referring to the territories covered by social networks or the catchment areas served by public facilities. But the purposes implicit in these definitions are evidently not the ones that local residents have in mind when they form their own conceptions of the neighborhoods where they live. The evidence does not yet reveal just what the residents' purposes may be, only that they are detached from some of the reputed social attributes of neighborhood communities. Yet there is emerging agreement that the residents' construction of a sense of neighborhood identity is in fact purposive. The fact that neighborhoods in general are seldom fellowships of friendship means not that people have ceased to have friends but that they are able to choose their friends from a wider area than the neighborhood, relatively unhampered by the imperative of geographic proximity. Social networks are now seen as products of voluntary choice, not determined by the primordial ties of kinship, ethnicity, or race or dictated by propinquity.[24] In a similar way, neighborhood identities may also become matters of choice—not natural and insensible by-products of localized friendship networks but results of conscious decision. The "natural" communities hypothesized by the Chicago school of urban sociology have been replaced by instrumental, artificial, "ideological communities," deliberately constructed and consciously advocated.[25]

But the sources of these constructions remain obscure. In part, as the evidence in Chapter 2 indicated, the sense of neighborhood identity may reflect the idiosyncratic influence of the neighborhood itself—a singular mixture of distinctive geographic features, past experience, and current leadership. Indeed, neighborhood identity seems more sensitive to the impact of such things than any of the other aspects of neighborhood politics that we have considered. But it is also a product of the residents' social characteristics, and it is not yet apparent how these attributes lead people to form conceptions of the neighborhoods where they live. We know that some of these social characteristics are unrelated to the sense of neighborhood identity. We do not know what kinds of characteristics encourage its development or what purposes it serves.

Perceiving the Neighborhood and Its Problems

Because they seldom exhibit the social solidarity of traditional communities, urban neighborhoods are frequently described as partial or incomplete communities — "communities of limited liability,"[26] "symbolic communities,"[27] or the like. The designations emphasize the social limitations of residential communities in cities, and they reflect a long-standing view that urbanism tends to undermine communalism. A generation of sociological commentary has elaborated on the theme that urban neighborhoods must amount to something less than communities in the traditional sense. Why they amount to anything at all has not been so fully explained. The reason for their functional deficiencies have been more completely specified than the reasons for their existence, and the unexpectedly persistent sense of neighborhood identity stands in special need of an explanation.

Although friendship ties and facility use do not seem to account for the existence of a sense of neighborhood identity, there are other factors that may tell us more about the social foundations for people's conceptions of the places where they live. Race and social class appear to be the most important of these other elements. Both are closely associated with the likelihood that neighborhood residents will assign names to their residential areas. As the findings reported in Table 3.3 indicate, the two factors have independent

Table 3.3. Race, socioeconomic status, and the sense of neighborhood identity (Percentage of respondents in each category who said that the neighborhood had a particular name)

| Race | Socioeconomic status | | |
	High	Medium	Low
Black	82.4 (115)	56.7 (428)	35.8 (395)
White and other nonblack	96.0 (403)	88.5 (480)	70.6 (174)

effects on the sense of neighborhood identity. The effects of race, for example, cannot be explained away completely by referring to socioeconomic status. Even among people of similar socioeconomic levels, black residents are consistently less likely to give names to their neighborhoods than whites.

Race and social class, of course, explain the development of neighborhood identity only in a statistical sense. Each of these social factors represents a complex ensemble of characteristics and experiences, any one of which might actually be responsible for the propensity to conceive of one's residential area as a distinct place with a name. To account for this propensity in something more than a formal way, we must consider just what it is about being black or poor that tends to obstruct the development of a sense of neighborhood identity, and what it is about being white or prosperous that encourages such developments.

One line of explanation, neglected in the past, is suggested by the recent emphasis on the voluntary and "artificial" character of urban subcommunities: perhaps black residents and poor residents are less likely than others to acquire a sense of neighborhood identity simply because they do not care so much for such acquisitions. Being black and being poor are not themselves matters of voluntary choice, but they may give rise to interests that condition people's choices. Residents who are black or poor may simply not be so interested as others in developing conceptions of the places where they live.

Explanations along these lines are implicit in the results of recent research, which suggest that a resident tends to form community attachments not only because the social environment of the neighborhood supplies an opportunity to develop these attachments but also because of some personal "vested interest" in the neighborhood that engenders a motivation to identify oneself as a community member. Homeownership, for example, appears to be one of the most important sources of this vested interest,[28] and it may also be a factor that helps to explain why race and social class are so closely associated with the sense of neighborhood identity. People who are black or poor are less likely to own their homes than those who are white or prosperous, and the absence of this economic stake in neighborhood society may help to explain why blacks and people of low social status are relatively disinclined to acquire a sense of neighborhood identity. Homeownership does account for a portion of the effect that race and social class have on the sense of neighborhood identity.[29] But an even more substantial part of their influence remains unexplained.

To account for the unexplained remainder, it is probably necessary to look beyond such individual attributes as homeownership. The evidence presented in Chapter 2, after all, has indicated that the sense of neighborhood identity may be more a product of neighborhood environment than of personal attributes like age or ethnicity or type of dwelling unit. In fact, it is more sensitive to the impact of the neighborhood setting than most of the other attitudes and perceptions that people have concerning the places where they live (see Table 2.1). Whether individual residents themselves are black or poor, in other words, will probably be insufficient to explain their sense of neighborhood identity, unless we also take account of the kinds of residential areas in which black or poor people tend to live. The survey results reported in Table 3.4 show that the type of area in which a person lives can be just as important for the sense of neighborhood identity as the individual resident's own characteristics. A comparison of the figures in each row of the table will show how much the sense of neighborhood identity varies with differences in the racial or social class composition of neighborhoods. A comparison of the figures in each column indicates how the propensity to name one's neighborhood varies with individual differences in race or socioeconomic status. In general, the results show that the racial composition of the neighborhood makes just about as much difference for the likelihood that residents will give names to

Table 3.4. Neighborhood racial and social class composition and the sense of neighborhood identity (Percentage of respondents in each category who said that the neighborhood had a particular name)

Race of individual respondents	Racial composition of neighborhood	
	Predominantly black	Predominantly white
Black	48.0 (828)	73.7 (114)
White	71.5 (31)	88.9 (1,030)

Socioeconomic status of individual residents	Socioeconomic status of neighborhood		
	High	Medium	Low
High	94.4 (400)	82.4 (285)	76.9 (54)
Medium	94.7 (76)	83.2 (390)	63.5 (220)
Low	79.7 (49)	47.9 (240)	29.2 (302)

their residential areas as does the race of the individual respondents themselves. In a similar way, variations in the socioeconomic composition of neighborhoods make differences for the sense of neighborhood identity that are roughly as large as the ones associated with socioeconomic variations among individual residents. In short, it is not simply being black or poor that inhibits the development of a sense of neighborhood identity; rather, it is something about living in black neighborhoods or poor neighborhoods.

Previous research is helpful in identifying some of the critical neighborhood conditions that may be responsible for strengthening or weakening the sense of neighborhood identity. Concerning the impact of neighborhood racial composition, for example, Donald I. Warren's study of black residential areas in Detroit suggests one possible line of explanation. The spatial segregation of blacks in American cities, says Warren, has resulted in the "social compression" of black residential communities. For the black urban population, this means that people who might otherwise live apart from one another — city dwellers of different social classes, values, or life-styles — may involuntarily become neighbors because of the residential restrictions imposed by racial discrimination. One consequence of this residential compression is that black neighborhoods may exhibit more internal heterogeneity than white neighborhoods, and Warren suggests that such social diversity may represent a serious handicap for effective community consensus and organization.[30] Although Warren does not make the claim himself, this internal heterogeneity could conceivably impede the emergence of a sense of neighborhood identity. Residents may be less likely to think of their residential areas as identifiable neighborhoods when the local population is not united by social similarity.

The survey evidence provides some support for this line of argument but also introduces some complications. With respect to the socioeconomic status of the residents, for example, black neighborhoods do seem to exhibit somewhat more internal diversity than white neighborhoods, but only if racially mixed residential areas (those where fewer than 90 percent of the respondents are of the same race) are considered separately from both other types of neighborhoods. Within these racially mixed areas, socioeconomic diversity is far more pronounced than it is in either the black or the white neighborhoods. An additional difficulty is that the relationship between socioeconomic diversity and the sense of neighborhood identity is not so consistent as might have been expected. If internal heterogeneity does inhibit the development of neighborhood identity, then one might anticipate that those black neighborhoods where socioeconomic diversity is most pronounced would also be the ones where the sense of neighborhood identity is least evident. But they are not. In fact, just the opposite is true. It is the most homogenous black neighborhoods where the sense of neighborhood identity is least widespread, and in general there is only a weak negative relationship between the socioeconomic diversity of neighborhoods and the likelihood that their residents will assign names to the places where they live.[31]

Variations in socioeconomic status, of course, do not represent the only possible source of social diversity within neighborhoods, and the conventional indicators of status may not have the same meaning in black neighborhoods as they do in white neighborhoods.[32] The evidence at hand may therefore be insufficient to reveal the full impact of social heterogeneity on the sense of neighborhood identity. But the evidence is at least sufficient to suggest that arguments about the effects of social diversity stand in need of a more comprehensive formulation. Socioeconomic diversity can help only in a limited way to account for the relative impairment of neighborhood identity in black residential areas, and it contributes even less to an understanding of this phenomenon in poor neighborhoods. There is certainly reason to suppose that the social dissimilarities in an area's population must have something to do with the inhabitants' ability to arrive at a coherent definition of the place where they live. But perhaps variability in status provides too narrow a conception of social diversity.

A somewhat more general view is implicit in Gerald Suttles's account of "defended neighborhoods" in the inner city. The emergence of these distinct residential areas, says Suttles, is a response to the disorder, uncertainty, and insecurity characteristic of urban life — all of which reflect social diversity of a sort. It is not simply a heterogeneity of social status, but a more broadly conceived behavioral and moral diversity originating partly in the fact that cities bring people of different types into close proximity and partly in the deficiencies of the social mechanisms for regulating relations among these people. These conditions are most pronounced in the inner city, where "ethnic and racial cleavages are still most apparent, undiluted, and irreconcilable. It is also that part of the city," says Suttles, "where population density and transiency are highest and together promote high levels of anonymity." This combination of anonymity and sharp social divisions tends to reduce the predictability of people's behavior. Conformity with legal or customary norms can seldom be taken for granted, and reliable expectations about the conduct of fellow citizens are further eroded by the concentration of the poor near the heart of the city. The apprehension that they will be "rather unruly, predatory, and unprincipled" seems to be shared even by the poor themselves.[33]

To maintain order and personal security under these circumstances, city residents have need of "cognitive maps" by which to regulate their movements and so minimize the frequency of encountering conflict, danger, or the unexpected. The defended neighborhood is likely to be the central feature of any such map. It marks the territory "within which people retreat to avoid a quantum jump in the risks of insult or injury that they must take in moving about outside that area."[34] The limits of the defended neighborhood define the area of greatest familiarity and security for its residents, an enclave of relative predictability in an unpredictable and untrustworthy environment. The size of the defended neighborhood, says Suttles, tends to vary according to the degree of disorder and uncertainty. In the low-income areas of the inner city, where mutual distrust is likely to be severe, the borders of the defended neighborhood may shrink to a single block or apartment building — an area that may be too small to carry its own distinct name.[35] When black or poor residents of the inner city fail to assign names to their neighborhoods, therefore, it may not always be the case that they are unable to define their residential territories. What we have regarded as evidence of an impaired sense of neighborhood identity may actually reflect a recognition of neighborhoods so diminutive that they do not qualify for any designation more specific than "my block" or "the street." If Suttles is correct, these nameless, miniature neighborhoods should be most common in precisely those inner city areas where black and poor people are numerous, and the concentration of these anonymous patches of territory in the inner city may help to explain why black and poor people are less likely than others to assign names to places where they live.

There is much evidence that lends substance to Suttles's account. Studies of neighborhood definitions among city residents show that the inhabitants of the inner city do tend to draw the boundaries of their neighborhoods much more narrowly than people who live in other parts of a metropolitan area.[36] This tendency to restrict the size of one's neighborhood may be echoed in patterns of community organization. In the present investigation, for example, interviews with panels of knowledgeable informants in each of the sample neighborhoods indicated that small block clubs are both more common and more influential in black residential areas than they are in white areas. Residents of the black areas sometimes seemed aware themselves that their images of the places where they live are drawn on a smaller scale than are the neighborhood conceptions of people elsewhere. A respondent in one low-income black area acknowledged the contrast succinctly: "There's no neighborhoods around here, just streets."

This is a way of viewing residential territory that may help to explain not only the failure to name the neighborhood but also the occurrence of disparities between "official" definitions of neighborhoods and the definitions used by residents. It may be significant, for example, that among the five sample neighborhoods where residents tended to ignore the standard names for their communities, four areas had predominantly black populations, and the remaining case was a low-income neighborhood with a white majority. In all these places, the use of idiosyncratic names or no names at all may reflect a tendency to disaggregate the territory of the official neighborhood into separate streets or blocks that enjoy no official recognition as distinct units. In fact, the residents themselves may not recognize these areas as authentic neighborhoods — they are "just streets." Yet even the acknowledgement of these fragmentary residential areas may be said to represent a sense of neighborhood identity — a conception of one's home territory drawn on a small scale so as to exclude as much of the inner city's disorder and insecurity as possible.

One significant difficulty stands in the way of this interpretation. Although such narrowly defined residential areas might remain unnamed, they cannot do without boundaries. According to Suttles, in fact, boundaries are among the most important and persistent characteristics of the defended neighborhood, and in parts of the city where social uncertainty, behavioral diversity, and insecurity are greatest, the definition of boundaries can be expected to assume special importance. Their prominence may be reflected, for example, in the territorial sensitivity of the inner city's juvenile gangs.[37] The problem is that this particular regard for neighborhood boundaries does not seem to be widely shared by the black or poor residents of the inner city. Just as these respondents were less likely than others to assign names to the places where they lived, they were also less likely to specify boundaries.[38] For these city dwellers, in other words, the failure to assign a name to the neighborhood is associated not simply with a tendency toward diminutive definitions of residential territory but with the general effacement of neighborhood identity itself. Their images of the places where they live tend to be shapeless as well as nameless, and it is questionable whether these constitute images at all.

The idea of the defended neighborhood probably captures the territorial conceptions of many city residents, but the survey results suggest that this notion may not be sufficiently comprehensive to portray the processes of neighborhood definition that operate in black or poor sections of the inner city. Perhaps a more general formulation is needed in order to explain not only the shrinkage of the neighborhood into a defensible fortress but the complete disappearance of the fortress itself. Although one response accentuates the distinction between domestic and foreign territory and the other erases it, both ways of viewing the residential area tend to occur side by side in predominantly black or low-status neighborhoods, and it is necessary to consider how the conditions of life in such areas might produce both points of view simultaneously.

For some black and low-status residents of the city, perhaps, the sense of insecurity is so overwhelming that it prevents the recognition of any safe territory at all beyond the front doorstep. Extreme anxiety of this kind could conceivably explain why black and poor people were less likely than other respondents to specify clear neighborhood boundaries. The same sort of disorder and uncertainty that causes the defended neighborhood to shrink in size may, in cases of intense insecurity, cause it to vanish entirely. One shortcoming of this theoretically economical explanation is that personal insecurity, although associated with a failure to define one's neighborhood by either name or territorial limits, is only weakly related to the obliteration of neighborhood identity. Respondents who said that it was unsafe to walk the local streets at night, for example, were only a little less likely to specify the names or boundaries for their neighborhoods than residents who felt secure on the streets after dark.[39] Considerations of security and social predictability may therefore be too limited to account for the processes of neighborhood definition.

Residents of poor and black neighborhoods are likely to have other pressing concerns, in any case. The same inner-city areas in which residents are most likely to experience threats to safety or social harmony are also places whose inhabitants usually confront a broad spectrum of irritations, inconveniences, affronts, and anxieties. Concentrated disproportionately in the older portions of the central city, urbanites who are black or poor may be also be exposed disproportionately to the problems of deteriorating neighborhoods where housing, sanitation, recreation, and schools all present difficulties just as vexing to the residents as the threat of crime or public disorder. One kind of response to such accumulations of neighborhood problems is to restrict the perceived scope of one's neighborhood, or to define the neighborhood itself out of existence. An inhibited sense of neighborhood identity may represent an important means for minimizing or avoiding the uncomfortable recognition of severe neighborhood problems. A house in the next block that has become an eyesore may seem less offensive if the next block can be placed beyond the limits of one's own neighborhood. When problems are more pervasive or closer to home, the failure to perceive any neighborhood territory at all beyond one's front door may allow for a degree of personal detachment from unpleasant surroundings. In urban areas where the streets are lined with abandoned buildings, drug addicts, or uncollected garbage, the sense of neighborhood identity may become another of the many things that local residents cannot afford to have.

The conditions that diminish the apprehension of a neighborhood identity are reflected in the survey evidence. Residents of poor or predominantly black neighborhoods tend to express an estrangement from their surroundings. They were more likely than other respondents to offer unfavorable evaluations of the general physical appearance of their residential areas, and they were also more likely to hold the opinion that their fellow residents were not good neighbors. Both expressions of distaste for the local environment were closely associated with the failure to specify the boundaries, the standard name, or any name at all for the neighborhood.[40] In short, the impairment of neighborhood identity among black and poor people may represent an understandable response to generally unappealing residential surroundings.

People who would find it infeasible to flee to the suburbs seem to develop other ways for escaping the aggravations of inner-city residential areas. Although the mental effacement of the neighborhood is certainly a less effective technique of avoidance than moving to a distant split-level, it belongs to the same family of strategies for dealing with undesirable situations. Exit — the simple abandonment of an enterprise where things are going badly — is one of the most common responses to perceived neighborhood deterioration. For some city residents, however, abandonment may be no simple matter. Poverty and race are encumbrances that sometimes make residental mobility impossible, or they only permit movement to areas of the city where refugees from a problem-ridden neighborhood would merely encounter more of the same. For many poor and black residents, therefore, exit may not be a practical means of coping with the afflictions of a declining neighborhood, and their handicaps in this respect are widely recognized. What may be recognized less clearly is the character of the alternatives to actual exit. One of them is psychological departure. If residents cannot get away from an undesirable neighborhood, they may be able to make the neighborhood go away instead, by denying the existence of a distinct and identifiable residential aggregate to which they belong. Though such expedients can hardly provide a successful defense against the discomforts of living in an unhappy residential area, they have considerable practical significance for the operations of neighborhood polities, because exit — even in its subjective form — is a substitute for the use of political action or "voice" as a response to undesirable conditions.[41] Those who do not detach themselves from their neighborhoods will be available to protest its problems.

Previous research has found that the propensity to resort to political action may be closely linked to people's prospects for residental mobility. City residents whose exit opportunities are restricted — blacks, for example — are more strongly inclined than others to regard political action as a corrective for neighborhood problems.[42] But it is also important to note that an inhibited sense of neighborhood identity makes them less likely to perceive the problems in the first place. Apart from its importance in defining a neighborhood polity, the sense of neighborhood identity provides a framework in which residents may begin to construct personal agendas of local problems and issues. When this framework is absent, the development of the agendas may be seriously impeded, and the likelihood of corrective action will decline. In fact, the inability to see any prospects for corrective action could itself inhibit both the emergence of neighborhood identity and the capacity to perceive neighborhood problems. No matter what the causal sequence, however, one implecation remains: though the relationship may sometimes seem paradoxical, a sharp sense of neighborhood identity is often accompanied by a sharp sense of neighborhood ailments and shortcomings.

A Framework for Defining Local Issues

In Coldstream-Homestead-Montebello, a three-day conference on local grievances provided the occasion for recognizing a new neighborhood definition. The circumstances may have seemed inauspicious for inaugurating a sense of neighborhood identity, but there is probably a close and general connection between forming a conception of the place where one lives and forming complaints about it. Mrs. Johnson perceived that bringing local residents together to discuss such common problems as sanitation or the cleaning of alleys might be an appropriate way to celebrate the emergence of a common identity.

Neighborhood problems themselves, of course, do not usually contribute to the residents' awareness of their neighborhoods. If they did, we might expect that residential areas with the most numerous and grievous difficulties would also be the ones whose inhabitants express the clearest conceptions of the places where they live. But we have already seen that this is not the case; in fact, just the opposite seems to be true. Neighborhoods that appear to suffer from the most severely unfavorable conditions are places whose inhabitants seem least likely to develop sharp images of their home territories. The presence of potentially troubling conditions in a residential area tends to dim the sense of neighborhood identity. But if this impairment of neighborhood identity provides a defense against the recognition of local troubles, it follows that a clear conception of the neighborhood should heighten the perception of trouble.

Because it can be related in such contrary ways to neighborhood problems, on the one hand, and to the perception of these problems, on the other, the sense of neighborhood identity may give rise to a peculiar disjunction between the existence of apparently undesirable local conditions and the residents' awareness of them. Where circumstances seem to warrant the most severe complaints, an impairment of the sense of neighborhood identity can be expected to limit the residents' recognition of what there is to complain about. But in more pleasant neighborhoods with fewer apparent reasons for discontent, a strong sense of neighborhood identity is likely to sharpen the inhabitants' sensitivity to possible objects of dissatisfaction.

This is not a case of false consciousness, but simply of variable consciousness. People's perceptions of neighborhood problems are not uniformly related to the underlying conditions that they supposedly reflect. The sense of neighborhood identity seems to influence this relationship in ways that could help to explain a common but poorly understood occurrence in neighborhood politics — the fact that even when they seem to face the same kinds of undesirable conditions, residents of different neighborhoods may nevertheless have sharply different ideas about the nature of local problems. Examining the role of neighborhood identity in the recognition of neighborhood problems may also help to confirm the part that its impairment can play in dulling peoples' awareness of unpleasant surroundings.

To detect the influence of neighborhood identity, of course, it is necessary to distinguish the impact of other factors. The most important of these other elements are the observable conditions to which people refer when they complain about neighborhood problems — trash on the streets, the run-down and abandoned buildings, crime and disorder. If neighborhood identity has an independent effect on recognition of such local problems, then its influence on peoples' perceptions of these underlying conditions should be evident even when the conditions themselves are held constant. Unfortunately, the measurement of these conditions has not reached a state of refinement that permits them to be held constant statistically with any precision. But relatively effective measurements were possible for two types of local problems.

The first of these was crime. All respondents were asked whether they or any members of their households had experienced any thefts in the neighborhood during the past year or so. Theft surely does not exhaust the full range of crime and disorder to which city residents are likely to be exposed, but it is a rather widespread sort of crime and one striking enough to be memorable yet seldom personal enough to be worth concealing from an interviewer. Previous criminal victimization surveys indicate that theft is one of the offenses for which the police receive relatively accurate reports.[43] This record of substantially reliable reporting was one of the reasons for choosing theft as an index of neighborhood crime problems for the present study. In the minds of the respondents at least, it seems to be associated with more general manifestations of crime and disorder. There is a positive relationship, for example, between the reported frequency of theft in a neighborhood and the prevalence of the belief that "crime or vandalism by young people or adults" has become a local problem.[44]

Physical deterioration was the second type of neighborhood problem for which at least approximate measurements could be obtained. Although no public agency makes frequent and systematic efforts to assess the condition of buildings in the city's neighborhoods, the local Department of Housing and Community Development conducts a periodic inventory of abandoned houses throughout Baltimore. A building, of course, need not have been abandoned in order to become deteriorated, but abandonment is generally regarded as a decisive symptom of disinvestment in neighborhoods. Abandonment is usually a response to the decline of a residential area; it contributes to further decay; and a deserted structure usually becomes a neighborhood liability itself soon after it has been abandoned.[45] Using data collected by the city government, all aban-doned houses were located for a probability sample of twenty census blocks in each of the neighborhoods under study — the same blocks from which the respondents had previously been selected for the survey of local residents. The data drawn from the municipal re-cords made it possible to determine whether individual survey re-spondents lived in the immediate area of an abandoned building. The areas under consideration are in most cases identical with indi-vidual city blocks. By aggregating information from all twenty of these blocks in a residential area, it was also possible to arrive at an estimate of the extent of abandoned housing in each of the sample neighborhoods. As in the case of theft, this measure of a specific lo-cal symptom was closely associated with people's perceptions of the more general problem. There was a strong relationship between the percentage of abandoned housing units in an area and the preva-lence of the opinion the "run-down houses and buildings" had be-come a local problem.[46]

But the findings in Table 3.5 show that exposure to "objective" conditions does not account fully for people's perceptions of neigh-borhood problems. The respondents have been divided into categor-ies here according to the degree of their exposure to potentially troublesome local conditions. In part A, for example, the left-hand column includes those residents whose households actually experi-enced thefts themselves. Next are people whose households have not had anything stolen but who live in neighborhoods where the rate of theft is high. Finally, there are those respondents whose households have not been victims of theft and who do not reside in high-theft areas. In part B, the respondents have been divided in a similar way to distinguish different degrees of exposure to neighborhood deterioration.

Comparing the figures across each row shows how the degree of actual exposure to potentially bothersome conditions influenced the likelihood that people would feel bothered by them. Not surprisingly, the results indicate that the greater people's exposure to theft or hous-ing abandonment, the more likely they are to complain about prob-lems of crime or physical deterioration of their neighborhoods. The finding is notable only because of the persistent view that residents of disadvantaged neighborhoods somehow get used to the conditions under which they must live, and that even a slum neighborhood may actually express its residents' tastes, preferences, or chosen style of life. The lower-class inhabitant of a slum, the argument goes, "is not troubled by dirt and dilapidation and does not mind the inadequacy

Table 3.5. The sense of neighborhood identity and perceptions of local problems, controlling for exposure to problem conditions

A. Crime (Percentage of respondents in each category who said they were bothered by crime or vandalism)

	Household's exposure to theft		
Respondent's sense of neighborhood identity	Victim	Nonvictim, but lives in high-theft neighborhood	Nonvictim, lives in low-theft neighborhood
Identifies neighborhood by name	75.5 (306)	46.3 (540)	30.5 (592)
Cannot identify neighborhood by name	61.2 (90)	33.5 (191)	23.6 (304)

B. Physical deterioration (Percentage of respondents in each category who said they were bothered by run-down houses or buildings)

	Household's exposure to deterioration		
Respondent's sense of neighborhood identity	Abandoned building on same block	High abandonment rate in neighborhood, but none on block	Low abandonment rate in neighborhood, none on block
Identifies neighborhood by name	56.5 (238)	52.0 (215)	15.1 (986)
Cannot identify neighborhood by name	57.4 (287)	33.2 (174)	13.0 (122)

of public facilities such as schools, parks, hospitals, and libraries."[47] The present evidence, on the contrary, suggests that city residents who are exposed to such problems tend to mind it very much.

But the survey results also indicate that such concern about neighborhood problems can be modified somewhat by the sense of neighborhood identity. Once the actual exposure to theft or abandoned buildings has been taken into account, there remain variations in people's conceptions of neighborhood crime or physical deterioration that are associated with their ability to assign particular names to the places where they live. In part A, for example a comparison of the two percentage figures in each column will show that even among those who are similarly exposed to theft, residents who cannot identify their neighborhoods by name are consistently less likely than others to believe that crime is a local problem. Though the size of its effect is not especially large, the sense of neighborhood identity appears to heighten city dwellers' sensitivity to the threat of crime and disorder.

Having a conception of one's neighborhood probably increases the ability to augment personal experience with the aggregated experience of an identifiable part of the city. In the case of the crime problem, this is apt to sharpen the residents' awareness of the robberies, attacks, or disorders that occur beyond their own doorsteps or their own blocks, and their impressions of the local crime problem will tend to grow accordingly. A sense of neighborhood identity increases the supply of raw material from which a person might construct an idea of local crime.

The situation is slightly different, however, with respect to ideas about local deterioration. The findings in part B of Table 3.5 show that the sense of neighborhood identity affects the awareness of local decay for only one group of respondents — those who live in areas where the rate of building abandonment is high but whose own blocks do not contain any abandoned buildings. An ability to identify one's neighborhood under these circumstances carries with it an ability to notice the physical deterioration that exists in the territory beyond one's immediate surroundings. But in other circumstances the sense of neighborhood identity does not have the same effect. The findings in the first column of part B show that when physical deterioration invades the block itself, the residents' perceptions of the neighborhood decay are essentially unaffected by their ability to identify the neighborhood. For people directly exposed to run-down buildings, in other words, this ability seems to have less influence on the perception of problems than it does for people directly exposed to theft. The reason, perhaps, is that an abandoned building a few doors away is simply not the same as a mugging a few doors away. Instances of crime are fleeting and extraordinary and usually not visible, and people's responses to them are likely to depend on the contexts in which they perceive these occurrences. But a derelict building is a more tangible and durable presence. If you have one on your block, it is likely to bother you whether you have a sense of neighborhood identity or not.

What may be the most notable implication of the survey findings, however, is that even if there are no abandoned buildings on one's block, the sense of neighborhood identity can make those in the next block or further away seem almost as objectionable as if they were just a few doors down the street or around the corner. For people

who were able to identify their neighborhoods by name, it made little difference whether derelict buildings were in the same block or
more distantly distributed around the neighborhood. Complaints
about neighborhood deterioration were just about as frequent in one
situation as in the other. Among people who lived on the same block
as an abandoned structure, 56.5 percent of those who could identify
the neighborhood by name said they were bothered by rundown
houses or buildings. The proportion declines only slightly, to 52.0
percent, when deserted buildings lay somewhere in the neighborhood beyond the respondent's own block. By contrast, when
residents could not identify their neighborhoods by name, distance
made for a much sharper decline in sensitivity to deterioration, from
57.4 percent to 33.2 percent.

A sense of neighborhood identity seems to extend the scope of personal concern. Having a conception of one's neighborhood may not
mean that a person is "public-regarding,"[48] but it does at least imply
a rather broad definition of private interests — a capacity to perceive
neighborhood problems that do not impinge on one's own immediate surroundings. It may be argued, of course, that this expan-
sive view actually has nothing to do with the sense of neighborhood
identity. The evidence has already indicated that social status is one
of the factors that seems to lie behind the propensity to form distinct
conceptions of neighborhoods, and it could also be responsible for
the effects that have been attributed to the sense of neighborhood
identity. High-status occupations and high levels of education may
be accompanied by conceptual skills and by public-regarding sentiments that contribute simultaneously to conceptions of the neighborhood and to conceptions of neighborhood problems. In that case,
the relationship that we found between the sense of neighborhood
identity and the perception of neighborhood problems might be only
an artifact of other things, and it could be explained away by referring to social status.

The obvious test for such possibilities is to examine the relationship between neighborhood identity and the perception of local
problems while controlling not only for the degree of exposure to
bothersome conditions but also for social status. Unfortunately, this
would require us to subdivide the respondents into so many categories that some of the subdivisions would be empty or nearly empty.
High-status residents of deteriorating areas who have no sense of
neighborhood identity are not likely to be very numerous, after all.
The number of respondents is sufficiently large, however, so that it is
possible to find out whether social status might explain variations in

the perception of local problems for people who are similarly exposed to potentially troublesome conditions. The results indicate that after the degree of exposure to theft or abandoned buildings has been taken into account, the relationship between social status and problem perceptions is so weak that it would be mathematically impossible for variations in status to explain away the association between the sense of neighborhood identity and the perception of such problems as crime or local decay.

In general, the evidence is consistent with the line of interpretation that has been pursued here: socioeconomic status is important chiefly because it determines what kind of neighborhood a person lives in, and therefore plays a leading role in deciding the kinds of neighborhood problems to which a city resident will be exposed. These neighborhood conditions, and not just individual social status itself, seem to have considerable influence on the development of a sense of neighborhood identity. In neighborhoods beset with problems, residents tend to have an attenuated sense of neighborhood identity or none at all. Abstaining from the recognition of a distinct residential territory is probably a way of obscuring undesirable neighborhood conditions. The failure to form a conception of one's neighborhood may therefore represent a defensive measure taken against a troubling or unattractive residential environment. Its insulating effects are evident in the survey results. They show that even when people are exposed to the same kinds of troublesome conditions, those who lack a sense of neighborhood identity are less likely than others to perceive these conditions as problems.

Residents who do perceive neighborhood problems, on the other hand, may become aware of other things at the same time. When they acknowledge that they are bothered by conditions beyond their own doorways, they implicitly recognize that the places where they live are parts of a larger residential territory that is not entirely private or personal, and they acknowledge that this public domain has become an object of concern. The concern itself may not represent a selfless regard for the public good, only a private interest in personal comfort or property values. But it is a private interest that takes shape within a conception of the neighborhood as a public area — a territory shared in common with neighbors.

People who form conceptions of their residential areas as distinct neighborhoods have also formed a kind of political covenant or social contract with their fellow residents. The terms of this implicit convention do not include the traditional Lockean agreements to abide by the decisions of a common authority or to surrender the rights enjoyed in some hypothesized state of nature. But they do imply the common recognition of a public space — both the physical sort of space and the metaphorical kind that political theorists sometimes discuss.[49] Public space is the medium in which one may address concerns that extend beyond the privacy of one's own living room or backyard.

Apart from creating the common ground for public action and discussion, the sense of neighborhood identity also helps to sustain one element essential to any polity — an agenda. It supplies the framework within which local residents arrive at definitions of local troubles. It is this aspect of neighborhood identity that reveals the insufficiency of the view that what city dwellers seek in their neighborhoods is primarily a place of refuge from the disturbances and impersonal insults of urban life, a secure haven that shields its inhabitants from the unfamiliar and the unpleasant. In fact, it is precisely the failure to develop a sense of neighborhood that actually seems to serve these ends and permits residents to retreat to the privacy of their personal domains. The sense of neighborhood identity, on the other hand, brings a sharper recognition of unpleasant or unsettling conditions. It is not simply a device for excluding what is alien or unattractive; it mediates between the personal concerns of private citizens and the more general problems of the city at large.[50] Rather than enabling residents to avoid trouble, the sense of neighborhood identity may lead them to embrace it.

Some rather eccentric results may seem to follow from this. It may offend a social scientist's sense of fitness, for example, that instead of reducing people's anxieties about local crime and disorder, neighborhood identity can actually inflate worries about these dangers. More important, results of this kind make it difficult to imagine why anyone would want a sense of neighborhood identity in the first place, since few people are inclined to add to the worries they already have.

The reason, perhaps, is that the same definition of the neighborhood that sharpens the perception of things to worry about may also carry at least the prospect of reducing these worries. The beginnings of local political order that are evident in neighborhood identity may eventually culminate in the emergence of a leadership stratum — a set of unofficial authorities who deal with their community's public business and whose role is recognized by local residents. To find out about residents' perceptions of these local authorities, respondents were asked whether they thought there were "some real leaders living in this neighborhood who can bring the neighbors together to get things done." The findings reported in Table 3.6 show that people who saw effective leadership in their neighborhoods were less likely to be bothered by crime or neighborhood decay than residents who did not perceive such leaders. The difference between these two types of respondents persisted even when they were similarly exposed to theft or derelict buildings. A belief in the existence of people and arrangements capable of handling neighborhood problems apparently makes potentially troublesome conditions seem less worrisome or noticeable. Perhaps the mere sense that there is someone else to worry about these matters relieves local residents of the responsibility of worrying so much themselves.

The belief in local leadership, of course, could be groundless; it may simply reflect a general inclination to think favorable thoughts about one's neighborhood. The same inclination could also lead residents to overlook such local problems as crime or physical deteriora-

Table 3.6. Perceived leadership and perceptions of local problems, controlling for exposure to problem conditions

A. CRIME (Percentage of respondents in each category who said they were bothered by crime or vandalism)

Respondent's perceptions of neighborhood leadership	Household's exposure to theft		
	Victim	Nonvictim, lives in high-theft neighborhood	Nonvictim, lives in low-theft neighborhood
Perceives "real leaders"	70.9 (200)	42.6 (416)	25.2 (409)
Perceives no "real leaders"	72.5 (178)	47.8 (284)	34.7 (434)

B. PHYSICAL DETERIORATION (Percentage of respondents in each category who said they were bothered by run-down houses or buildings)

Respondent's perceptions of neighborhood leadership	Household's exposure to deterioration		
	Abandoned building on same block	High abandonment in neighborhood, but none on block	Low abandonment in neighborhood none on block
Perceives "real leaders"	48.8 (262)	34.9 (217)	13.8 (544)
Perceives no "real leaders"	68.8 (242)	51.6 (172)	17.3 (479)

tion, and it would therefore account for the relationship between the perception of effective local leadership and failure to perceive local problems. But there are two indications that the respondents' impressions about neighborhood leadership reflect an institutional property of the neighborhood itself and not just their own personal inclinations. First, the leadership perceptions of the people living in a particular neighborhood tend to be consistent with the reports of the knowledgeable informants who were subsequently interviewed concerning the same neighborhood. There was an association of moderate strength, for example, between the percentage of residents in a neighborhood who perceived effective local leadership and the prevalence of the same assessment among the informants.[51] An even stronger relationship was found between the leadership perceptions of the residents at large and the extent to which local informants agreed that "when it comes to the handling of community issues and activities, the people who live in this area are very well organized."[52]

A second piece of evidence also suggests that there is some basis for the respondents' assessments of local leadership. In neighborhoods where high proportions of residents have positive impressions about local leadership, the tendency to be untroubled by crime or deteriorated buildings is evident, not just for those residents who express confidence in community leadership, but also for the minority who do not share this belief. The implication here is that something in the neighborhood environment itself, rather than just the imaginations of individual respondents, helps to soothe the worries of people who live in areas where effectiveness of local leadership is widely recognized. There are obvious grounds for the presumption that this environmental factor is to be found in the political and leadership arrangements of neighborhoods.

The process of transforming a neighborhood into a political society is one that not only heightens the sensitivity to local problems and issues but also holds out the promise of institutions that can cope with these difficulties. The development of a sense of neighborhood identity among local residents does not lead in any reliable way to the creation of these political arrangements, but it defines an element of commonality among neighbors that can provide the foundation and the justification for common processes of governance. And it serves as a framework for defining the problems and issues that may preoccupy those who govern. Just who governs and what they do about neighborhood problems are issues that the mere emergence of neighborhood identity does not resolve.

In general, the evidence helps to clarify what it means for a neighborhood to become a political society. In the first place, it does not necessarily mean that the local residents are especially fond of one another. John Locke's lonely primitives may have been moved to form polities by "the love, and want of Society," but friendship and sociability do not figure prominently in the process by which modern city dwellers come to regard themselves as members of identifiable residential communities. Nor are residents drawn to acknowledge their neighborhoods by the magnetic attraction of neighborhood churches, stores, or work places. In short, the sense of neighborhood identity is not a collective ratification of private friendship and neighborly solidarity among the inhabitants of a residential area. Instead, it seems to be a cognitive container for the definition of neighborhood issues and problems. People who live in "bad" neighborhoods can insulate themselves from the recognition of local troubles by failing to develop a conception of the neighborhood. People who live in more fortunate neighborhoods are more likely to form such conceptions, and (other things being equal) they are also more likely to perceive the problems that they encounter in their communities. "Good" neighborhoods, it seems, prompt residents to recognize what is bad about them, because they foster the sense of neighborhood identity and so sharpen sensitivity to local aggravations and inconveniences.

In the process, private residential areas begin to acquire political status. Those who define the neighborhood's problems, after all, are also supplying the raw material for neighborhood politics. The sense of neighborhood identity itself implies the recognition of a public sphere, shared in common with fellow residents. Those who acknowledge it have elected not to exercise their options for psychological exit from the local domain; they are potential users of "voice" as an instrument for dealing with neighborhood concerns. In fact, most forms of neighborhood political action that we shall subsequently consider turn out to be associated with the ability to arrive at a definition of one's neighborhood.[53]

In other words, the sense of neighborhood identity not only heightens sensitivity to local problems and issues but also holds out the promise of actions and arrangements to cope with these difficulties. The development of a sense of neighborhood identity among residents does not lead in any reliable way to the creation of local political arrangements, but it defines an element of commonality among neighbors that can provide the foundation and justification for common processes of governance. These processes, and not merely the conception of neighborhood itself, convert residential areas into fully functioning neighborhood polities. In order to constitute a political society, residents must not only think of themselves as politically related, they must act as though they are.

4.
Informal
Governance

*Lombard Street, Union Square. Photograph by
Charlotte Crenson.*

A bout seventy-five residents of the Union Square area marched through the streets of their neighborhood on a pleasant day in June 1977, carrying a mock coffin. When the procession reached the shady, green precincts of Union Square Park, the imitation casket would undergo a figurative burial (literal excavations being prohibited in the park), and a simulated funeral ceremony would symbolize the marchers' wish that a recently proposed historic preservation ordinance for the neighborhood might soon be laid to rest by the City Council. For participants in the demonstration, the legislation represented a new source of anxiety about the future of their community, and it created particular uncertainty about their own places in it. Historic preservation might help to ensure the permanence of the area's buildings, but it was the staying power of their inhabitants that worried the protesters. Tenants of "historical" structures might have to pay higher rents than those who lived in buildings that were merely old, and homeowners on fixed incomes might face sharply higher property tax assessments once their neighborhood became quaint and not just obsolete. In time, the place could become too expensive for many of its current residents, and it was this apprehension that moved the imitation mourners at the mock funeral. They were trying to convince their neighbors that things were not what they seemed: in Union Square, preservation meant change.

The process of change had actually started almost ten years earlier, when the neighborhood had begun to attract a new group of residents — young, well-educated, and usually childless people who saw possibilities in the block-square park and the graceful nineteenth-century townhouses that bordered it. At first, longtime residents, who had seen the neighborhood undergo steady decline for more than twenty years, had not put much store by these possibilities. A restoration of respectability seemed impossibly remote to people who had watched the neighborhood park as it had been gradually given over to derelicts, or neighborhood homes as they had fallen from scrubbed gentility to decay to abandonment. A seventy-three-year-old resident from nearby Lombard Street, interviewed in 1967 on a park bench in Union Square, had held out little hope for improvement: "All of the hoodlums in this part of the city hang out in the square . . . There used to be wonderful, good, middle-class people here who worked hard, were proud of their home and kept it clean. Ladies would go out there [in the park] and sit and no one would bother them. Some of these stumble-bums now have no more respect for a lady than for a dog. I think America's gone to hell, my kind of America. There are no ideals left around here."[1] Not far away, a twenty-four-year-old newcomer to the neighborhood was working with his wife to renovate three of the brick rowhouses that faced the park. Robert and Joanne Whitely had recently graduated from college, where he had majored in French and she had majored in English. Now he was a milkman and she was a waitress. They had moved into the neighborhood a year earlier. "The Square struck me as being unusual and extraordinary," said Whitely, "the best of what was left in a decaying inner city area." And he was determined not to let it decay any further: "I'm just interested in preserving all of Baltimore. If you lose this, you lose the real character of the city. With all the modern steel and glass in cities, you're losing your identity. Every city will look the same; there'll be nothing unique or all its own."[2]

The Whitelys' plans extended beyond the three houses that they had already begun to salvage. At their request an architect had produced a rendering of an entirely restored, derelict-free Union Square, with an ornate iron fountain to replace one that had been removed long before. Later in 1967 Joanne Whitely became a founder of the Union Square Association, along with other new and old residents who were interested in neighborhood restoration. In 1970 the group successfully urged the City Council to declare the blocks immediately adjacent to the square a historic preservation district. In 1975 the city completed a $250,000 program of improvements in Union Square Park, and a private fundraising campaign sponsored by the Union Square Association generated enough money to pay for a new $9,000 iron fountain. By 1977 the association's leaders were lobbying for an enlargement of the preservation district that would triple its size. It was this proposal for expansion that had prompted dissenting residents to launch their funeral procession through the square.

The protesters assembled on Mount Street west of the park and marched eastward on Hollins Street along the northern edge of Union Square, carrying their signs past some of the neighborhood's most notable examples of renovated gaslight-era architecture, singing their own version of the "Battle Hymn of the Republic" ("Our eyes have seen the renters as they're thrown out in the street . . . "). From the front steps of several restored buildings, homeowners watched the procession pass, sensing that the demonstration was directed as much at them as at the City Council. They complained of being "persecuted" and "abused." "We are not exactly rich people," said one of them. "We moved in with nothing down and a 7 percent loan and worked hard to restore a home. We feel we have contributed to the neighborhood."[3] Leaflets being distributed by the protesters suggested that the contributions of preservationists might eventually drive neighbors from their homes, and they expressed a suspicion that restoration might contribute more to the incomes of real estate speculators than to the collective good of the neighborhood.

The distinction between private gain and public good had never been especially clear in Union Square. The neighborhood's birth in 1846 was the result of a philanthropic gesture. Three brothers from a prosperous Baltimore mercantile family donated a square of land west of the city's business district for a public park. But the brothers also owned all of the real estate for some distance around it, and their next task was to bring into being the public that would benefit most immediately from their act of generosity. By 1847 the philanthropists were subdividing the fields around Union Square into building lots, constructing homes, and selling them to Baltimoreans who fancied life near a city-maintained park.

The homebuilding business continued to draw profits from the environs of Union Square until the late 1880s. Since the empty lots were gradually filled with brick rowhouses over such an extended time, the area today includes a broad cross-section of mid to late nineteenth-century building styles. Architectural diversity has provided one of the chief arguments for historic preservation of the neighborhood. It is a part of the city that reflects not only the progressive variations in mid-Victorian domestic taste but variations in social class as well. The finer houses of prosperous Baltimore families faced one another across the square and lined up along the main thoroughfares nearby. On narrow side streets were diminutive homes for the families of working men, many of them employed by the Baltimore and Ohio Railroad, whose shops and yards once lay only a short distance away. City administrators reviewing the proposal for an expansion of the preservation district in 1977 found in the area's varied housing stock an accurate reflection of "the economic, social, and racial heterogeneity which characterized Baltimore's neighborhood villages before the advent of motor transportation."[4] A house on Hollins Street, along the route of the 1977 funeral march, represented a further claim to historic distinction. The parents of H. L. Mencken bought it when the future Sage of Baltimore was three years old, and except for an absence of half a dozen years, he continued to occupy it until his death in 1956. Union Square and its vicinity figure prominently in his autobiographical recollections of childhood in the 1880s, when the neighborhood "was still almost rural, for there were plenty of vacant lots nearby, and open country began only a few blocks away."[5]

It would be almost as difficult to imagine vacant lots and open country in the Union Square of the late 1970s as to conceive of H. L. Mencken in childhood. Vacant buildings, however, were much in evidence. A sample survey in 1979 indicated that approximately 6 percent of the structures in the neighborhood were abandoned, and the people of the neighborhood had not fared much better than the buildings. As in Mencken's youth, most of the local residents — about 90 percent — were white, but 49 percent of those interviewed reported annual family incomes of less than $5,000. The neighborhood preservation movement may help to account for the fact that an area with so many low-income households also included a relatively high proportion of prosperous ones. About 19 percent of the local respondents reported yearly family incomes higher than $20,000. Other peculiarities of the inhabitants may be related to this economic disparity. In particular, the residents interviewed in Union Square were more likely than people in any other area studied to report that many of their neighbors did not get along with one another. They were also more likely to say that they had been personally annoyed with at least some of their neighbors during the preceding year, and they were more likely than residents elsewhere to say that they had recently argued with a neighbor. Compared to Baltimoreans interviewed in other parts of the city, the people who live around Union Square seem to be more contentious, more argumentative, and more irritated with one another than residents anywhere else. Mencken would be proud.

The social and political divisiveness of the neighborhood could be seen in the protest against enlargement of the historical preservation district — and not just in the division between preservationists and their opponents. Each of these factions exhibited its own internal variations of interest and opinion. In the procession that marched past H. L. Mencken's house, for example, there were at least three distinct contingents. One of them had been mobilized by Brendan Walsh, an activist in the Catholic Worker movement who had moved to Union Square from New York in 1968. He and his wife had established a shelter for homeless men on Mount Street about a block west of the park. Unsupported by public funds, their work was financed by private contributions, drawn in large part from his income as a school teacher and hers as a nurse. Upstairs in the house on Mount Street the Walsh family lived; downstairs there was soup and a place to sleep for the vagrants and drifters who collected in the park or the vacant buildings in its vicinity.

In 1976 Walsh distributed the first in a series of leaflets and pamphlets concerning the issue of neighborhood preservation. It protested the expenditure of $250,000 for cosmetic improvements to Union Square Park. The broadside argued that the park had already been adequate for most residents of the neighborhood, and that the funds for its improvement might have been spent more usefully to provide deprived people in the surrounding area with "food, clothing, and the supplies necessary to repair houses in need of repair." As for the preservationists, Walsh charged that the "concern of these individuals is not historical preservation; it is 'bank book preservation.'" A more extensive pamphlet distributed early in 1977 attempted to back up this accusation. Based on an examination of real estate records, it reported that some of the leading neighborhood preservationists were actually property speculators who stood to gain financially if the expansion of the historic district were approved. Walsh charged that one local family in particular, whose members had bought thirty-eight buildings, stood "as an example of speculators . . . They urge us to raise the question: Is 'historical preservation expansion' really concerned with the preservation of history *or* is it more concerned with profit and human greed?"

Robert and Joanne Whitely, together with two sisters of Mrs. Whitely, were the family in question. In less than ten years' time, their effort to salvage neighborhood houses had matured into Robert E. Whitely and Company, Realtors, and Mrs. Whitely was now the leading proponent of an expanded preservation district. Walsh used two mimeographed pages to inventory the family's real estate transactions in the neighborhood, and in a later broadside he added tax advantages to speculative gain as a motive for expanding the preservation area. Under new federal tax legislation, owners of income-producing properties in historic districts became eligible for special tax benefits if they had spent more than $5,000 on the exterior restoration of a structure. Homeowners who restored the buildings where they lived were not eligible for similar benefits.

Walsh distributed his pamphlets door-to-door around the neighborhood, provoking "a lot of reaction" in the process. The responses ranged from talk of a lawsuit against him to expressions of interest and support. He began to hold meetings in the house on Mount Street to discuss a course of action against the preservationists. Among the thirty or thirty-five residents who usually attended was Mary Avara, a figure of recognized authority in neighborhood affairs who had never before led her followers into an alliance with those of Walsh. Mrs. Avara had grown up in the neighborhood and lived there for all of her sixty-seven years. Her family had been established in the area even longer; Mrs. Avara's mother had run a local grocery store whose income had helped to support Mary and her seventeen brothers and sisters. Later Mrs. Avara herself, a widow for many years, had supported her own family as a bail bondswoman, an occupation that had made her almost as well known among the city's judges, lawyers, and politicians as she was among her neighbors. These far-flung networks of acquaintanceship had contributed to her qualifications as a neighborhood leader in Democratic party politics, and in the mid-1940s she had founded her own organization—the Sixth District Women's Civic and Welfare League—which she continued to lead long after retiring from the bail bond business.

Disdainful of government-sponsored antipoverty and community action programs, she was proud of the grass-roots support elicited by her own efforts at community organization:

> I'll tell you. I don't care who's involved with any of these [other] organizations—the urban whatever-they-call-it down here. They cannot get people anywhere like I can. I can pack St. Peter's hall, packed and jammed, with the Sunday afternoon bingo. They have to find chairs to seat them if Mary Avara's behind it. They know that I will not rip them off. I will not lie to them. And I notarize papers free. I do not charge for the notary. I never charge nobody for nothing. I

will get up in the morning and go to court with them—
wherever . . .

I do more for the people in this neighborhood than any
other program that you have . . . I have a club here. They
play bingo for two cents or five cents a game. I take them to
Atlantic City and places. We have prayer meetings here. We
have people here who are in dire need of help. They come
here to me. They have nowhere to go to get their yards
cleaned, or how about the welfare, or if they're out of food.
They come here exactly to my house.

While Brendan Walsh's house west of the square offered shelter
and food for destitute men in the area, Mary Avara's on the east was
a place where neighborhood women, usually elderly, could find advice and support. Unlike the Walsh home, however, one could also
register to vote there. "I put more people on the books to vote than
anybody," says Mrs. Avara. "They put people on to vote, then they
vote my ticket . . . I keep their names and addresses and I write to
them with my envelope—not on anything that looks political, 'cause
that goes in the garbage, but with my handwriting. It's a personal
letter: 'This is me.'"

According to independent observers of neighborhood politics,
Mrs. Avara's personal touch can produce approximately three hundred votes for any political candidate who manages to befriend her.
The terms of friendship are usually straightforward. When aspiring
officeholders request her support, says Mrs. Avara, "we don't talk
politics—never. I just say, 'What are you going to give us? So much
toward a bus trip?'" The only visible personal reward for Mrs.
Avara's political labor has been her appointment as a part-time
member of the State Board of Movie Censors, where her spirited attacks on pornography and her discreetly vivid descriptions of the
films from which she and her board have protected the public have
made her a minor celebrity in places far from Union Square.

Her views about the historic preservation of the neighborhood
were expressed in terms almost as strong. It was a "money-making
racket" that raised rents so high for many of her neighbors that
"these poor people can't even *exist* . . . When there started to be the
historical area, they threw these people out." The residents who
moved in to replace them were often uncongenial strangers ("These
are the kind of people . . . you say something about them, they get
a lawyer"), not the sorts of neighbors who were likely to show up for

the Sunday bingo at St. Peter's hall or lend much support to the Sixth District Women's Civic and Welfare League. And the historic pretensions of the preservationsists did not impress Mrs. Avara. "We knew H. L. Mencken," she says, without awe. "He dealt with my mother. All these stories that you hear building up about H. L. Mencken. He used to wear a coat — I still remember — and a slouch hat, and he'd put his hands in his pockets, and he'd come in my mother's store. My mother spoke broken English, you know. And he'd pick up all her tomatoes. My mother hated that . . . If there was a nail, he'd pick it up. And he didn't like children . . . He didn't want nobody on his pavement."

Accompanied by a sizable delegation of friends and supporters, Mrs. Avara joined Brendan Walsh to march across H. L. Mencken's pavement in the funeral procession. Walking with them were a few members from another group that had been internally divided on the question of expanding the historic preservation district. Communities Organized to Improve Life (COIL) was a coalition of more than forty neighborhood associations, churches, PTAs, and other groups scattered over an area of Southwest Baltimore much larger than Union Square. For more than a year, representatives of the coalition had participated, along with members of the Union Square Association, in a study of the proposed addition to the historic preservation district. They had agreed to join the delegates of the Union Square Association in this enterprise, according to one COIL leader, on the understanding "that when the time came for them to expand [the historic district], they would sit down in advance with all the community groups and explain exactly what they were doing and have a dialogue with them." COIL's representatives were still waiting for the "dialogue" in December 1976, when leaders of the Union Square Association persuaded the city's Commission on Historical and Architectural Preservation to endorse the enlargement of the Union Square historic district. This first step toward City Council approval of the expansion caught COIL at an awkward moment. "We were in the process of just developing the concept of a housing service," explains one COIL activist, "because we saw what was happening [in Union Square], and we were two years behind the times as it was, and we wanted to get in here and work with tenants to try to keep them from being displaced and also encourage homeownership. That was the goal at the time. Then it hit the fan in December."

Although under pressure from some of its member organizations to oppose extension of the historic district's boundaries, COIL's board of directors initially declined to join Brendan Walsh and Mary Avara in their protest against the proposal. The organization sought instead to occupy a middle ground. Uncompromising resistance to historic preservation was rejected, says one leader, "because you won't get anything accomplished that way . . . That's not trying to develop solutions. The goal of that [protest] was to make people aware of a problem — not to come up with solutions and work on the problem, just to make a lot of noise. There are those who make noise — the grandstanders — and there's the workers . . . We figured ourselves to be the workers." But COIL needed time to do its work, and its board of directors decided to recommend a one-year moratorium on any expansion of the preservation district, so that interested groups and organizations might negotiate a new proposal for extending the historic area — one that would be acceptable to a broader cross-section of local residents. COIL proposed itself "as a facilitator in developing this working relationship among the organizations involved, since one of the goals of COIL is to help develop a stable community."[6]

The middle ground proved to be the most unstable. In a community already polarized, COIL's leaders found that it was difficult to gain a hearing for their position: "Common sense does not prevail. You're either for it or you're against it. If you're in the middle, you don't have a stand." Perhaps just as important was the influence of a recently enacted city ordinance that COIL's board had not been aware of. It required that municipal legislation be acted upon within one year of its introduction; any proposed ordinances that were still pending after a year's time would automatically die. In the eyes of the preservationists and city officials, therefore, COIL's "compromise" moratorium was indistinguishable from Brendan Walsh's demand that the preservation ordinance be dropped. COIL's board of directors apparently agreed, and after a reconsideration of the subject, its members voted to oppose passage of the ordinance "as it now stands." A few COIL members joined Brendan Walsh and Mary Avara in their protest march through the neighborhood, but others were still reluctant to surrender their role as agents of neighborhood compromise.

Reflecting this desire for accommodation, COIL's board of directors balanced their statement of opposition to the preservation ordinance with several proposals that would cushion its effects on local residents if it happened to pass. One of their suggested amendments to the ordinance would have limited the expansion of the historic district so as to exclude approximately eighteen hundred homes

originally slated to fall within its boundaries. Another set of proposals called for the city government to support COIL's planned housing service through public programs that would help some of the
area's renters to become homeowners, together with government
financial assistance that would enable other low-income tenants to
pay their rising rents. While Brendan Walsh continued his protests
against the preservation ordinance, COIL representatives negoti-
ated with city officials concerning the components of a neighborhood housing program. At least some of the COIL negotiators perceived that Walsh's demonstrations increased their own bargaining
power: "When they were outside picketing City Hall, we were inside talking to City Councilman 'Du' Burns and those people . . .
Brendan was great for us. The majority of us were moderates, so we
said [to the city officials], 'Do you want us to react like that? If you
want us to do that, we'll go out and do whatever needs to be done.'
We were saying that there is a rational approach to all this, still trying to get the moratorium, but also pushing for the housing service."

As his protests continued, Walsh saw the distance widening between his own position and COIL's. "It's my opinion," he says, "that
they got their money for their housing program and stuff like that [in
return] for playing ball." Municipal agencies interested in neighborhood revitalization had already been moving to the support of
the preservation ordinance. Following the endorsements of the
Commission on Historical and Architectural Preservation and the
City Planning Commission, the local Department of Housing and
Community Development announced its official backing for the legislation at public hearings in July 1977. Walsh's chief ally, Mary
Avara, did not appear at this session, though she had been a conspicuous opponent of the preservation ordinance at previous public
meetings; most of her followers were absent as well. Continued
opposition, she had decided, was hopeless: "I had started out with
those poor people, but you can't fight City Hall . . . I worked on it
till we lost. I knew we lost and I told them." The reasons for such a
pessimistic assessment of the situation were growing steadily more
apparent, but in addition to the gathering bureaucratic support for
the historic preservation ordinance, Mrs. Avara had also received a
telephone call from an influential state senator and party politician
inquiring about the reasons for her displeasure with the legislation.
Neighborhood activists in Union Square had their own interpreta-
tions of her withdrawal from the controversy. "She comes with a
good heart." one of them commented later, "but I think when the

politicians come in, they tell her how they want her to act, and that's how she acts."

Brendan Walsh continued to act on his own. In October, not long before the City Council was to vote on the preservation ordinance, he appeared at City Hall in a clown suit, carrying a new supply of leaflets, in order to publicize some questionable real estate transactions on the part of an important local politician who supported the legislation. On the evening of the vote itself, a brief scuffle occurred when one exasperated council member vented his temper against Walsh. Finally, in a City Council that was almost as sharply divided as the neighborhood itself, the Union Square preservation ordinance won approval. An amendment pared the size of the proposed historic area to exclude some territory, though not as much as COIL had recommended. In addition, COIL representatives reached a subsequent agreement with officials of the Department of Housing and Community Development on measures to forestall the displacement of current Union Square residents. There would be subsidies for some low-income renters and assistance for others who wished to become homeowners. Residents who already owned their houses might receive financial help with needed home improvements.

Three years later COIL activists acknowledged that city officials had generally lived up to their agreements but estimated that about 20 percent of the preservation area's former residents had been displaced all the same. And one of them predicted that more would be leaving in the future: "Most of the people who are renting there now, unless they have a good income, will not be there in ten years. They'll be gone." There is no evidence to confirm or refute either the estimates or the predictions. Even if they are correct, of course, one might observe that they reflect a more gradual and less disruptive rate of neighborhood change than might have occurred in the absence of measures to cushion the impact of historic preservation.

In some respects Union Square seemed to change hardly at all. Two years after the resolution of the historic preservation issue, little progress had been made toward resolving the differences among the neighborhood's various leaders and organizations. When interviewed at the end of 1979, almost three-fourths of a panel of informants who were knowledgeable about Union Square believed that "different factions of residents often seem to disagree with one another about what's best for the area," and the remaining informants all conceded that this statement was at least "partly true." In no other sample neighborhood were perceptions of factionalism so prevalent. At the same time, however, there were scarcely any other neighborhoods where the discussion of local issues was so widespread. Although the debate about historic preservation may not have fulfilled COIL's plans for a "dialogue" on the subject, it did stimulate deliberations that engaged the attention of representatives from most of the groups in Union Square's unlikely collection of neighborhood sects.

The fact that local residents were fighting with one another should not obscure the fact that they were also talking to one another about matters of common concern, and it was the persistence of disagreement that probably helped to sustain and expand neighborhood discourse. A working relationship between Brendan Walsh and Mary Avara — hardly to be expected in the normal course of things — was a readily understandable by-product of neighborhood conflict. Moreover, while the controversy revealed previously unrecognized areas of agreement between local factions, it also prompted discussion between factions that disagreed. Although COIL's directors rejected the position represented by Brendan Walsh, for example, and although his group did not belong to the coalition, COIL's leadership and Walsh regularly "contacted each other back and forth" during the course of the neighborhood controversy about historic preservation. Political discourse spanned even wider differences than this one. Responding to charges of real estate speculation, for example, Joanne Whitely acknowledged that some opponents of historic preservation might be genuinely concerned about the welfare of poor people in the neighborhood. She and Brendan Walsh, she said, "simply represent two entirely different views of life. I happen to believe in free enterprise. There's nothing wrong with it."[7] But the recognition of such fundamental disagreements seems not to have obstructed a continued exchange of opinions. "The funny thing," observes Brendan Walsh, "is that we can talk to Whitely . . . I don't think she hates us or anything like that. We just have a difference of opinion with regard to making money versus not making money."

The Neighborhood as a Setting for Political Discourse

It is more difficult to recognize political discourse when it takes place among the residents of a neighborhood than when it happens on the floor of the U.S. Senate. Even the casual conversations about candidates and parties that occur among voters prior to election day seem to have a more obviously political character than the parochial deliberations of neighbors about trash on the street or unruly children. But neighborhood discourse shares at least some of the politically relevant attributes of other more plainly political discussions. It represents an occasion for the formation and articulation of opinions about matters that are not merely private or personal. The functional parallel between such "extemporaneous assemblies" in the neighborhood and the more explicitly political assemblies of representative government was clearly evident to Alexis de Tocqueville. Neighborly deliberation may not make for a neighborhood government, but the more frequently neighbors "form themselves into a deliberative body," the more they acknowledge the status of their neighborhood as a public forum and a political society.

In at least one important respect, however, neighborhood discourse may differ from some of the more commonly recognized political deliberations that occur among citizens at large. Studies of voting behavior, for example, have indicated that citizens' preelection political discussions tend to occur between people who already share the same political attitudes and preferences, and the absence of debate from these exchanges has led some observers to question their value as political discourse.[8] But the experience of Union Square suggests that neighborhood discussions, unlike election-time dialogues, may frequently be accompanied by large differences of opinion. This does not prove that deliberations about neighborhood problems represent a higher order of political discourse than the campaign conversations of voters. It does indicate, however, that the conditions for neighborhood deliberation are generally consistent with the conditions under which neighborhoods develop some of the other attributes that mark them as political societies. Just as the sense of neighborhood identity need not depend on the existence of personal solidarity among neighbors, the conduct of neighborhood discourse does not seem to depend on the existence of consensus among them.

The character and extent of political discussion in neighborhoods may not be accurately reflected, of course, in debates between neighborhood leaders like Brendan Walsh and Joanne Whitely, or in the deliberations of organizations like COIL. To find out about the more general flow of spontaneous political talk among neighbors, respondents in the sample survey of residents were asked several questions about their participation in community discussions of community matters that took place without the sponsorship of formal organizations or official political leaders. After reporting on their contacts with city officials and with community associations, residents indicated whether, "apart from contacting city government or specific organizations," they had spoken with neighbors during the past year or so "about any neighborhood problems or needs." Residents of different neighborhoods exhibited sharply different propensities for informal neighborhood discourse. Such talk was most widespread in one neighborhood where 76 percent of the respondents reported recent conversations about community matters; it was least common in another residential area where only 19 percent of the inhabitants said they had engaged in informal discussions of neighborhood needs or problems. For all twenty-one sample neighborhoods, the median rate of participation in informal talks about community matters was 38 percent, and the most frequent subject of conversation was trash and sanitation, though other topics like crime and neighborhood deterioration were almost as popular.

Although the conduct of these neighborly conversations obviously requires social contact among local residents, it does not seem to imply personal friendship or solidarity. Residents who engaged in neighborhood discourse were just about as likely to say that most of their friends lived outside the neighborhood as those who did not (gamma = .10). Whether one's "really good friends" lived on the same block, in the same residential area, or further away was similarly unrelated to participation in discussions about community conditions (gamma = .06). It did make some difference, on the other hand, whether respondents regarded most of the people on their own blocks as personal friends, merely acquaintances, or strangers (gamma = .21). Residents who saw mostly strangers in their immediate surroundings were less likely than others to engage in informal conversations about the state of the neighborhood, but those who reported mere acquaintanceship with the people on the block were almost as likely to participate in such conversations as those who professed personal friendship. There is no evidence here, in other words, for a connection between neighborhood discourse and neighborly intimacy.[9]

Neighborhood discourse resembles the sense of neighborhood identity in this respect: neither of these attributes of the local polity has much to do with communal solidarity. They have considerably more to do with one another. There is a relatively strong association, for example, between the ability to assign a distinct name to one's neighborhood and the informal discussion of neighborhood problems with fellow residents (gamma = .44). Earlier findings suggest a possible explanation for this connection. The sense of neighborhood identity, as we have seen, helps to heighten the perception of neighborhood problems, and people who perceive neighborhood problems, perhaps, are more likely to discuss them informally with fellow residents than those who do not. The link between the sense of neighborhood identity and the tendency to engage in neighborhood discourse may therefore be explained by the fact that respondents with well-defined conceptions of their residential areas also have an enhanced propensity to perceive neighborhood problems that require discussion.

The survey results presented in Table 4.1 are designed to test this line of explanation. The respondents have been divided here into three groups according to the number and intensity of their complaints about neighborhood problems. The survey findings show that even among respondents with similar impressions about the severity and extent of neighborhood problems, those who thought that their residential areas had names were more likely to talk with their neighbors about local problems than those who did not. Among residents who were not especially bothered by any community problems, for example, 34.8 percent of those who could name their neighborhoods, but only 11.0 percent of those who could not, reported that they had engaged in informal conversations about neighborhood matters.

People who can name their neighborhoods may have an enhanced propensity to perceive neighborhood problems, but this awareness of things to complain about does not fully explain the

Table 4.1. The sense of neighborhood identity and participation in neighborhood discourse, controlling for problem perceptions (Percentage of respondents in each category who talked to neighbors about neighborhood problems or needs)

Sense of neighborhood identity	Number of problems named that bothered respondent a lot		
	None	One or two	Three or more
Identifies neighborhood by name	34.8 (616)	50.1 (506)	62.5 (315)
Cannot identify neighborhood by name	11.0 (204)	29.0 (260)	39.3 (122)

tendency to participate in neighborhood discourse. A comparison of the percentage figures across each row of Table 4.1 does show that the more problems residents perceive, the more likely they are to engage in neighborhood discussions. But a comparison of the figures in each column shows that controlling for these variations in people's problem perceptions does not account for the difference in political loquacity between people who can identify their neighborhoods and those who cannot.

Other factors—like socioeconomic status[10]—also failed to explain away this difference. The association between neighborhood identity and neighborhood discourse, it appears, does not depend on the operation of other variables, and it is not difficult to understand why such intervening factors should be unnecessary to the relationship. Residents who have formed a conception of the place where they live are simply more apt to make it a subject of conversation than people who have not developed such conceptions. Conversely, people who engage in discussions about the places where they live are probably more apt to form conceptions of their neighborhoods than people who do not participate in conversations of this sort. The survey findings show only that the sense of neighborhood identity is associated with participation in neighborhood discourse, not the sequence in which these things occur. The results could indicate that a sense of neighborhood identity helps to promote the informal discussion of local problems, but they could also support an alternative interpretation that is just as plausible: the discussion of neighborhood problems may enhance the sense of neighborhood identity.

Table 4.2 has been designed to illustrate this plausible alternative. The findings here have been presented so as to give explanatory priority to neighborhood discourse and to show how participation in informal discussions of neighborhood problems may affect the sense of neighborhood identity. The influence of another variable—participation in personal discussions with neighbors—has also been taken into account here. Considering this additional kind of conversation among fellow residents helps to clarify the relationship between political discourse and neighborhood identity. Residents who talk with their neighbors about local needs and problems, for example, may also be inclined to talk to them about private matters or things in general. The mere occurrence of conversations among neighbors—and not the fact that they sometimes happen to discuss neighborhood problems—could be responsible for sharpening the respondents' ability to identify their neighborhoods.

Talking about neighborhood problems is in fact closely related to

Table 4.2. Participation in neighborhood discourse and the sense of neighborhood identity, controlling for the discussion of personal problems (Percentage of respondents in each category who said that the neighborhood had a particular name)

Personal conversation with neighbors	Neighborhood discourse	
	Discussion of neighborhood problems	No discussion of neighborhood problems
Discussion of personal problems	82.8 (446)	69.1 (344)
No discussion of personal problems	81.1 (364)	61.5 (865)

talk about personal problems (gamma = .51). But the findings reported in Table 4.2 permit us to distinguish the effects of personal conversations from those of political conversations, and these results indicate that there is a special relationship between the discussion of neighborhood problems and the sense of neighborhood identity. A propensity for political talk, not personal talk, distinguishes those residents who have developed conceptions of the places where they live. A comparison of the percentage figures across the rows of Table 4.2 shows that those who discuss community problems with their neighbors are more likely to give names to their residential areas than those who do not discuss such issues, and this difference persists whether the respondents reported personal conversations with their neighbors or not. A comparison of the figures within each column shows, on the other hand, that talking about personal problems with neighbors is scarcely associated with the ability to name one's neighborhood. Once the respondents' participation in neighborhood discourse has been taken into account, their involvement in personal discussions with fellow residents makes only a slight difference for the likelihood that they will be able to assign names to the places where they live.

The survey results again reflect the distinctly political predispositions that lie behind city residents' ideas of neighborhood. Those who can identify their neighborhoods are inclined to use them as forums in which to discuss neighborhood concerns. They show no special tendency to employ their neighborhoods as personal havens in which to exchange sympathy and advice about private matters. In general, the survey results have shown that the personal ties that may bind neighbors together are not responsible for sustaining neighborhood identity or neighborhood discourse, nor do they contribute to the relationship between these two aspects of the neighborhood polity.

In the case of neighborhood discourse, the distinction between personal solidarity and neighborhood political life becomes especially pronounced. People who take part in informal discussions of neighborhood matters not only fail to exhibit any special tendency toward friendship with fellow residents; they actually seem to display a degree of antagonism toward their neighbors. Respondents who reported that they had talked about community matters with their fellow residents were much more likely than those who did not to say that they had recently been annoyed with the conduct of their neighbors (gamma = .50). Participants in the informal deliberations of the neighborhood were also more likely than the nonparticipants to report that they had argued during the past year with at least some of their neighbors. (gamma = .51).

The relationship between neighborhood discourse and neighborhood disagreement is not peculiar to Union Square. When people talk to their neighbors about community matters, they generally tend to fight with their neighbors as well. Contention may seem an improbable accompaniment for neighborly conversation. While there is no reason to assume that conversation between neighbors will always be neighborly, it is odd that the signs of hostility should be concentrated disproportionately among those who engage in neighborhood discourse. Perhaps the statistical association between these things is misleading. The discussion of neighborhood issues, in itself, may not actually be connected with the occurrence of antagonism. Two alternative possibilities need to be considered.

In the first place, the neighborhood problems that the respondents have discussed with their fellow residents may frequently be problems for which they hold their neighbors responsible. In these cases, a conversation with fellow residents about community conditions readily becomes an occasion for complaining to neighbors about the trouble that they have caused. Neighborly animosity may obviously precede such conversations, and arguing could easily be the result. But the discussion, the animosity, and the arguing may all be reflections of the local problems that are irritating the participants in neighborhood discourse. These underlying problems, and not the hostility that they generate, could actually explain the tendency to discuss neighborhood issues. In fact, the respondents' hostility may not even be directed at the same neighbors with whom they discuss local issues. It is possible, after all, to talk to one neighbor about the reasons for displeasure with some other neighbor. In any case, antagonism may accompany the discussion of neighborhood problems only because the problems themselves tend to generate both the antagonism and the talk, not because hostility alone tends to produce political conversations.

A second possibility is that antagonism results from neighborhood discussions simply because any kind of personal contact among fellow residents may supply an occasion for personal friction. Neighbors who never speak with one another, after all, never have the opportunity to fight with one another. People do not become angry with their neighbors because they discuss neighborhood issues, perhaps, but merely because any encounter with neighbors increases the chances for conflict.

Reduced to its essentials, therefore, the first explanation suggests that animosity is simply a by-product of the same neighborhood problems that are also responsible for generating political conversations among neighbors. The second explanation is that animosity results not from political conversations themselves but from the mere fact that conversations involve contact, and contact of any kind promotes friction.

If the first explanation is correct, then controlling for people's perceptions of local problems should remove the reason for the relationship that we have observed between neighborhood animosity and neighborhood discussion. Among people with similar impressions of neighborhood problems, animosity should make little difference for the likelihood of participation in neighborhood discourse. The problems are presumably responsible for triggering this participation, and the antagonism is merely another result that they generate along the way. The findings reported in Tables 4.3 and 4.4 permit us to examine this possibility, and they suggest that the explanation is insufficient. No matter how slight or severe the respondents' assessments of local problems, those who reported either arguments or annoyance with their fellow residents were consistently more likely to engage in neighborhood discussions than those who did not report these signs of friction. The connection between neighborhood animosity and neighborhood discourse does not originate in an underlying irritation about community problems. In Table 4.4, for example, the results show that even when residents were not especially bothered by

Table 4.3. Participation in arguments and in neighborhood discourse, controlling for problem perceptions (Percentage of respondents in each category who talked with neighbors about neighborhood problems or needs)

Arguments with neighbors	Number of problems that bothered respondent a lot		
	None	One or two	Three or more
Argued	43.9 (43)	68.5 (93)	69.4 (88)
Did not Argue	27.4 (806)	39.4 (733)	50.6 (371)

Table 4.4. Annoyance with neighbors' behavior and participation in neighborhood discourse, controlling for problem perceptions (Percentage of respondents in each category who talked with neighbors about neighborhood problems or needs)

Annoyance with neighbors	Number of problems that bothered respondent a lot		
	None	One or two	Three or more
Annoyed	47.6 (254)	55.7 (363)	59.2 (274)
Not annoyed	20.0 (594)	32.5 (464)	46.6 (184)

any neighborhood problems at all, those who were annoyed at their neighbors were more than twice as likely to discuss neighborhood matters as those who had not been annoyed. The implication, of course, is that this annoyance cannot have been a mere reflection of the same problem perceptions that prompted neighbors to talk with one another about local conditions. An awareness of neighborhood problems seems to increase the likelihood of such conversations, but it does not explain why people who participate in these conversations also tend to be angry at their neighbors.

The second explanation may offer a more straightforward way to account for this tendency. Participants in neighborhood discourse may express animosity toward their neighbors simply because any sort of social contact among residents increases the opportunity for friction and contention. Respondents who discuss personal problems with neighbors may be just as prone to annoyance and argument as those who engage in deliberations about community problems. This is a line of explanation that seems to be partly supported by the survey results presented in Tables 4.5 and 4.6. Neighborhood discourse has been considered here as a source of annoyance and argument rather than as a result. The presentation of the evidence is therefore similar to its arrangement earlier, when neighborhood discourse was treated as a possible contributor to the sense of neighborhood ident-

Table 4.5. Participation in neighborhood discourse and arguments with neighbors, controlling for the discussion of personal problems (Percentage of respondents in each category who said they had argued with neighbors during the past year)

| | Neighborhood discourse | |
| | Discussion of neighborhood problems | No discussion of neighborhood problems |
Personal conversation with neighbors		
Discussion of personal problems	21.9 (453)	11.5 (368)
No discussion of personal problems	11.3 (388)	4.1 (924)

Table 4.6. Participation in neighborhood discourse and annoyance with neighbors, controlling for the discussion of personal problems (Percentage of respondents in each category who said they were annoyed with neighbors' behavior in the past year)

| | Neighborhood discourse | |
| | Discussion of neighborhood problems | No discussion of neighborhood problems |
Personal conversation with neighbors		
Discussion of personal problems	62.3 (453)	36.6 (368)
No discussion of personal problems	52.5 (387)	29.3 (923)

ity (see Table 4.2). As in that case, we can compare the impact of neighborhood conversations with the effects of personal conversations. The results in Table 4.5 indicate that the two types of discussion are related in about the same way to the likelihood that respondents would report arguments with their neighbors. Of those who had discussed only personal problems with neighbors, 11.5 percent had been involved in arguments. Among those who had discussed only neighborhood problems, the proportion was almost the same — 11.3 percent. The chance of an argument was no greater for residents who engaged in neighborhood discussions than it was for those who engaged in personal discussions. Both kinds of conversations contributed about equally to the prospects for argument among neighbors. This evidence lends weight to the contention that any sort of social contact between neighbors adds to the likelihood of friction.

But the evidence presented in Table 4.6 suggests something different. The results here show that residents who participated in neighborhood discourse were more likely to be annoyed at their neighbors' conduct than those who engaged in personal conversations. Among respondents who had discussed only neighborhood problems, 52.5 percent reported such annoyance, but the proportion was only 36.6 percent for those who had confined themselves to conversations about personal matters. Even more striking is the disparity that exists between the apparent impact of neighborhood discourse and the effects of personal discussion on the respondents' sense of annoyance. A comparison of the percentage figures across each row indicates how much difference it made whether or not the respondents engaged in discussions of neighborhood problems. A comparison of the figures within each column shows how much difference was made by participation in personal conversations. The results clearly show that whether residents engaged in neighborhood discussions made a greater difference for the likelihood of annoyance than whether they participated in personal discussions.[11] Annoyance with neighbors is more closely related to informal deliberations about community problems than to discussions of personal problems. In this respect at least, mere social contact and discussion do not seem to provide an adequate explanation for the occurrence of friction. The likelihood of irritation depends in addition on the kinds of subjects that people discuss with their fellow residents, and deliberations about the neighborhood's political business seem to account for more of this aggravation than do discussions of private or personal matters.

Actual arguing—as opposed to mere aggravation—seems to follow a different pattern. It results just as much from personal conversations as from discussions of neighborhood problems. Assuming that arguments with neighbors arise out of annoyance with neighbors, this means that people who engage in personal conversations can produce the same amount of arguing as those who engage in political conversations, but from a smaller reservoir of annoyance. Some indication of their superior capacity to generate arguments becomes evident if the percentage figures in Tables 4.5 and 4.6 are compared with one another. Among residents who participated only in neighborhood discussions, 52.5 reported annoyance with neighbors, but only 11.3 percent reported actual arguments—a ratio of nearly five to one. For people who engaged only in personal conversations, however, the ratio of annoyance to argument is just slightly over three to one—36.6 percent reporting annoyance as compared to 11.5 percent reporting arguments.

People who engage in personal conversations with their neighbors seem to convert their annoyances into arguments more readily than those who participate in discussion of community problems, and this rough impression was substantiated by a more detailed analysis of the evidence.[12] The explanation, perhaps, is that neighbors who discuss personal matters with one another also tend to personalize any disagreements or annoyances that arise to disturb their relationship. Under these circumstances, differences of opinion might easily become sore points, more explosive and more difficult to contain than they would be if the disputants had not become so close to one another. The result is that animosities erupt with into arguments more readily for neighbors who discuss personal matters with one another than for those who do not. In discussions of neighborhood rather than personal problems, there may not be the same tendency to personalize disagreements, and the antagonisms that accompany these less intimate conversations may therefore represent a less potent source of open conflict.

But even though antagonism may become more manageable under these circumstances, it remains more plentiful. The likelihood of neighborly annoyance and aggravation is greater for participants in neighborhood discourse than it is for people who engage in personal discussions or for residents who abstain from either kind of conversation with their neighbors. Neighborly deliberations about neighborhood issues seem to be surrounded by an air of irritation, and it appears that the acrimonious spirit accompanying these discussions cannot easily be explained away. The aggravation is not simply an incidental by-product of the same perceived neighborhood problems that provide the subject matter for community discourse. Even among people who have similar impressions about the severity of neighborhood problems, those who are annoyed with their neighbors are still more likely to talk with fellow residents about local problems and needs than those who are not annoyed. Nor does this annoyance seem to be the simple result of personal contact among residents — a sign of the social friction that comes from social engagement. Personal conversations, though they are just as likely to be accompanied by arguments as neighborhood conversations, are less likely to be linked with feelings of annoyance.

Neighborly aggravation, it seems, is simply one of the conditions that tends to accompany neighborhood discourse. Whether it is a source of communal discussion or a consequence remains uncertain. But one thing at least is reasonably clear: neighborhood political life does not have its beginnings among those who love their neighbors. The sense of neighborhood identity, as we found earlier, is largely unrelated to the existence of personal warmth or friendship among neighbors. Neighborhood discourse is not only divorced from these signs of personal solidarity but also associated with a certain degree of animosity toward fellow residents. In short, the foundations of the neighborhood polity do not seem to lie in a village like communalism that has somehow managed to survive the depersonalizing forces of urbanization. Although some observers have seen the communal warmth of the neighborhood as a promising basis for political community,[13] this fellow feeling does not seem to support the kinds of actions that help to create a neighborhood polity. Many city dwellers may be bound to their neighbors by ties of close personal friendship or mutual regard, but these urbanites are generally not the ones who contribute to the elementary political capabilities of their neighborhoods. The residents who do make these contributions are often people who exhibit some of the symptoms of the loss of community that is alleged to occur in an urban environment; informal deliberations about matters of community concern occur in an atmosphere of neighborly tension, not neighborly solidarity.

Translating Political Talk into Political Action

Mere talk, of course, may not constitute politics — even when the common good is the subject of conversation. In the deliberative assemblies of governments, discussion qualifies as political discourse

not only because of its content but also because of its political results. The debates of the legislators acquire something of their political character from the simple fact that they can lead to legislation.
The election-time conversations of voters may qualify as political
events for a similar reason — because they lead to the selection of political authorities. Political action in general has been defined by reference to its outcomes. According to one formulation, it is social behavior that contributes to the authoritative allocation of valued
things for a society.[14]

In a similar way, the political status of neighborhood discourse
may depend at least in part on the kinds of results that it produces,
and on whether it produces any results at all. Respondents who reported that they talked informally about local problems or needs
with their neighbors were asked, therefore, what kinds of subjects
had been discussed most often in these conversations and whether
they or their neighbors had subsequently tried to do anything about
these matters. A sizable majority of those who had engaged in neighborhood discourse said that action of some kind had resulted from
their discussions. For the twenty-one sample neighborhoods, the
median proportion of respondents reporting that discussion had led
to action was 31 percent; the median rate of participation in neighborhood discourse, at 38 percent, was only slightly higher than this.
When neighbors talk informally about local needs or problems, the
chances are quite good that something will come of it.

Respondents who said that their discussions had led to action were
next asked what kinds of action had been taken. In general, the measures reported by the respondents could be grouped in three different categories, though residents who recounted a series of steps that
they had taken were sometimes given credit for more than one kind
of activity. The most common upshot of neighborhood discourse was
that one or more of the discussants would approach government
authorities (usually municipal authorities) concerning the subject
that had been discussed. Among the neighborhoods studied, the median proportion of residents who reported that neighborhood discourse had resulted in contacts with public officials was 18 percent
(58 percent of the discussants who said that some action had been
taken).

Presenting a problem or a request to a formal, nongovernmental
organization was another recourse for participants in neighborhood
discussion. The organization approached was most frequently a
community association, and the median proportion of all neighborhood residents who reported that such steps had been taken was 8

percent (26 percent of those who claimed that they or their neighbors had taken action as a result of informal discussion).

The third general outcome of neighborhood discourse was that neighbors would take matters into their own hands. Instead of referring the subjects of informal discussion to municipal authorities or to formal organizations, neighbors took direct action in an effort to resolve these issues on their own. Without official assistance or sanction, neighbors might clean the debris from an unsightly alley or vacant lot, or they might consult with one another concerning the coordination of informal crime-prevention measures. The median proportion of neighborhood residents using this direct approach for dealing with local needs and problems was 10 percent, and in the median neighborhood they made up 31 percent of all those who reported that discourse had culminated in neighborhood action.

This reliance on do-it-yourself expedients in coping with local issues is an especially striking expression of neighborhood political capabilities. It reflects the same kind of impromptu "executive power" that Tocqueville saw rising from the "extemporaneous assembly" of the neighborhood — a capacity to resolve local issues and problems "before anybody has thought of recurring to a pre-existing authority superior to that of the persons immediately concerned." In some cases, of course, the authority of the persons immediately concerned seems almost an extension of governmental power itself. In Union Square, for example, the judgments and pronouncements of Mary Avara enjoy nearly official status for a portion of the local population. She frequently exercises her authority in order to resolve matters that might otherwise become the business of municipal courts or city agencies. In one typical case, for instance, a young man was seen breaking into parking meters not far from the street where Mrs. Avara lives. Some of the neighbors brought her a petition about the matter; it demanded that the culprit be arrested and prosecuted. They asked her to sign it and then present it to the appropriate authorities. Instead, Mrs. Avara decided to handle the case herself. Through her neighbors, she issued an unofficial summons for the accused. He was to present himself at her house for a talk. "I do it all the time," she says. "They won't talk to nobody else. They'll talk to me . . . I tell them, 'You don't fool with Mary. You know Miss Mary likes you, but don't you fool with me. Now I got the petition. I know you did it. Now either you stop or you're going to jail. And don't say "Miss Mary's going to be behind me . . . "' I can take him to court. Those judges know me. When he comes over, I will not embarrass him in front of anybody. But he will not do that again, because the judges downtown know that if Mary Avara comes in, that's it."

Few neighborhood residents, of course, have the kind of informal authority that Mrs. Avara has among her neighbors or the notoriety that she has among the city's judges. Far more typical of the attempts to invoke the unofficial executive power of the neighborhood is the action taken by one of Mrs. Avara's fellow residents in Union Square, a woman who was troubled by household pests. She and several of the people on her block had been talking about a widespread cockroach problem. Their individual efforts to exterminate the bugs seemed to have been ineffective. Each time a resident tried to drive out the roaches with poisons and sprays, the insects temporarily retreated into the neighboring homes, only to return when someone else launched an offensive against them. The neighbors decided to cope with the problem by coordinating their roach-extermination efforts. Now they all arrange to spray their homes at the same time so that the roaches will have no sanctuary. The respondents report that this new collective arrangement has been noticeably more effective than the earlier individual attempts.

There is no evidence that anyone with the informal authority of a Mary Avara stands ready to enforce this arrangement or that the practice itself enjoys any particular legitimacy. It depends instead on the voluntary actions that neighbors take to produce collective benefits, and in this respect it is similar to most of the other cases in which Baltimoreans reported that they had dealt with neighborhood needs or problems by taking matters into their own hands. In an upper-income white neighborhood, for example, the residents of one street, dissatisfied with the snow-removal services of city government, contribute money to a common fund that they use to hire their own snowplow. In a low-income black neighborhood, residents disturbed by the garbage that flows into their street from torn trash bags contribute money toward the purchase of proper garbage cans for neighbors who do not own them. Coercion, legitimate or otherwise, does not appear to play a part in these arrangements. There may be sanctions for noncooperation — the disapprobation of neighbors, perhaps — but they are not political sanctions, and the political status of such neighborly practices may be called into question as a result. Like more conventional political actions, these neighborhood measures lead to an allocation of valued things such as money or cleanliness, but the allocations do not have the "authoritative" or binding character that seems to be required by some definitions of political behavior.[15]

What lends a political character to these unofficial measures of neighborhood governance is not the manner in which they are executed or enforced but rather the quality of the valued things that are being allocated. Hiring a snowplow and purchasing garbage cans for neighbors may not be authoritative acts backed by the force of legitimate coercion, but they are not instances of merely private conduct either. They represent efforts to produce indivisible, or public, goods—"public" because they are benefits that can be enjoyed by neighbors in general, or in fact by anyone who happens to walk down the street. The advantages of a block that is free of trash or cleared of snow are accessible not just to the people who bear the costs of cleaning or clearing but to everyone in the vicinity. One person's "consumption" of neighborhood cleanliness or snow-free thoroughfare does not diminish the supply available for others. These are the characteristics that distinguish public goods.[16] Most of the official public services provided to neighborhood residents by municipal authorities exhibit these attributes, and the unofficial public services that the residents provide for themselves meet the same specifications. Such improvised services may not be the acts of a neighborhood government, because they are not necessarily endowed with the kind of authority that governments exercise. But they are public undertakings all the same—measures taken to promote the general welfare on behalf of a neighborhood public. Their occurrence reflects an emerging political society whose members are prepared to assume responsibility for some of the arrangements that can help keep a civil society civil.

Taken together, the unofficial public services that arose from informal neighborhood discussions accounted for only a minority of all the efforts that residents made to deal directly with local problems. People frequently took matters into their own hands without seeking the advice and consent of any fellow residents. In fact, some of the evidence to be presented later indicates that most of the cases in which people kept watch to protect their neighbors' homes or attempted to police the conduct of neighborhood children were not accompanied by any reports of neighborhood discourse. But the cases under consideration now are only those in which an informal attempt to handle a neighborhood problem occurred against a background of neighborhood deliberation about the issue. These are the instances in which the unofficial conduct of neighbors approximated the behavior that might be expected among the members of a functioning polity, because the exercise of informal executive power was linked to an extemporaneous assembly of residents in which the opinions of at least some neighbors might be aired and aggregated.

Apart from this shared trait, the informal measures resulting from neighborhood discourse had only a few things in common with one another. Like the informal neighborhood discussions from which they emerged, many of these unofficial actions had to do with problems of public sanitation. In Reservoir Hill, for instance, where neighbors struggled to restore public order and public services during the great blizzard of 1979, they have also labored — sometimes only in twos and threes — to maintain the cleanliness of streets, alleys, sidewalks, and other public spaces. One resident who reported having planted grass and flowers to beautify the neighborhood noted more generally that "me and my neighbor downstairs try to do what we can to clean up." In another predominantly black neighborhood with a somewhat higher income level than Reservoir Hill, one respondent told of launching several ambitious alley-sweeping campaigns — but with a pitifully small army of helpers. "My next-door neighbor and I," she explained, "work closely together."

Many of the unofficial public servants who act to maintain public sanitation do so in tiny groups or all by themselves. Occasionally, however, participation in these efforts became more general. One respondent told of organizing groups of children to go through the neighborhood cleaning up yards and alleys. Another reported that "all the old women in the neighborhood get out there with brooms and pails." And in at least one case, a sizable team of neighbors set itself the task of cleaning up a public park.

After public sanitation, the most common object of unofficial action was public order. Informal discussions of neighborhood problems frequently led to arrangements for the policing of neighborhoods. The arrangements were often simple understandings by which neighbors agreed to watch one another's homes in an effort to prevent break-ins, theft, or vandalism. But if it had already become too late to prevent neighborhood crimes or other disturbances, residents sometimes intervened more actively to restore public peace. Occasionally they acted on their own. In a typical case of this kind, a man bothered by noise on his street asked a young neighbor to stop running his motorcycle late at night. This was one of a few instances in which a respondent did not distinguish between a neighborhood discussion and the action that resulted from it. In this case and a handful of others, unofficial action was reported as a consequence of a discussion about local problems because the discussion itself *was* the action. An informal talk with the neighborhood motorcyclist was also an unofficial act designed to meet a neighborhood problem. The conversation amounted to the presentation of a demand for peace and quiet. The occurrence of such conversations — where residents register complaints with their neighbors — could help to account for some of the antagonism that accompanies neighborhood discourse. But these cases would have to be far more numerous than they are in order to explain away the connection between neighborhood discourse and neighborhood friction.

Neighborhood discourse did sometimes result in the making of complaints to neighbors about public disorder, but the process of deliberation was generally distinct from the actual delivery of the complaint. Although a lone resident might take responsibility for transmitting the grievance to its intended destination, the complaint itself was likely to have passed through prior consultations that involved at least two neighbors and often more. In Reservoir Hill, for example, an apartment dweller reported having talked with neighbors about the inconvenience and anxiety created by "teenagers [who] come into our hallway and smoke reefers." The upshot of this preparatory discussion was a subsequent conversation with the teenagers themselves, in which the young people were asked to go elsewhere. Respondents who reported that neighborhood discourse had led to neighborhood action regularly distinguished between the discussion itself and the action that resulted from it, even when the ensuing action was simply a further discussion in which grievances or demands were transmitted to neighbors. Such complaints were most often aimed at the maintenance of public peace and order.

But perhaps the most striking aspect of unofficial public service in neighborhoods was the very diversity of the aims pursued. Although public sanitation and public order were the most common objects of informal direct action, they were only two of a variety of causes for which neighbors took matters into their own hands. When a street began to deteriorate in one all-white neighborhood of Northeast Baltimore, the residents "got out there with shovels and patched it up." When elderly residents in a low-income black area were anxious about walking home from a neighborhood center after dark, some of their neighbors informally arranged to escort them through the streets to their front doors. And when the residents of another neighborhood become concerned about the physical deterioration of their community, they contacted the owners of run-down buildings to demand improvements.

There are few types of neighborhood problems that seem incapable of provoking informal neighborhood action. A variety of local inconveniences could set the executive powers of neighborhoods in motion. Some of these efforts to deal directly with local problems were collective undertakings that involved relatively large numbers of people, but many of them were joint actions of only two or three residents, and some were carried out by solitary citizens after discussions with a few of their neighbors. Finally, unofficial action was occasionally a matter of complaining to fellow residents and thus converted neighbors into potential adversaries, but these cases were a small minority of those reported.

One of the few constant elements in the respondents' accounts of their unofficial public services is that they consistently acted to increase the supply of public goods within their neighborhoods. Their attempted contributions to public sanitation, health, order, and safety would result in collective benefits that they could not avoid sharing with fellow residents. Precisely for this reason, their behavior may seem problematic, defying explanations based on conventional notions of rational self-interest or the commonsense assumptions of the free market. Since indivisible public goods can be enjoyed by many people in a neighborhood — including those who have contributed nothing to the production of these goods — strictly rational and self-interested residents will wait for some civic-minded neighbor to go to the trouble of sweeping the alley or policing the street and will then consume the benefits of public order and public sanitation free of expense or exertion. Rational self-interest does not rule out the possibility of cooperative ventures to share the costs of collective benefits. Under certain conditions — where the number of potential beneficiaries is very small and where the process of group decision making itself does not impose any costs — self-interested actors may find it profitable to contribute to the production of public goods. But since these conditions are rarely found in practice, the verdict of classical economic theory is that public goods will tend to be produced in less than optimum quantities. This means that the costs of cleaning an alley, for example, may be lower than the costs that a dirty alley imposes on the people who live near it. But even though there is something to be gained by cleaning up, no resident will lift a broom. The collective gains that come from cleanliness can be enjoyed just as easily if someone else does the work.[17]

Classical economic reasoning does not deny that anyone will ever volunteer to do this work; it suggests, however, that the amount of such "public" work performed will usually be insufficient to maximize public gains. The value of the public benefits achieved through an additional hour of alley sweeping will almost always exceed the cost of the additional labor, but the benefits are spread across all the residents of a neighborhood or a block, and the costs fall on just a few public-spirited residents who are willing to do the sweeping. It is no surprise that they tend to stop their work before the value of its benefits to the neighborhood in general is balanced by the cost that it has imposed on them in particular. That is why the voluntary production of public goods in neighborhoods will tend to remain below its optimum level.

Since we rarely have any way of knowing exactly what "optimum" is in these matters, there is no way to test this line of explanation. But one of its shortcomings should be evident without any tests. The economic theory of public goods tells us why the voluntary production of public services in neighborhoods is likely to remain below the optimum level, but it does not explain why anybody bothers to produce them at all. One obvious explanation suggests itself almost immediately. Since rational self-interest is supposed to discourage people from contributing to the production of public goods, the people who generate unofficial public services for their neighborhoods may be less driven by self-interest than most other city dwellers; they may be more generous, altruistic, or open-hearted than their neighbors.

Self-interest, of course, can be anything that a person chooses to be interested in. A resident who pursues the gratitude of neighbors through good works is just as self-interested as one who aims to maximize personal income and leisure time by avoiding any unpaid work. In this sense, everyone is equally driven by self-interest. But some people may exhibit more regard for fellow residents, more concern for the welfare and happiness of neighbors at large. It is possible, in other words, to define one's self-interest more generously and charitably than other people do, and such magnanimous conceptions of self-interest may lie behind voluntary attempts to deal with neighborhood problems.

If they do, there is little evidence of these conceptions among the respondents who said that informal discussions with neighbors had culminated in unofficial efforts to produce public goods or eliminate public harms. Hostility toward neighbors was just as evident for those who reported impromptu public services as for those who participated in informal neighborhood discourse — and in some respects, more evident. People who reported that their informal discussions of neighborhood problems had led to unofficial attempts at solutions were more likely than other residents to say that they had been annoyed with their neighbors (gamma = .42) and more likely to have argued with their neighbors (.33). Beyond this, they were also somewhat less likely than others to rate their fellow residents as "good neighbors" ($-.23$), and there was little evidence of personal solidarity between unofficial public servants and their neighbors. They were no more likely than other people to report that their friendship ties were concentrated inside the neighborhood ($-.01$) and slightly less likely than other respondents to say that they lived in "the kind of neighborhood where people are very friendly" ($-.14$). In fact, there were some signs that the producers of neighborhood public goods regarded their residential areas as rather inhospitable places. They were not inclined to believe that it was safe to walk on the local streets after dark ($-.24$), and they seem to have been especially worried about neighborhood crime problems (.48).

Unofficial public services, like the neighborhood discussions from which they emerged, do not seem to depend on the existence of good feeling among neighbors or on the magnanimity of the unofficial public servants. Instead, the evidence again suggests that neighborhood political life develops against a background of neighborhood antagonism. The residents who produced public goods for their neighborhoods tended to be people who did not get along with their neighbors. The two plausible explanations for this parallel the ones that we considered earlier in the case of neighborhood discourse. First, the very process of generating public goods may generate antagonism. Second, the neighborhood problems that prompt residents to take matters into their own hands may also make them angry at their neighbors. In both cases, we would find an association between neighborly antagonism and neighborhood public service, but in neither instance could the antagonism be said to have caused the unofficial services.

The first explanation, for example, suggests that hostility is a by-product of these public service activities. Policemen, schoolteachers, and other municipal employees officially charged with the delivery of public services frequently encounter hostility in the course of performing their duties, because one of their responsibilities is to impose community standards on citizens who do not adhere to them. Unofficial public servants may often face similar circumstances within their neighborhoods. One of the services that they perform, after all, is to deliver complaints to neighbors who do not seem to adhere to acceptable standards of cleanliness or propriety. Such "public services" could easily turn into arguments. Similar kinds of occurrences were proposed in order to explain the connection between neighborhood antagonism and neighborhood discourse, and they need to be considered here too. Arguing with neighbors may be one of the principal means for dealing with neighborhood problems, and this would account for the relationship between reports of unofficial public service and expressions of hostility toward neighbors.

While this line of explanation cannot be dismissed entirely, two difficulties reduce its plausibility. In the first place, the impressionistic evidence already presented indicates that most instances of informal direct action did not seem to involve the delivery of complaints to neighbors. This potential source of argument and antagonism, therefore, was absent from the vast majority of cases in which residents performed unofficial public services. Second, although unofficial action may sometimes have entailed the delivery of complaints to neighbors, such interchanges with fellow residents do not seem to have represented special occasions for contention. In fact, delivering complaints to city officials was accompanied by a slightly stronger propensity to argue with one's neighbors (gamma = .50). Contacting city government was another possible outcome of neighborhood discourse (an alternative to unofficial actions taken by the neighbors themselves), one that would not have required residents to confront their neighbors with complaints. Yet the absence of this need to create the circumstances for an argument seems not to have made the respondents any less argumentative. In other words, the conditions for neighborly contention appear to have existed whether residents attempted to handle local problems on their own or referred these problems to municipal officials.

The implication, perhaps, is that the tendency to argue is not inherent in either method of dealing with neighborhood problems but is produced instead by exposure to the problems themselves. The line of explanation is similar to one considered earlier in order to account for the association between neighborhood discourse and neighborhood animosity. In this case, it could help to explain the connection between neighborhood hostilities and unofficial attempts to produce neighborhood public services: unofficial public servants may tend to be angry with their fellow residents simply because the same local problems that prompt them to take informal direct action also make them irritated at the neighbors who cause or tolerate these problems.

This is another instance in which controlling for people's perceptions of community problems may help to explain away an apparent relationship between neighborhood antagonism and neighborhood political action, and this time the proposed explanation is at least partly supported by the survey evidence. The findings in Table 4.7, for example, show that once the problem perceptions of neighborhood residents have been taken into account, there is no longer a noticeable relationship between the respondents' evaluations of their neighbors and the likelihood that they will engage in informal direct action.[18] Among respondents who had similar impressions about the severity of local problems, people who thought they had good neighbors were just as likely to become unofficial public servants as those who believed they were surrounded by bad or mediocre neighbors. The relationship that we observed earlier between having a low opinion of one's neighbors and taking direct action to deal with local problems is apparently a reflection of variations in people's problem perceptions. Residents who perceive many severe problems in their neighborhoods are more likely than others to take informal direct action to cope with these problems. Possibly because they do have such troubled perceptions of their neighborhoods, they are also more likely than others to believe that they live among fellow residents of inferior quality.

A similar explanation seems to account — at least in part — for the tendency of unofficial public servants to argue with their neighbors. The same perceived local problems that stimulate their informal efforts at public service may also lead them into arguments with the neighbors whom they hold responsible for these problems. But if such processes are at work here, they do not account fully for the relationship between arguing and informal direct action. The evidence in Table 4.8 shows that even among people who have similar impressions about the severity of neighborhood problems, the arguers are still somewhat more likely to engage in direct action than those who do not argue.[19] Finally, the survey results reported in

Table 4.7. Evaluation of neighbors and informal direct action, controlling for problem perceptions (Percentage of respondents in each category who reported unofficial efforts to deal with local problems directly)

Evaluation of neighbors	Number of problems that bothered respondent a lot		
	None	One or two	Three or more
Good	6.5 (742)	12.4 (619)	21.5 (268)
Bad or in between	8.9 (87)	14.4 (176)	23.6 (169)

Table 4.9 indicate that the relationship between being annoyed with one's neighbors and acts of unofficial public service is even less affected by controlling for the respondents' problem perceptions.[20] In short, some of the neighborly antagonism associated with the activities of neighborhood public servants cannot be explained away as a mere by-product of the same local problems that prompted these residents to take matters into their own hands.

Nor does this hostility seem to be a simple result of the friction generated by neighborhood public service itself — an incidental outcome of inharmonious encounters that occur when neighbors attempt to handle local difficulties among themselves. The evidence already presented suggests the unofficial public service may, in a minority of cases, provide an occasion for discord among neighbors, but these occurrences are probably not sufficient to account for the fact that unofficial public servants tend to display more antagonism

Table 4.8. Arguments with neighbors and informal direct action, controlling for problem perceptions (Percentage of respondents in each category who reported unofficial efforts to deal with local problems directly)

Arguments with neighbors	Number of problems that bothered respondent a lot		
	None	One or two	Three or more
Argued	12.7 (43)	17.3 (93)	26.0 (88)
Did not argue	6.3 (808)	11.7 (736)	20.4 (371)

Table 4.9. Annoyance with neighbors and informal direct action, controlling for problem perceptions (Percentage of respondents in each category who reported unofficial efforts to deal with local problems directly)

Annoyance with neighbors	Number of problems that bothered respondent a lot		
	None	One or two	Three or more
Annoyed	12.7 (254)	15.8 (365)	24.2 (274)
Not annoyed	4.0 (596)	9.6 (465)	17.4 (184)

toward their neighbors than other respondents do. In general, the survey findings imply that a certain measure of neighborly hostility may actually strengthen the inclination to assume personal responsibility for maintaining public order, health, and safety within one's neighborhood. This antagonism is not just a reflection of other conditions that may accompany unofficial efforts to cope with neighborhood problems—the perceptions of the problems themselves or the frictions that may arise when neighbors take matters into their own hands. Both the problems and the frictions can provide only partial explanations for the animosities displayed by neighborhood public servants. To some extent, these animosities actually seem to create the conditions for both informal neighborhood discourse and the informal exercise of the "executive power" that sometimes results from these deliberations. John Locke, after all, saw the beginnings of political society in the "inconveniencies of the state of nature."[21] The unpleasantness that come from sharing a residential area with uncongenial neighbors may play a similar role in generating some elements of the neighborhood polity.

It is probably no coincidence, therefore, that Union Square, the most contentious of the twenty-one sample neighborhoods, is also the community in which residents were most likely to report informal efforts at neighborhood public service. Not far behind is Reservoir Hill, where looting and civil disorder could disrupt the tranquillity of a winter snowfall. Its inhabitants rank fourth among the residents of the twenty-one neighborhoods in the likelihood that they would report instances of informal direct action. Coldstream-Homestead-Montebello, where the past battles of local politicians have given way to several years of relative peace and organizational unity, stands considerably lower in this ranking—two places behind the median neighborhood. And the residents of Canton, with their well-established sense of neighborhood tradition and order, come last of all in the propensity for unofficial public service. Neighborhoods that seem "strong" by conventional standards are rarely places where informal deliberations among residents lead to the unofficial production of public services. In fact, such signs of neighborhood political life are frequently accompanied by some of the conventionally recognized infirmities of a "weak" neighborhood.

Neighborhood Diversity and Unofficial Public Service

Perhaps it takes an unconventional interpretation of neighborhood social processes to understand why symptoms of political vitality should emerge so often in apparently disorganized communities. Such a singular perspective seems to be implicit in Jane Jacobs's attempt to find the sources of neighborhood order in the very diversity, confusion, and incoherence of city life.[22] Even after twenty years her point of view has not been fully assimilated to the conventional wisdom in urban social analysis, but her dissenting opinions about city planning and neighborhood organization seem to anticipate the connections that we have observed between neighborhood discord and the unofficial production of neighborhood public services.

The "ubiquitous principle" from which Jacobs's argument proceeds is "the need of cities for a most intricate and close-grained diversity of uses that give each other mutual support."[23] As applied to neighborhoods, the principle calls for a variety of public attractions—shops, offices, and other gathering places—to be intermingled with closely spaced private residences along each street. Such tightly packaged samples of urban diversity will bring many different kinds of activities and enterprises within the compass of the neighborhood, not simply for the sake of variety, but in order "to give people reasons for crisscrossing paths."[24] The densely woven flows of street traffic that result will help to ensure that the neighborhood's public places are kept under constant surveillance. The steady procession of passersby becomes an unofficial force of watchers whose foot patrols through the neighborhood are supplemented by local residents at their windows and doorways, their attention drawn to the street by the varied steams of human activity concentrated there. It is this informal army of watchers, says Jacobs, and not just the local police department, whose services are essential to the maintenance of public peace and order in neighborhoods. These unofficial services become all the more essential in Jacobs's view because she regards the security of neighborhood streets as "the bedrock attribute of a successful city district."[25]

The discordant heterogeneity of city life is not necessarily a source of disorganization. "Under the seeming disorder of the old city," Jacobs says, "wherever the old city is working successfully, is a marvelous order for maintaining the safety of the streets and the freedom of the city." "Intricate minglings of different uses in cities," she insists, "are not a form of chaos. On the contrary, they represent a complex and highly developed form of order."[26] And she leaves no doubt concerning the fundamentally political character of this street-level regime. "We shall have something solid to chew on," Jacobs suggests, "if we think of city neighborhoods as mundane organs of self-government. Our failures with city neighborhoods are, ultimately, failures in localized self-government."[27] The successes, on the other hand, have their beginnings in the "casual public sidewalk life" of the locality, which supplies the necessary support for a community's formal public organizations by "mediating between them and the privacy of the people of the city."[28]

In Jacobs's distinctive line of argument, local political order grows out of apparent social disorder. This seeming contradiction could offer a means for understanding why public service and personal animosity tend to go together in urban neighborhoods. "Close-grained diversity" and the jostling life of the sidewalk that results from it may help to create the conditions that encourage citizens to take charge of public order, health, and safety in their neighborhoods, but they are also conditions for personal friction, irritation, and animosity. This, at least, is one way to make sense of the curious link that we have found between neighborhood tension and neighborhood political life. As an interpretation of the evidence, however, it remains incomplete. Jacobs's observations about the makeup and layout of neighborhood land uses may help us to understand the circumstances that create opportunities for the informal policing of the neighborhood, but they do not explain why city dwellers feel the impulse or the obligation to pursue these opportunities. More generally, Jacobs does not give us a full account of the kinds of social attitudes and social relationships that are likely to be engendered by neighborhoods that compress a rich variety of activities and enterprises within their boundaries.

These are the matters to which Richard Sennett has devoted most of his attention in *The Uses of Disorder*.[29] There he adds an important social-psychological dimension to the argument that Jane Jacobs has begun to develop. Jacobs concentrates her fire on those physical arrangements that tend to impoverish the public street life of an urban neighborhood — arrangements that preclude a close-grained diversity of work and amusements, that seal off the residents from the stream of sidewalk events, and that turn public places into empty ones. Sennett directs his criticism at the social conceptions that encourage and reinforce these physical arrangements. He attacks in particular the "myth of purified community," an image of emotional cohesion that rests merely on the social sameness that exists within a group, and not on its members' joint activities or actual social experience together. Such "images of communal solidarity," Sennett argues, "are forged in order that men can avoid dealing with one another."[30] They are visions that help to maintain a sense of social coherence and security by enabling people to dispense with the sometimes disturbing experiences that are necessary in order to learn what they actually have in common with their neighbors. By encouraging people to believe that they are the same as their neighbors, this myth of community can create a sense of social solidarity in the absence of social contact.

It is a belief that can also make community participation unnecessary. People convinced that they are surrounded by citizens who resemble themselves can confidently leave the affairs of their neighborhoods to others. When neighbors are pretty much alike, after all, there is little to distract them from minding their own business — in part because it does not make much difference who is minding the neighborhood's business. In order to turn their attentions from their own isolated and private affairs to the public concerns of the neighborhood, says Sennett, the sense of sameness among neighbors must be replaced by an exposure to social differences, frictions, and conflicts.[31] An internally heterogeneous neighborhood of the sort endorsed by Jane Jacobs can provide the setting for these experiences of social diversity. Living in such a neighborhood means having neighbors who seem unfamiliar, unpredictable, and probably untrustworthy. It also means that one cannot afford to remain inattentive to the public business of the locality, because the neighbors cannot be depended upon to deal with these matters so as to suit one's taste. To ensure that their own interests are represented and protected in the management of their streets and communities, the residents of such neighborhoods must inject themselves into the "casual public sidewalk life" of the area. They are driven to take matters of public order into their own hands because they trust no one else to do so — or perhaps because they are apprehensive that someone else might do so. As Sennett explains it, "the very diversity of the neighborhood has built into it the obligation of responsibility; there would be no way to avoid self-destruction in the community other than to deal with the people who live around the place. The feeling that 'I live here and I count in this community's life' would consist, not of a feeling of companionship, but of a feeling that something must be done in common to make this conflict bearable, to survive together."[32] A resident's sense of being at odds with the neighbors, therefore, might lead to unofficial acts of public service precisely because the neighbors do not share one's own conceptions or concerns about the public order, health and safety.

Taken together, Jacobs and Sennett offer a way of understanding why people who dislike or mistrust their neighbors might also tend to become the informal public servants of their neighborhoods.

What they suggest is not a specific hypothesis about the conditions for neighborhood governance but a general point of view that could yield a variety of hypotheses about the origins and operations of neighborhood polities. Their perspective encompasses a broad and largely unspecified range of unofficial activities that help to keep urban neighborhoods clean, safe, and orderly. These informal measures of local governance are not restricted to the kinds of informal direct actions that we have already considered, the ones that result from impromptu deliberations among neighbors. They also seem to include the efforts of individual residents to produce public goods on their own, without prior discussion. The diversity of these efforts and their unstandardized character make it difficult to ask residents about their public service activities in general. Instead, the respondents in Baltimore were questioned about several different kinds of neighborhood public services that seemed likely to occur with some frequency. These activities also seem representative of the behavior that Jacobs and Sennett would regard as signs of public life in urban neighborhoods. Residents were asked, for example, whether during the past year or so they had ever kept an eye on a neighbor's home when the neighbor was away. They were also asked whether they had tried to stop a neighbor's children from doing something they shouldn't be doing, and whether they had worked together with other neighbors to improve the appearance of their street.

People who engaged in any of these three neighborhood activities were also more likely than other residents to report informal direct action of the kind that we have already discussed.[33] Some residents, in other words, seem to exhibit a fairly general inclination toward more than one type of unofficial public service — even though the services in question call for several different kinds of behavior. Watching a neighbor's home, for instance, does not necessarily require any consultation among neighbors. But policing the neighborhood children calls for at least some momentary contact with young neighbors, and even more extensive contacts are implied by the informal direct actions that were considered earlier. They were always preceded by discussions with fellow residents. Working with neighbors to improve the appearance of the street required coordinated action as well as discussion. Our inquiries about the respondents' performance of unofficial public services cannot exhaust every possibility for the informal production of public goods in urban neighborhoods, but they do span a range of activities — from solitary observation of a neighbor's home to cooperative ventures undertaken with neighbors. And yet the evidence indicates that these public services tend to be associated with one another in spite of the variations.

The findings suggest that certain types of people or neighborhood environments may lend themselves to public service activities in general. The observations made by Jacobs and Sennett contain several different sorts of implications about the kinds of local conditions and personal attitudes that might encourage these activities. The most obvious of these is neighborhood diversity: Jacobs and Sennett both assert that heterogeneity is an encouragement to public life in urban neighborhoods. But if diversity does stimulate unofficial public service, it does not do so in any obvious way. Although several different indicators of local diversity were used, none of them was associated at a significant level with any of the informal public service activities under consideration.

Unfortunately, diversity is difficult to pin down, and some forms of diversity could not be measured directly. It was infeasible, for example, to find out how closely the sample neighborhoods approximated the close-grained diversity of uses envisioned by Jane Jacobs, in which a variety of activities are intermingled on each block. But it was possible to capture some imperfect reflections of neighborhood variety. Where relatively high proportions of the local residents reported that they worked, shopped, or worshipped within their own localities, for example, it is reasonable to infer that their neighborhood contained not only residences but also places for worship, working, or shopping. None of these signs of variety in neighborhood uses was related to such public service activities as policing the neighborhood children or watching a neighbor's home. Nor were public service activities related to a composite measure of the extent to which the work, shopping, and worship of local residents were combined within their own neighborhoods. Several other measures of neighborhood heterogeneity — diversity in racial composition, socioeconomic status, and the mixture of single-family and multi-family housing units — were similarly unrelated to the residents' reports of unofficial public service.[34]

This does not necessarily mean that Jacobs and Sennett are mistaken when they attibute important effects to neighborhood diversity. The measures used here, after all, may not isolate the particular forms of diversity that are critical for the public life of urban neighborhoods. It is also possible that heterogeneity plays a role in neighborhood polities that is more indirect than anticipated. The nature of this influence may become evident if we first consider some of the factors that are more directly related to neighborhood public service activities.

One of the most notable of these is the kind of building in which a person lives. People who live in single-family homes are consistently more likely to engage in unofficial services of all kinds than are people who live in multi-family buildings. Of course, differences in type of residence may have this effect simply because they reflect variations in the respondents' vested interests in their neighborhoods. Residents of single-family dwellings are more apt to own their homes than those in apartments, and homeownership may help to foster a proprietary interest in maintaining the public order, health, and safety of one's neighborhood. The influence that we attribute to the kind of building that a person lives in may actually represent the effect of homeownership. In order to take account of this possibility, Table 4.10 presents the survey results so that we can distinguish the effects of living in a rented single-family home from the effects of owning one's single-family home. Comparing the two figures in each column of the table shows that homeowners are in fact more likely than renters to report some types of unofficial public service,[35] but even after the effects of homeownership are taken into account, whether a person lives in a single-family building or a multi-family building still makes a difference — as is shown by a comparison of the figures across each row of the table. In fact, the effect of living in a single-family building is just as large and sometimes larger than the influence of homeownership.

The propensity for unofficial public service exhibited by people who live in single-family homes helps to illustrate another of the precepts of neighborhood design advanced by Jacobs and Sennett. Both of them emphasize the importance of removing barriers between people's living quarters and the life of the street. Sennett, for example, is concerned about multiplying the "points of contact" among neighbors, and Jacobs obviously wants to focus as many eyes as possible on the events that take place in the street. Single-family homes, although they may seem more "private" than apartment houses, actually lend themselves more easily to such links between public and private spaces because they make the public life of the street more accessible to their inhabitants. When looking out from the windows of an apartment, a resident, may be several stories removed from the business of the street, and the front door opens on a usually empty hallway. But the windows and doors of a single-family home bring its residents into closer contact with the public domain of the neighborhood and may lead them to appropriate a

Table 4.10. Type of residence and informal public service activities, controlling for homeownership

	Type of residence	
Tenure	Single-family	Multi-family
A. WORKING WITH NEIGHBORS TO IMPROVE THE APPEARANCE OF THE STREET (Percentage of respondents in each category who said they worked with neighbors)		
Own	60.8 (977)	47.2 (94)
Rent	52.6 (360)	33.3 (684)
B. TRYING TO STOP NEIGHBORHOOD CHILDREN FROM DOING WHAT THEY SHOULDN'T (Percentage of respondents in each category who said they tried to police local children)		
Own	51.7 (966)	44.1 (90)
Rent	61.1 (359)	48.3 (668)
C. WATCHING NEIGHBORS' HOMES WHEN THEY ARE AWAY (Percentage of respondents in each category who said they watched neighbors' homes)		
Own	80.9 (976)	67.1 (94)
Rent	64.7 (359)	54.5 (702)
D. INFORMAL DIRECT ACTION (Percentage of respondents in each category who reported unofficial efforts to deal with local problems directly)		
Own	15.4 (980)	9.4 (94)
Rent	10.8 (362)	8.2 (704)

stretch of street frontage as their own. In this area they may exercise responsibility for the maintenance of order and cleanliness. This ease of transition from the private to the public sphere appears to have the kinds of consequences that Jacobs and Sennett would predict. These results are reflected in the survey findings, which show that living in a single-family home encouraged joint efforts to upgrade the appearance of the street, and individual attempts to police the neighborhood children and to keep the neighbor's homes under surveillance. What is more, these tendencies toward public service were at work even among people who rented their single-family homes rather than owning them.

In Baltimore the influence of single-family occupancy may have special importance. The city's large supply of rowhouses — amounting to an estimated 50 percent of the local housing stock[36] — undoubtedly helps to bring single-family homes within the reach of many moderate-income families who would not otherwise be able to afford them, and this sizable stock of rowhouses may also increase the supply of single-family housing that finds its way into the rental market. The results become visible on almost any warm evening, when families in many of Baltimore's rowhouse neighborhoods furnish "their" sidewalks with lawn chairs and convert these areas into open-air living rooms. The survey findings suggest that the public street lives of neighbors may be affected by single-family occupancy in more fundamental ways as well. Efforts at unofficial public service are likely to be commonplace in areas where single-family homes are numerous. If Baltimore's neighborhood polities are as strong as their reputation portrays them, the plentiful supply of single-family rowhouses may account for some of the strength. More generally, the evidence implies that homeownership — often recommended as a foundation for well-ordered neighborhoods — may not be the only basis for the development of self-governing capacity in a residential area.

Single-family homes facilitate a mixture of public and private activities, creating a kind of diversity in urban neighborhoods — an intricate mingling of different uses such as Jane Jacobs has recommended. In that limited sense, neighborhood diversity may contribute to the emergence of neighborhood public order, and there is another sense in which its contribution may not be quite so limited. An analysis of the survey evidence reveals that the socioeconomic diversity of a neighborhood may be one of the background factors that determines whether single-family occupancy will influence the public life of a residential area. The relevant data are in Table 4.11. The figures here are partial gamma coefficients — measures of association that show how strong the relationship is between living in a single-family home and engaging in various unofficial public services, once the effects of homeownership have been taken into account. For three of the four kinds of public service activities, these coefficients are much stronger in socially homogeneous neighborhoods than in diverse ones. In other words, single-family occupancy does not make nearly as much difference for public service activities in high-diversity neighborhoods as it does in low-diversity ones. An inspection of the data on which the coefficients are based would show why. In socially homogeneous neighborhoods, residents of sin-

Table 4.11. Relationship between single-family occupancy and unofficial public service activities in neighborhoods of varying socioeconomic diversity, controlling for homeownership (Partial gamma coefficients)

Neighborhood socioeconomic diversity	Public service activities			
	Working with neighbors to improve street	Policing neighborhood children	Watching neighbors' homes	Informal direct action
High	.18	.09	.36	.15
Medium	.42	.10	.26	.15
Low	.42	.42	.24	.46

gle-family homes are much more likely than apartment dwellers to engage in unofficial public services. For apartment dwellers, tendencies toward public service become more widespread as the social diversity of the neighborhood increases. For the occupants of single-family homes, however, the extent of public service remains just about the same in high-diversity neighborhoods as in low-diversity ones. In effect, the more diverse the neighborhood, the more nearly the apartment dwellers close the "public service gap" between themselves and the residents of single-family homes. In the high-diversity neighborhoods there is scarcely any difference at all between the two groups, and the coefficients in Table 4.11 therefore indicate that single-family occupancy is scarcely associated with public service activities in these residential areas. The single exception to this pattern appears in the third column of the table, where it is evident that the relationship between single-family occupancy and keeping the neighbors' homes under surveillance is not substantially affected by variations in neighborhood diversity. Perhaps it is significant that watching the homes of fellow residents is the only kind of public service under consideration that does not require social interaction among neighbors.[37]

As for the other forms of neighborhood public service, one possible implication of the survey results is that neighborhood social diversity somehow helps apartment dwellers to overcome the obstacles that stand in the way of their attempts at public service. Separated from the public life of the street by elevators and stairways, they are generally less likely than residents of single-family homes to police the local children or join their neighbors in efforts to make their streets attractive. But there is something about neighborhood social diversity that increases either the willingness or the ability of apartment dwellers to neutralize the disadvantages they face and to take part in the public lives of their neighborhoods.

Richard Sennett has already suggested why neighborhood diversity should have an influence of this kind. When dissimilar sorts of people live together in the same neighborhood, they tend to mistrust one another's capacities for maintaining the order and appearance of the residential area that they share. The result, perhaps, is not a simple and general increase in the individual residents' determination to take care of these matters themselves, but a greater tendency for certain politically "disadvantaged" subgroups (like the apartment dwellers) to brush aside the obstacles that might otherwise prevent them from equaling the public service efforts of their fellow residents. There may be an understandable reluctance to concede a dominant role in the management of neighborhood affairs to these fellow residents when so many of them are so different from oneself. It may also be difficult to believe that these socially alien neighbors will actually discharge their responsibilities for neighborhood governance. People who live in socially diverse neighborhoods, lacking confidence in the political reliability of their fellow residents, may convince themselves that if public order and public appearances are to be maintained in their communities, they will have to do it themselves.

If Sennett's interpretation is correct, we should find that people tend to engage in public service activities when they lack confidence in the public service activities of their neighbors. Some (but not all) of the survey evidence seems to support Sennett's explanation.

The residents interviewed in Baltimore were asked several questions about their perceptions of public service efforts among their neighbors. In addition to asking them whether they themselves had watched their neighbors' homes, for example, interviewers also asked them whether they thought that there were a lot of other people in their local communities who tried to "prevent crime in their neighborhoods by keeping an eye out for strangers around their neighbors' homes or cars." Besides inquiring whether the respondents themselves had tried to police the neighborhood children, the interviewers also asked them whether they thought that other people in their neighborhoods tried to "keep neighborhood children from getting into trouble, even when their own children aren't involved." When it came to the matter of joint efforts to improve the appearance of one's street, the question about personal activities had to be less closely connected with the question about perceptions of the neighbors' activities. Respondents were asked whether they thought that there were a lot of people in their residential area who tried to "clean up trash and debris in their neighborhood, even when it's not their own property."

The line of argument derived from Richard Sennett's observations suggests that public service activities should be most widespread in neighborhoods where residents generally think that they cannot rely on the public service activities of their neighbors. Sometimes this is just what we find. When the respondents from each neighborhood are considered as a group, it is evident that residential areas where relatively large numbers of people attempt to police the local children are also areas where relatively small numbers of people *believe* that anyone is policing the local children. The greater the proportion of local residents who engage in child-policing activities, the smaller the percentage who perceive that such things are being done. Conversely, the more people there are in a neighborhood who perceive that such things are being done, the fewer there are who have actually been doing them.[38]

Though anticipated, the results are still curious, and they are not isolated. The same pattern is found with respect to informal direct actions of the kind that we have already considered — unofficial public services preceded by informal deliberations among neighbors. The fewer people there are in a neighborhood who perceive that their fellow residents are keeping an eye on suspicious strangers, policing the local children, or cleaning up street trash, the more there are who report that they have engaged in informal direct action themselves. Here again, relatively widespread efforts at neighborhood public service tend to be accompanied by widespread lack of confidence in the public service activities of fellow residents. This contradictory pattern does not hold consistently, however. The percentage of people in a neighborhood who keep local homes under surveillance does not vary much depending on the prevalence of local beliefs about the surveillance activities of neighbors. Nor do reports of cooperative efforts to improve the appearance of local streets become more widespread when perceptions of voluntary street-cleaning efforts decline.

There is another inconsistency in the evidence. Our attention has been limited so far to the respondents from each neighborhood taken as a group. We know that child-policing activities tend to become widespread in neighborhoods where many residents are skeptical of their neighbors' efforts along these lines. But we do not know whether the individual residents who actually police the neighborhood children are also the same ones who think that their neighbors are not engaged in policing. The data reported in Tables 4.12 and 4.13 allow us to compare survey findings for individual residents with those for neighborhoods. Table 4.12's three rows represent different kinds of neighborhoods — communities where high, medium, and low proportions of residents perceived that a lot of their neighbors were policing the local children. Comparing the figures in the three rows illustrates what we have already found: child-policing activities are most widespread in neighborhoods where the perception of these activities is least prevalent. The percentages in the third row of the table are substantially larger than the comparable percentages in the top row, indicating that the level of child policing tends to be relatively high in precisely those neighborhoods where there is a low level of belief in the child-policing efforts of fellow residents.

But when respondents within each type of community were considered individually, child-policing activities and the perception of these activities were no longer inversely related to one another. The two columns in Table 4.12 distinguish the individual respondents in each type of neighborhood who thought that their fellow residents were trying to police local young people from those who did not think so. Comparing the figures in the two columns shows that individual residents tend to engage in child-policing activities when they believe that their neighbors are similarly engaged. But those who doubt their fellow residents' efforts to preserve public order

Table 4.12. Policing local children and individual perceptions of local child-policing activities, controlling for prevailing neighborhood beliefs about the policing of children (Percentage of respondents in each category who said they tried to police local children)

Prevalence of beliefs about child policing in neighborhood	Individual respondent believes that lots of neighbors police local children	
	Yes	No
High	47.5 (262)	38.2 (419)
Medium	64.7 (188)	55.2 (521)
Low	72.5 (132)	53.5 (534)

against unruly children are less likely to take measures against such children themselves.

An examination of the survey results concerning informal direct action yields the same kind of mismatch between the findings about individual residents and the findings about neighborhoods. The relevant data are presented in Table 4.13. The results indicate that, for neighborhoods, reports of informal direct action become somewhat less widespread as beliefs in the child-policing activities of fellow residents become more widespread. For individual respondents, however, the likelihood of informal direct action seems to increase when people perceive that their neighbors are policing the local children. At the neighborhood level, in short, preceptions and activities are inversely related; for individual respondents, they are positively related to one another. Moreover, the same inconsistent pattern also appears when informal direct action is considered in connection with other kinds of beliefs about the public service activities of neighbors—not just child-policing efforts, but voluntary efforts to clean up neighborhood trash or debris and to keep the homes of fellow residents under surveillance. In all these cases, the survey results indicate that individual respondents are more likely to take informal direct action when they believe that their neighbors are performing unofficial public services as well. But people who live in neighborhoods where such beliefs prevail tend not to engage in informal direct action.

There is no obvious explanation for results of this kind. It is clear,

Table 4.13. Informal direct action and individual perceptions of local child-policing activities, controlling for prevailing neighborhood beliefs about the policing of children (Percentage of respondents in each category who reported unofficial efforts to deal with local problems)

Prevalence of beliefs about child policing in neighborhood	Individual respondent believes that lots of neighbors police local children	
	Yes	No
High	13.5 (281)	9.0 (437)
Medium	15.8 (191)	9.8 (523)
Low	23.4 (134)	12.0 (538)

however, that they cannot be accommodated by the explanation originally proposed — that residents would be driven to unofficial public service when they perceived that their neighbors were not performing these services. In fact, individual respondents who do not believe that their fellow residents are performing neighborhood services tend not to perform these services themselves. This much, at least, holds true for all four types of public service activities under consideration — child policing, street improvement, neighborhood surveillance, and informal direct action. In every case, individual residents who engaged in these activities tend to believe that their neighbors are performing similar activities.[39] What is true for individual residents, however, does not hold true so consistently for neighborhoods. The complications arise in connection with efforts at child policing and informal direct action, because in neighborhoods where these two types of public service activities are most common, there is a tendency to *disbelieve* that local residents are engaged in such efforts.

In some respects the neighborhood results and the individual results follow contradictory patterns, and any interpretation of the findings must succeed in reconciling this apparent inconsistency. Concerning the neighborhood findings, some additional pieces of evidence suggest a starting point for an explanation. Specifically, an analysis of the survey results shows that neighborhoods where high proportions of the respondents report that they try to police the neighborhood children are also communities in which the number of children per household is relatively high. Residents in these neighborhoods are also more likely than people elsewhere to say that local children play together in large groups rather than small ones, and they are more likely than residents elsewhere to report that local children played in public places (streets and shopping areas, for example) rather than in private ones.[40] In other words, neighborhoods where child-policing activities are widespread tend to be residential areas where there might be numerous occasions for the policing of young people, simply because the local population of children is relatively large and because the circumstances under which they amuse themselves might be expected to make them a nuisance to the adults of the neighborhood. At the same time, the very fact that so many occasions arise for disciplining local children might tend to convince local residents that their neighbors are not exercising much discipline. The result is that communities where child-policing activities are most extensive also tend to be areas where people do not *believe* that child-policing activities are extensive. The disbelief and the activity both reflect the magnitude of the public order problem presented by local young people.

The problem, of course, is that this explanation for the behavior of neighborhoods does not account for the behavior of individual residents. Neighborhoods produce a high level of child-policing activities when they exhibit a low level of belief in these activities. But within these "disbelieving" neighborhoods, the individual residents who actually tend to engage in child-policing activities are not the disbelievers; they are the ones who think that many of their neighbors are making efforts at child supervision. Why should individual beliefs and prevailing neighborhood beliefs be related in such different ways to child policing?

One explanation is that individual residents who believe that their neighbors are unofficially supervising local children may enjoy a sense of social support for their own activities in this direction, and so they exhibit a tendency toward child-policing activities themselves. People who have confidence in the order maintenance efforts of their neighbors can respond more readily to the problems created by local juveniles than people who lack this confidence. A more plainly political interpretation is that these confident people have a kind of power in relation to fellow residents who are more doubtful about neighborhood support for public order and public safety. Their power is reflected in the public services that they perform — "services" that may frequently involve efforts to punish or control perceived misconduct on the part of the neighbors or the neighbors' children. The belief that there is neighborhood support for such public service activities helps to promote this exercise of power. This belief, of course, does not confer any significant political advantages when most of the people in a residential neighborhood share the same sense of political confidence. Power, after all, is a relational phenomenon; an advantage shared by everyone is no longer politically advantageous. But the fewer people there are in a neighborhood who think that local norms encourage the unofficial maintenance of order, the greater the political edge that they will enjoy over their less confident fellow residents, and we can expect this edge to be reflected in their public services activities.

That is just what the results reported in Tables 4.12 and 4.13 seem to show. People who believe that there is social support for their child-policing activities are consistently more likely to engage in these efforts than people who do not hold this belief. But it is precisely when their belief is least widely shared within the neighborhood that they outdo the child supervision efforts of their less confident fellow residents by the widest margin. In neighborhoods where the level of belief in child policing is low, the believers are much more likely to engage in child policing than the disbelievers. But where the belief in child supervision is more widespread, the size of this difference is not so great.

In general, it appears that two kinds of factors help to stimulate efforts at public service. The first of these is a local condition or problem — such as a large juvenile population — that presents a reason or a need for unofficial attempts to maintain public order, safety, or cleanliness. All residents are more likely to take action when they are confronted with such conditions than when they are not. But the capacity to act may be just as important as the need to act, and some residents are endowed with more of this capacity than others. Their advantage becomes most pronounced when it is shared with only a few of their fellow residents, because it is here that they enjoy the greatest superiority over their neighbors. Where the belief in social support for child-policing is least widespread, for example, the handful of believers enjoys its greatest political advantage.[41]

Perhaps a more vivid illustration of the conditions for neighborly power is offered by the findings in Table 4.14. The survey results reported here have to do with each kind of informal political action that we have considered so far — from participation in neighborly discourse to keeping the neighbors' homes under surveillance. The findings show how the different sorts of unofficial political action are related to the socioeconomic status of the individual respondents and to the socioeconomic composition of the neighborhoods in which they live. Comparing the figures across each row in the various sections of the table indicates, with only a few exceptions, that high-status residents are more likely than lower-status residents to participate in the unofficial political lives of their neighborhoods. Informal neighborhood politics is in this respect no different from most other varieties of politics. But a comparison of the figures within each column in the various parts of the table adds a distinctive dimension to the situation. The variations here reflect the different kinds of neighborhood social environments to which the respondents are exposed. The first column of percentages in each section of the table shows, with only one exception, that high-status people are more apt to engage in informal political action when they live in low-status neighborhoods than when they live in the midst of other high-status people. In part, their tendency to become politically active in low status neighborhoods may represent a

Table 4.14. Socioeconomic status and public service activities, controlling for socioeconomic composition of neighborhood

Socioeconomic status of neighborhood	Socioeconomic status of individual residents		
	High	Medium	Low

A. PARTICIPATION IN NEIGHBORHOOD DISCUSSIONS (Percentage of respondents in each category who talked to neighbors about local problems or needs)

High	53.3 (412)	36.5 (297)	31.1 (57)
Medium	52.7 (84)	41.1 (398)	20.9 (239)
Low	68.9 (52)	43.9 (258)	26.6 (330)

B. INFORMAL DIRECT ACTION (Percentage of respondents in each category who reported unofficial efforts to deal with local problems)

High	15.4 (402)	7.1 (294)	1.8 (57)
Medium	27.5 (84)	13.8 (399)	6.1 (238)
Low	24.9 (51)	15.0 (259)	8.1 (321)

C. WORKING WITH NEIGHBORS TO IMPROVE THE APPEARANCE OF THE STREET (Percentage of respondents in each category who said they worked with neighbors)

High	49.0 (405)	41.5 (284)	42.4 (56)
Medium	58.7 (84)	54.7 (398)	47.5 (238)
Low	73.2 (52)	58.7 (259)	43.8 (331)

D. TRYING TO STOP NEIGHBORHOOD CHILDREN FROM DOING WHAT THEY SHOULDN'T (Percentage of respondents in each category who said they tried to police local children)

High	36.4 (390)	43.3 (280)	61.8 (57)
Medium	65.9 (84)	54.7 (397)	47.3 (230)
Low	65.0 (52)	66.9 (256)	58.9 (329)

E. WATCHING NEIGHBORS' HOMES WHEN THEY ARE AWAY (Percentage of respondents in each category who said they watched neighbors' homes)

High	74.1 (410)	71.6 (295)	80.7 (57)
Medium	69.5 (84)	65.7 (399)	60.0 (238)
Low	72.7 (52)	71.6 (257)	65.6 (331)

response to the local problems that are likely to be characteristic of these neighborhoods. Living conditions in low-income neighborhoods, after all, are seldom as pleasant as they are in residential areas where prosperous households are concentrated. The result, perhaps, is that low-status neighborhoods confront their inhabitants with more reasons for informal political action than high-status neighborhoods, and therefore stimulate more widespread public service activities.

The difficulty with this explanation is that it cannot be extended very far beyond the high-status respondents. People of low status, for example, do not exhibit any general tendency to become politically active when they are exposed to the problems of low-status neighborhoods. An examination of the third column of percentage figures in each section of the table shows that low-status residents are usually no more likely to engage in unofficial political action when they live among other low-status people than when they live in high-status neighborhoods. The only exception to this pattern occurs in part B, where it is evident that low-status residents are more likely to engage in informal direct action when they live in low-status rather than in high-status neighborhoods.

Low-status neighborhood almost certainly suffer from more severe problems than high-status neighborhoods, but low-status residents who are exposed to these problems are usually no more likely to respond to them by taking informal political action than low-status respondents who are not exposed to these problems. It is among the high-status residents, paradoxically, that we find the strongest indication of an informal political response to the problems of low-status neighborhoods. They differ from low-status people in this respect probably because they enjoy the political advantages conferred by relatively high incomes, high levels of education, and prestigious occupations. By themselves, in other words, the problems experienced by low-status residential areas are not sufficient to stimulate political action; the individual inhabitants must have a capacity to take action, and the skills, attitudes, and social connections associated with high socioeconomic status evidently provide this capacity. The result, stated simply, is that unofficial political activity is most widespread among relatively rich people who live in relatively poor neighborhoods.

Such residents enjoy an especially sharp political edge over their low-status neighbors. It is not simply that they are endowed with the personal resources of high-status people, but that they live in residential areas where these resources are in short supply, and the political resources that accompany high socioeconomic status seem to confer more significant political advantages when their possessors are surrounded by other people who do not enjoy them. The survey data in Table 4.14 show not only that high-status people generally tend to outdo their low-status neighbors when it comes to unofficial activism but that this tendency is more consistent and pronounced within the relatively poor neighborhoods than it is in the rich ones. When rich people are surrounded by other rich people, the political advantages of being rich are diluted. But when rich people live among poor people, the political value of their wealth, education, and occupational prestige tends to be enhanced.

This, at least, is the interpretation of the evidence that seems most nearly suited to the survey data. It suggests that neighborhood diversity does play some part in triggering the informal executive powers of a neighborhood polity, but this diversity is of a particular sort; it is more limited than the social heterogeneity recommended by Richard Sennett or the close-grained mixture of activities envisioned by Jane Jacobs. It is the kind of diversity that results when a socially advantaged minority finds itself in the midst of a less fortunate majority. In this form of diversity the advantaged minority faces a distinctive combination of circumstances. First, they are exposed to the problems and aggravations that come from living in a socially disadvantaged community. Second, they enjoy personal resources that increase their ability to respond to these problems by taking informal political action. Third, the political value of these resources is not reduced by the presence of many other people who enjoy the same resources. This mixture of circumstances appears to create a special propensity for unofficial political acts to maintain public order, safety, and sanitation in urban neighborhoods. The same circumstances may also help to account for the fact that neighborhood public servants sometimes seem to be irritated with their neighbors. Frequently, the residents who produce unofficial public goods for their neighborhoods are misfits within their residential areas. They are rich people in poor neighborhoods; they are people who think that there is local support for informal public services in communities where few of their fellow residents share this belief. In short, they tend to be at odds with most of their neighbors, and the experience of being an alien presence in one's neighborhood may contribute to a sense of friction or annoyance with one's neighbors.

One more set of survey findings may help to refine our understanding of the political role played by these neighborhood misfits. In particular, it may be important to consider not only the distinctive social characteristics that differentiate a local minority from their fellow residents, but the political ties that link them to the unofficial polity of the neighborhood. To find out about some of these ties, all respondents were asked the following question: "Suppose an important problem came up in your neighborhood and you felt it was necessary to get the whole neighborhood active in fighting the problem. Of all the people you know, who would be the best person to go to in order to get the neighborhood behind you?" Respondents who were able to name such a person were expressing the belief that they had social or political contacts through which it was possible to achieve the political mobilization of the neighborhood as a whole. In some neighborhoods almost everyone could name a political contact of this kind. In the extreme case, for example, less than 2 percent of the respondents in one residential area were unable to designate a person capable of mobilizing the neighborhood. At the other extreme, there were two communities where more than 40 percent of the respondents could not think of anyone capable of mobilizing their fellow residents — Union Square and Reservoir Hill. The relative scarcity of political contacts in these neighborhoods probably reflects a lack of local political cohesion. When people report that they do not know any leaders capable of mobilizing their neighbors, they are also indicating that they are beyond the reach of mobilization themselves, and out of touch with their neighborhood's leadership group. When these politically detached people are numerous in a neighborhood, it probably means that there *is* no leadership in the neighborhood capable of mobilizing the residents. It is a sign that the neighborhood has not achieved a high level of political integration.

The findings reported in Table 4.15 show what a difference it makes for a neighborhood to be politically integrated in this way, and for individual residents to be politically connected to local leaders. The evidence shows, first, that individual respondents who thought they knew leaders capable of mobilizing the neighborhood were always more likely to engage in informal political action than those who were not acquainted with such local political figures. Being politically connected may encourage individual residents to perform unofficial public services, or it could be that the performance of these public services brings residents into contact with locally prominent people who seem capable of mobilizing the neighborhood. In either case, it is evident from a comparison of the figures in the two columns of the table that residents who were acquainted with such neighborhood leaders were more apt to be informal public servants than those who were not.

Public service activities were related differently to the political integration of the neighborhood at large than to the political con-

Table 4.15. Acquaintance with neighborhood leaders and public service activities, controlling for political integration of the neighborhood

Proportion of politically connected residents in neighborhood	Individual respondents acquainted with leaders who can mobilize neighborhood	
	Yes	No

A. PARTICIPATION IN NEIGHBORHOOD DISCUSSIONS (Percentage of respondents in each category who talked to neighbors about local problems or needs)

High	48.0 (658)	21.5 (121)
Medium	41.0 (510)	20.0 (204)
Low	47.7 (397)	24.8 (237)

B. INFORMAL DIRECT ACTION (Percentage of respondents in each category who reported unofficial efforts to deal with local problems)

High	11.4 (659)	4.1 (123)
Medium	13.3 (511)	6.6 (204)
Low	17.8 (397)	10.4 (237)

C. WORKING WITH NEIGHBORS TO IMPROVE THE APPEARANCE OF THE STREET (Percentage of respondents in each category who said they worked with neighbors)

High	54.6 (650)	19.8 (121)
Medium	54.5 (504)	43.1 (200)
Low	57.5 (397)	37.4 (234)

D. TRYING TO STOP NEIGHBORHOOD CHILDREN FROM DOING WHAT THEY SHOULDN'T (Percentage of respondents in each category who said they tried to police local children)

High	40.9 (636)	32.4 (108)
Medium	63.0 (500)	46.9 (203)
Low	63.5 (394)	53.6 (233)

E. WATCHING NEIGHBORS' HOMES WHEN THEY ARE AWAY (Percentage of respondents in each category who said they watched neighbors' homes)

High	73. (658)	47.9 (121)
Medium	73.9 (511)	34.9 (204)
Low	56.9 (396)	50.9 (234)

nectedness of the individual residents. This is the second implication of the survey data, and it becomes evident from a comparison of the percentage figures in the different rows within each section of the table. The differences between these percentages are associated with variations in neighborhood political integration, and they suggest that there is sometimes a tendency for public service activities to occur in neighborhoods where relatively small numbers of local residents are connected with leaders capable of mobilizing the local population at large. In other words, unofficial political action is sometimes most widespread where the level of political integration is lowest. The explanation, perhaps, is that politically disjointed neighborhoods also tend to suffer from the kinds of local problems that might stimulate informal political action. Or perhaps it is precisely the absence of mechanisms for mobilizing the neighborhood as a whole that drives the residents to take matters into their own hands by policing the local children or joining their neighbors in unofficial street-cleaning efforts. The lack of political integration does not always encourage these unofficial expedients. In some cases it appears to have no consistent effect at all, but there is only one case where the results show that the opposite is clearly true. This exception occurs in the last section of the table, where it is evident that politically connected residents are more likely to watch their neighbors' homes when they live in politically integrated neighborhoods than when they live in politically disorganized communities. In all other instances, neighborhood political integration either discourages public service activities or has no consistent effect on them.

In this respect, the findings are consistent with others that we have already seen: unofficial political action tends to be more widespread in disadvantaged neighborhoods than it is in more fortunate residential areas. But there is one feature of the current results that represents a departure from the earlier pattern. Specifically, being politically connected does not seem to confer any special political advantage in neighborhoods where large numbers of fellow residents are politically isolated or detached. In fact, the findings in Table 4.15 indicate that it is usually in the neighborhoods with high levels of political integration that the "public service gap" between the politically connected residents and the politically unconnected residents is greatest. In other words, being politically connected seems to confer the greatest political advantages when one is surrounded by fellow residents who are also acquainted with community leaders capable of mobilizing the local population. The most obvious explanation is that being able to contact the neighborhood's political mobilizers does not represent any particular political benefit if most of the local population is beyond the reach of mobilization. This is one case in which the value of a political advantage increases when one's neighbors enjoy the same advantage.

The findings serve as a reminder that there is a kind of neighborhood power that does not consist of the influence that individual residents exercise over one another; it is a "non-zero-sum" kind of power. Political connectedness is an advantage that becomes more valuable the more widespread it is, and in this respect it is unlike some of the other politically advantageous resources that we have considered.

Apart from this dissimilarity, there is a general and consistent pattern in the evidence considered so far. Such signs of neighborhood political life as the sense of neighborhood identity, the occurrence of neighborhood discourse, and the production of unofficial public services have all proven to be independent of personal solidarity among neighbors. Even more notable is the fact that neighborhood political discussions and several other kinds of informal political activities are associated with neighborhood antagonism or friction, a friction that now seems more understandable. In part, friction appears to reflect the same local problems that arouse residents to informal political activity. People who are bothered by neighborhood problems are obviously the ones most inclined to do something about these aggravations. But they are also liable to blame some of the irritation on their neighbors, and this may help to explain why the people who take unofficial action to deal with perceived neighborhood problems tend to be irritated at their fellow residents.

Some portion of their displeasure may also originate in the unofficial activities themselves. A neighbor who intervenes to prevent juvenile misbehavior, for example, is sometimes rewarded with a dose of juvenile abuse. The experience can hardly increase the unofficial public servant's affection for the neighborhood young people or their parents. A pattern of similar experiences may help to explain why unofficial public servants as a group tend to be hostile toward neighbors.

These are certainly plausible explanations for the connection between neighborhood public service and neighborhood animosity, and they receive some support from the survey evidence. But the evidence also reveals the shortcomings of these explanations, and it suggests that another, more comprehensive explanation may lie behind them. Unofficial public service seems to reflect a particular sort of neighborhood diversity, the kind that arises when an advantaged minority happens to be present in a disadvantaged residential area. Members of local minorities are apt to experience some degree of friction with their less privileged neighbors simply because they are misfits within their residential communities. But their situation also makes them the most probable candidates for unofficial public service. Their inclinations toward informal political action arise, in the first place, because they experience directly the problems of poor and politically disorganized neighborhoods. This means not only that they are exposed to the kinds of "inconveniencies" that can drive people to political action but also that they may sense an especially sharp mismatch between these local disadvantages and the standards of comfort or convenience that their privileges have led them to expect. The apparent result is an especially strong tendency to engage in unofficial political action, and perhaps a tendency to be especially irritated at the neighbors who are blamed for causing these aggravations.

A further consideration is that the social advantages of these relatively privileged minorities may often be translated into political advantages that facilitate unofficial activities. Educational background, organizational skills, or simply the confident belief that one's actions make a difference for the neighborhood—any of these things may represent a political resource, and the people who control these resources possess the wherewithal to exercise political influence. This means that privileged people who live in underprivileged neighborhoods are likely to have the capacity, not just the reasons, for informal political action. Circumstances also boost their potential as political actors in a third way: few of their neighbors share their advantages. Political resources are more valuable in neighborhoods where almost no one has them than in neighborhoods where almost everybody does.

In general, it is the presence of privileged residents in underprivileged neighborhoods that seems to set the stage for the relationship between neighborly public service and neighborly antagonism. Exposed to the aggravations of life in disadvantaged neighborhoods, privileged people are apt to react with particular vehemence—both by taking action and by taking offense. When they attempt to deal directly with local irritations, their actions will bring them into contact with neighbors who do not share their own social backgrounds and characteristics, and such disparities among neighbors can be expected to intensify whatever friction is inherent in these encounters. Finally, the very fact that they are surrounded by people less educated or successful than themselves may help to increase the annoyance with which these privileged residents regard their less privileged neighbors. In short, the mechanisms that make unofficial public servants hostile toward their neighbors seem to operate with special force in neighborhoods where an advantaged minority lives surrounded by a disadvantaged majority. Considered individually, these mechanisms may be insufficient to account for the connection between animosity and informal political action. The sociopolitical structure of the neighborhood itself supplies the missing ingredient in the explanation and a possible framework for organizing its elements.

This structure also reveals something about the framework of a political society. John Locke and other theorists of our political beginnings have imagined that an equality of condition among men was the starting point for the political equivalent of the Creation. In Baltimore's neighborhoods, by contrast, it is precisely an inequality of condition that seems to strike some of the first sparks of political life. Perhaps this is the version of the political creation story suitable for big cities, derived from Jacobs and Sennett instead of Hobbes, Locke, or Rousseau. But it should also be remembered that even an inegalitarian version of the story could not accommodate all the facts. Its shortcomings become evident when we consider the political integration or connectedness of neighborhood residents. As a political resource, it becomes more valuable the more widely it is shared. The survey results also indicate that where political connectedness is most widespread, unofficial public service activities may sometimes diminish. In other words, it appears that in urban neighborhoods some of the elements of political society may be at odds with others. The evidence could compel us to draw a distinction between the capacity of neighborhoods to generate informal street-level politics and their ability to achieve neighborhood-wide political integration. The activities of the street and sidewalk need to be considered in relation to the political organization of the neighborhood as a whole.

5.
Community
Organizations

Whitelock Street, Reservoir Hill. Photograph by Charlotte Crenson.

In February 1979, while much of Baltimore stood immobile in deep snow, Reservoir Hill roused itself to collective action. Elsewhere, public institutions ceased operating and public gatherings were canceled; in Reservoir Hill, however, residents struggled through the drifts keen on public service or public disorder or some combination of the two. As congregations of looters formed outside the stores on Whitelock Street, Stephanie Hull, president of the Reservoir Hill Community Association, was activating her organization to meet the neighborhood's emergency needs. Before the plundering was over, she had seen to it that association members were distributing food and services to local residents. At least some of the looters had become born-again public servants and keepers of the peace by nightfall.

In Reservoir Hill, acts of civil disorder did not stand in clear opposition to efforts at order maintenance. Disruption and cohesion seemed to arise from the same circumstances. They were alternate responses to a single neighborhood crisis, and in fact the concurrence of neighborhood order and disorder may have reflected not just the passing influence of a winter blizzard but more durable elements in the unofficial constitution of the neighborhood polity. Unity and discord never seemed far removed from one another in Reservoir Hill. By June, for example, several of the same unofficial public servants who had responded so energetically to Stephanie Hull's wintertime call for assistance had joined to oust her from office in a factious election for the presidency of the Reservoir Hill Community Association. February's organizational cohesion had been transmuted into springtime strife.

More precisely, tendencies toward strife and cohesion existed side by side in Reservoir Hill. The tensions that led to the June rebellion had surfaced months before the presidential election took place. During the snowstorm, therefore, members of the Reservoir Hill Association had mobilized to perform prodigies of public service in an atmosphere already tinged by enmity and resentment. They were not unusual in this respect. Neighborly hostility, as we have already seen, often accompanies unofficial efforts to maintain public order, safety, or sanitation. But because this is the case, neighborhoods that exhibit a strong capacity for improvising their own informal public services may also have little capacity for achieving political unity and integration. The same circumstances that encourage residents to exercise their unofficial "executive powers" for the common good can also stimulate social animosities that impede the development of community-wide organizations for aggregating and articulating local opinion, or for coordinating local action.

The experience of Reservoir Hill seems to illustrate this potential dilemma of neighborhood politics. The neighborhood's capacity for informal public service and its propensity for factional conflict both seem to be associated with the same feature: the presence of relatively rich people in a relatively poor neighborhood. The survey evidence has already indicated that rich people display their strongest tendencies toward unofficial public service when they live in poor neighborhoods. But when the population of a relatively poor residential area happens to include a relatively rich minority, the neighborhood is apt to exhibit strong tendencies toward intramural strife. The strife and the public service are both evident in Reservoir Hill.

Like Union Square, Reservoir Hill has recently attracted middle-class home buyers and investors who see possibilities for restoration, rehabilitation, or profit in the neighborhood's nineteenth-century townhouses. As in Union Square, these relatively prosperous newcomers have clashed with the lower-income inhabitants who make up a majority of the local population and who are fearful that rising rents and taxes may force them to move elsewhere or require them to spend larger fractions of their incomes on shelter. In contrast to Union Square, however, this conflict is complicated and perhaps intensified by racial differences. Almost all of Reservoir Hill's lower-income residents are black; many, but by no means all, of its higher-income residents are white.

It was a "long-standing racial conflict" in the Reservoir Hill Community Association that Stephanie Hull saw contributing to her defeat for reelection as president of the organization. "There was the sense," she says, "that one who has more than others, i.e., middle-class whites, should lend skills and expertise [to the organization], but not expect any benefit or recognition. It was the same attitude that prevailed for white liberals in the civil rights movement of the 1960s, and maybe it's OK for a few months, but over a year or more, it just can't be sustained." Selfless community service might be expected for the duration of a snowstorm, or for short-term neighborhood projects, but eventually the dissimilarity between the interests of middle-class white residents and lower-class black residents was bound to force its way to the surface. Race itself was not the source of this difference. It originated, according to Stephanie Hull, in "the basic class conflict in the organization [which] was being masked by racial contention . . . The conflict is between low-income residents who want to stay in the area and other middle-class residents who want to attract outsiders."

The class-based nature of the conflict is one thing on which Mrs. Hull and her foul-weather friends seem to agree. "Everybody knows," says one of her leading springtime opponents, "that our fight is not a racial one. It doesn't make any difference if you are black or white or green, you must represent the people." And some of the people, at least, did not believe that they were adequately represented under the regime of President Hull. Her persistent efforts to find a basis for political unity between low-income and middle-income residents only succeeded in activating the latent suspicions of her less prosperous constituents, who were apprehensive that their own interests might be sacrificed to the neighborhood improvement efforts of their better-educated and better-off neighbors. The business of making Reservoir Hill a more attractive place to live, after all, had limited appeal for people who were worried that they might soon find it too costly to continue living there. For people struggling to hold their ground in the neighborhood, local improvement efforts seemed merely to distract attention from the most serious neighborhood issues. While Mrs. Hull had to search for common interests that promised to unite her neighbors, the conflicting interests that divided them were immediately evident to her opponents. Conflict seemed to be the natural condition of the neighborhood. "You know why? You know why?" thunders one of Mrs. Hull's most formidable critics. "Right now, you got what you call the middle class moving in. They're not any better than anyone else, just more fortunate. And poor people are being displaced. People don't have no place to go. They got no money to move, no decent housing . . . What these middle-class people want is their *trees*, and they want their back alleys paved. These are people who don't need anything. But we see the need of people . . . I like my back alley paved too, but I'm not going to put a back alley ahead of a person who doesn't have a place to live."

Some efforts had in fact been made to ensure that there would be places for poor people in the neighborhood. Before becoming president of the neighborhood association, for example, Stephanie Hull had joined with about a dozen other members of the group to organize a homeownership service for Reservoir Hill. Supported by funds from the city government, the service aimed to convert some of the neighborhood's low-income renters into homebuyers. A full-time director helped clients to negotiate sales contracts with landlords, find subsidized low-interest mortgages, and estimate the cost of needed home repairs. The program also made grants to cover both repairs and settlement costs. After two years the homeownership service had helped almost forty households to become Reservoir Hill homeowners. But rapidly rising real estate values in the neighborhood were making it more and more difficult for the program to find homes for low-income purchasers and to retain the support of low-income constituents. The three white activists who had most to do with the day-to-day operation of the program increasingly became targets of resentment. In time, some of the residents who had worked along with Stephanie Hull to establish the homeownership service would oppose her for reelection to the presidency of the Reservoir Hill Association.

Their animosity could not be understood simply as a reflection of disappointment with the homeownership service. The program had been preceded by a ten-year series of housing and rehabilitation projects in Reservoir Hill. All of them had promised additional homes for low-income residents, and none of them had been able to deliver as many housing units as the neighborhood's low-income residents had been led to expect. The Reservoir Hill Association, whose executive board served as the local planning advisory committee for the city's Department of Housing and Community Development, had participated in the design of publicly assisted housing programs for the neighborhood, and it was held partly responsible for what low-income residents regarded as repeated betrayals. They thought it suspicious that housing construction and rehabilitation efforts initially designed to benefit the area's disadvantaged families always seemed to attract more middle-class households to the neighborhood in the end.

The homeownership service readily fell under the shadow of long-established resentments. The fact that educated, white, middle-class residents were most active in the administration of the program did not help matters. "There's a demand," comments one of them, "for people who have the skills to get up there and do the job, and a resentment that they have the skills." Middle-class members of the association were expected to assume leadership responsibilities but aroused antagonism if they attempted to exercise leadership authority. "They feel used — used and abused," observes the same activist. "It's exhausting, draining, because there's constant abuse . . . It's a request that skilled members of the community be staff for people who cannot articulate their needs."

Low-income organization members, on the other hand, were likely to grow indignant when middle-class leaders — black or white — tried to define their needs for them. A long-time resident of the neighborhood, for example, recalls how she felt when she was elected to serve with better educated people on the community association's executive board: "I was the only one sitting up there with all those degrees. These are the angels flying through the community — educated fools. They was flaunting what they had . . . but they should have been playing a low key . . . They was saying, 'We know what you're supposed to have. We know what you want.'" Yet even though they frequently resented the leadership of their middle-class neighbors, the less fortunate members of the Reservoir Hill Association usually declined to fill leadership posts themselves. One of Stephanie Hull's critics in the 1979 election was asked on three occasions to serve as president — once by Mrs. Hull herself. She explains why she refused the office: "I just didn't think I was qualified. I didn't think I had what it took to be a president . . . I'm a low-income person, and touch base with a lot of low-income people. It sort of clues me in to a lot of things, but at the same time it doesn't give me the structure or maybe the education [to] deal with all these situations. I couldn't write a proposal. I could say what I'd like to see in it but then to actually write it . . . I couldn't do that. So I thought that that in itself would be a disservice to the community . . . I think I can deal with the grass-roots stuff, but not be able to do the proposal stuff. I can talk it, but I can't write it."

Better-educated residents who could do both the talking and the writing generally encountered difficulties when it came to the "grass-roots stuff." Reservoir Hill's middle-class leaders could not secure the trust and loyalty of the neighborhood's predominantly lower-class constituency. But lower-class residents who could command such grass-roots support were unwilling or unable to assume full leadership responsibilities as long as skilled, educated, middle-class residents were available to do the "proposal stuff." Under the circumstances, leadership in the Reservoir Hill Association was a precarious business — a wearing effort to preserve unity and to smooth over the class-based controversies that were almost always threatening to fracture the organization. Yet even the search for consensus itself could eventually exhaust the good will and patience of the association members. According to one neighborhood activist, both Stephanie Hull and the white attorney who preceded her as president of the Reservoir Hill Association "would resist putting on the agenda the real troublesome items that would make a messy, horrible meeting . . . and people didn't go for that." Tired by the struggle to maintain unity, says the same observer, the low-income women who were key members of the association finally lost patience with Mrs. Hull: "We had whole meetings devoted to planning the Fall Festival, because she thought it would be positive. Stephanie's a social worker, and she likes to create cohesive groups and create 'positive experiences,' and these women were not worried about the quality of their experiences. They were watching their friends leaving the neighborhood. So it seemed frivolous. It seemed they were always coming to meetings when there were very important issues [to discuss] and people getting kicked out . . . You face these problems day to day. Then you go to a meeting, and it's about the Fall Festival. It's just irritating. And you wonder *why* it's about the Fall Festival."

Perhaps even more worthy of wonder is the fact that in an organization where irritation threatened so frequently to erupt into open conflict, members could be mobilized for cooperative ventures designed to produce collective benefits for the community at large. The planning of the Fall Festival may have been exasperating for some local activists, but the neighborhood celebration was held all the same, and it was an occasion for widespread resident activity. Even more remarkable, of course, was the neighborhood's response to the snowstorm during the winter that followed. On these and other occasions, the local clash of private interests were interrupted by an outburst of informal public service. What lay behind the clash of interests was the confrontation between the neighborhood's middle-class minority and its lower-class majority. But as the survey evidence has already indicated, the same sort of confrontation may also contain the seeds of a neighborhood's informal "executive power." High-status people exhibit their strongest inclinations toward unofficial public service when they live in the midst of lower-status neighbors.

Such findings, of course, cannot explain the public service efforts of Reservoir Hill residents who do not enjoy high levels of income, education, or occupational prestige. It should be noted, however, that their efforts are limited in character. The survey findings show that Reservoir Hill's low-status residents are not notable for the frequency with which they try to police the neighborhood children or watch their neighbors' homes. But one thing that does distinguish them is a relatively strong tendency to engage in informal direct action, to deal with neighborhood problems after discussing the problems informally with fellow residents. This inclination to take matters into one's own hands may conceivably be explained by a simple inability to place matters in anyone else's hands. In a politically fragmented and factionalized neighborhood like Reservoir Hill, where lower-class inhabitants in particular do not recognize any leaders capable of mobilizing their fellow residents, it may also be difficult for them to recognize any neighborhood authorities or institutions to which they might refer their problems. They rely on their own efforts because they cannot identify anyone else on whom to rely, and they discuss problems informally among themselves because the formal institutions for conducting such deliberations are either inaccessible or paralyzed by conflict.

Given the conditions that prevail in Reservoir Hill, some such explanation for the public service activities of low-status residents seems at least plausible, and it may fit the circumstances of other neighborhoods too. In Union Square, for example, factional strife is also accompanied by a high level of informal direct action and by a relatively widespread inability to identify leaders capable of mobilizing fellow residents. Union Square's inhabitants, like those of Reservoir Hill, do not outclass people in most other neighborhoods when it comes to individual public service efforts — watching neighbors' homes, for example, or policing neighbors' children. But they do exhibit a strong tendency to generate their own improvised public services after discussing matters with fellow residents. In neighborhoods beset by strife, perhaps, one must construct an impromptu consensus before undertaking any public service initiatives. In communities where consensus can be taken for granted, on the other hand, residents may be more willing to exercise "executive power" on their own, without first consulting their neighbors. In any case, factional strife in a neighborhood may increase the likelihood that local residents will be left to their own devices, simply because other devices like formal community organizations have been destroyed or injured by conflict. The result, as in Reservoir Hill and Union Square, may be a heightened tendency to resort to informal direct action as a way of dealing with local problems.

The absence of political integration in a neighborhood like Reser-

voir Hill could actually encourage ventures in unofficial public service. After a teenage friend was stabbed to death in a street dispute,
for example, four Reservoir Hill residents in their early twenties
organized a community sports club to provide a recreational program for local young people who might otherwise be idling on street
corners. Without organizational sponsorship, outside financial assistance, or even a regular indoor meeting place, the four residents
established and coached basketball and softball teams, arranged for
games on a vacant lot, and organized a cleanup of the lot after each
game was over. Had there been adequate organized recreational
programs for the estimated six thousand children who live in Reservoir Hill, it is unlikely that such impromptu efforts would ever have
occurred.[1]

Reservoir Hill's failure to achieve organizational unity and political integration seems to drive its residents toward self-reliance. The
matters that they take into their own hands are most frequently
problems of trash and sanitation. Scattered throughout the neighborhood are tiny enclaves, each no bigger than a block or two,
where some local resident — almost always a woman — has established herself as unofficial sanitation commissioner. Mrs. Minnie
Williams, for example, presides over her block on Lakeview Avenue, where a perceived decline in local cleanliness drove her first to
exasperation and then to action. "Finally, in 1973," she recalls, "I
said I cannot stand this neighborhood." Instead of moving elsewhere, Mrs. Williams mobilized her fellow residents for periodic
cleanup campaigns and coordinated her own informal sanitation
program by means of persistent complaints directed at her neighbors, local landlords, and city officials. Backsliders can expect telephone calls or sharply worded letters from Mrs. Williams, and a
large sign posted on her front porch sternly exhorts her fellow residents to continue their exertions on behalf of neighborhood cleanliness.[2]

In Reservoir Hill even these informal, small-scale efforts to maintain public sanitation are frequently accompanied by friction among
neighbors. A lack of political integration and organization may
stimulate impromptu public services by unofficial leaders, but it can
also deprive them of the support they need to sustain or extend their
efforts. Mrs. Willie Mae Davis, for example, has taken charge of
trash problems in an area just a few blocks away from Mrs. Williams's territory. "There's a lot of volunteer in me," says Mrs. Davis.
"In the beginning, I swept both sides of the street on the block all by
myself. Depending on the way I felt, some days, I would work my
way down to Ducatel Street [two blocks away]. I was trying to get a

message across — to show people what was possible." Sometimes, however, the message was not well received. After recruiting some local children to assist her cleanup efforts, Mrs. Davis attempted to mobilize the area's adults for the same cause by distributing fliers door to door. "I had many insults," she recalls, "like 'You work for the city?' Lots of people threw the fliers down on the ground behind me. It was just the kids and I — except for two ladies over on Newington [Avenue], and they wouldn't go any further. There was no one to do the overall job."

To do the "overall job," Mrs. Davis finally turned to the Reservoir Hill Community Association, in which she had become an active member. Together with a committee of association officers, she helped to draft a proposal for a city-financed, neighborhood-wide sanitation program. The character of the program reflected the distinctive — and contentious — character of the neighborhood itself. Its peculiarities become evident if it is compared with a parallel program that was being designed across town in Coldstream-Homestead-Montebello at about the same time. Both programs were supported financially by city government, and both were launched in neighborhoods where the problem of trash and sanitation is the leading concern of local residents.[3] But while Coldstream-Homestead-Montebello's program made no secret of the intention to change the trash disposal habits of its constituents through education and social pressure, the Reservoir Hill program proceeded in a more subtle and indirect fashion. Recalling the rebuffs that she had experienced when trying to induce her neighbors to clean up the block, Willie Mae Davis observes that the current sanitation program "is trying to force education without using the word education, because that doesn't digest so well." A neighbor, also active in the Reservoir Hill Association, agrees with her assessment of neighborhood temperament. The neighbor explains that Mrs. Davis is "the type of person who may say to you, 'Hey don't put that out there without a top on it.' She's the type of person who can say that and get away with it . . . But maybe our fliers cannot say that, and maybe our [sanitation program] cannot say that . . . Education doesn't go down well." Instead of exhorting residents to clean up the neighborhood themselves, therefore, the Reservoir Hill sanitation program used its city grant to buy a truck and hire a part-time crew to go through the neighborhood cleaning up debris. Their job was not merely to pick up street trash, but to "project an image that it could be done" — in the hope that local residents would begin to do it themselves without preaching or scolding.

By contrast, the sanitation program of the Coldstream-Homestead-Montebello Community Corporation made a direct attempt to mobilize its constituents for the cause of neighborhood cleanliness, sometimes by embarrassing them. Mrs. Doris Johnson, executive director of the corporation, explains that her organization saw the sanitation problem as a "people problem":

> So we have attacked it as a people problem. We wrote up a sanitation program . . . and the first thing we told them was that we did not want a truck. We wanted a person to assist Mrs. Briscoe [a past president of the organization] to get leaflets and to educate people about the things that rats carry . . .
>
> People tend to want to do a little better than the guy next door, or just as good, or they'll feel inferior . . . So what we try to do is to put that peer pressure on them . . . I don't think any citation from downtown that somebody quietly gets when nobody's looking is going to do anything like what peer pressure is going to do.
>
> We ask the block captain to try to cite the habitual offender . . . She reports the house. We go out and see it, and the [other] block captains aid her in going through her block one Saturday . . . We'll make sure that we hit that bad person. We'll say, 'We're residents. We live here. We're not the city. We're not the cops. We want you to clean up.'

Reservoir Hill's sanitation program attempts to clean up the neighborhood; Coldstream-Homestead-Montebello's trash vigilantes pressure local residents to do the job themselves. The sharp variation in sanitation strategies may reflect the organizational differences that exist between two neighborhood polities in which the degree of consensus varies. After a period of sharp factional conflict, Coldstream-Homestead-Montebello had achieved a measure of organizational unity. Reservoir Hill had not yet overcome its internal divisions, and the absence of consensus is a clear handicap in any effort to exert peer pressure. Even more important, in socially divided neighborhoods like Reservoir Hill the neighborly friction that is almost certain to accompany such attempts at pressure may tend to activate larger conflicts — especially when the organizational leaders directing these pressures are mostly middle-class whites and the targets of pressure are mostly lower-class blacks.

In Reservoir Hill, the absence of organizational unity and political integration may drive residents to take matters into their own hands, but it can also reduce the scale of their efforts and limit the scope of community mobilization. When a neighborhood is split by social and factional differences, it may be possible for a grass-roots activist like Minnie Williams or Willie Mae Davis to upbraid her immediate neighbors for carelessness or indifference. But when such efforts are extended to the neighborhood at large through a formal community organization, they are apt to be confounded with broader racial, class, or factional conflicts that threaten to fragment the local population. Perhaps this is why the exhortation of local residents to greater cleanliness doesn't "digest so well" in Reservoir Hill as it does in Coldstream-Homestead-Montebello.

Reservoir Hill's cleanup campaign may also have fallen afoul of neighborhood conflict in another way: it created jobs. The sanitation program could provide employment for just a handful of unemployed men in Reservoir Hill, but many more than a handful of Reservoir Hill men were unemployed. The result was a series of squabbles about hiring. "Jobs," notes Stephanie Hull, "are a problem. There's terrible turmoil over jobs." More generally, the financial assistance that Reservoir Hill received from government agencies sometimes seemed only to supply the local residents with something to fight about. It was a factor that might help to explain the neighborhood's sudden shifts from public contention to public service and back again. "In the snow emergency," explains Mrs. Hull, "we had no other place to turn and we worked together. There was nothing to fight over. No one was pouring resources in, and there was no problem relating to outside agencies. But outside grants and aid seem to cause dissension." Another resident agrees: "It's like with pigs in a pen. You throw out some food, but it's not enough, and they get to fighting with one another."

Instead of providing the incentives that cement individual residents into a cohesive community organization,[4] financial resources sometimes appear to supply the grounds for organizational fragmentation. The Reservoir Hill Community Association often seemed to function most effectively as an institution of the neighborhood polity when it was cut off from external assistance and material resources. Like its constituents, the organization may have demonstrated its political capacities most impressively when it was left to its own devices. This does not mean that outside aid necessarily undermines formal community associations. It signifies, perhaps, that in a neighborhood constituted like Reservoir Hill, almost anything of value could become a source of contention.

The chief casualties of this propensity for conflict were political integration and political leadership. Reservoir Hill, as one local resident notes, seems to devour its own leaders. Stephanie Hull was one in a succession of them, and the sequence did not end with her. The conflict between low-income blacks and middle-income whites found a momentary point of compromise in the election of a middle-income, black public administrator who succeeded Mrs. Hull as president of the Reservoir Hill Association. He served a full one-year term but was impeached and removed from office by some of his former supporters midway through a second term. The pattern of leadership succession in Reservoir Hill aggravates tendencies toward political disintegration that are already strong. New leaders take office without the opportunity for regular consultation with their predecessors, whose good will toward the community association has usually been exhausted. Some of these ex-leaders also leave behind small factions of embittered followers whose presence in the neighborhood contributes to the difficulty of achieving unity. Political fragmentation may engender political self-reliance among local residents, whose capacity for informal public service becomes evident in neighborhood-wide emergencies. But the same fragmentation also reflects a failure to achieve political integration.

Participation in Neighborhood Groups

The attributes that make a neighborhood a polity do not necessary come in complete sets. The case of Reservoir Hill, in fact, suggests that some of the critical elements of neighborhood political life tend to appear only when others are absent. Where residents are inclined to exercise their unofficial "executive powers" to produce public goods, they may also be unable to achieve the political unity necessary for constructing institutions that express the will of the neighborhood. In Reservoir Hill, at least, the ability to produce unofficial public services seemed to be inconsistent with the ability to maintain political integration. Our task is to find out whether a similar mismatch of political capacities also appears in other neighborhoods.

In Baltimore's residential areas, the most noticeable signs of political integration are community organizations. Respondents in the sample survey of local residents were asked if they knew of any organizations or groups — even informal ones — where people from their neighborhoods got together to work on local problems. In every neighborhood studied, the most frequently mentioned groups were formal community associations. In one residential area, an ethnic organization was named by a significant number of respondents, and in another neighborhood, a church. But an even larger fraction of the respondents in both areas named a neighborhood improvement, civic, or homeowners association, a block club, or a community corporation. Only a handful of residents—nowhere more than 10 percent of the respondents interviewed—indicated that neighborhood business was transacted through informal groups that had no names. In all the neighborhoods studied, therefore, the institutions most frequently mentioned as mechanisms for dealing with local matters were organizations that not only were formal, but had been established for the specific purpose of handling neighborhood business. They were not "natural" groups embedded in a local network of informal relationships or unplanned offshoots of community institutions originally established to serve other purposes.

After being asked to identify groups that worked on neighborhood problems, respondents in each neighborhood were asked about their own relationships with these groups—whether they belonged to any of them, had attended any of their meetings, or had contacted any of them about neighborhood problems. The survey results indicate that such attachments are strongly associated with other signs of individual integration into the neighborhood polity. People who reported any kind of affiliation with community groups, for example, were much more likely than others to identify a fellow resident who could "get the whole neighborhood active in fighting [a local] problem." The ability to name such a person has already been noted as a reflection of residents' political connections in their neighborhoods. It suggests not only that they are in contact with some local leader who can mobilize their neighbors but also that they stand within the range of mobilization themselves. Respondents who exhibited this mark of political integration were far more likely than others to report that they belonged to community organizations (gamma = .77), had attended the meetings of such groups (.74), or had contacted these groups about local problems (.59).

The findings could signify that people's attachments with community groups are products of the preexisting contacts they have with community mobilizers in their neighborhoods. Residents who are politically connected tend to be drawn, as a result, into the activities of neighborhood organizations. Just as plausible, however, is the argument that the reverse is true—that organizational ties themselves help to generate political connections, or that they *are* the political connections. Some support for this view comes from the fact that repondents who named leaders capable of mobilizing the neighborhood often identified these mobilizers as officers of formal community associations. In fact, such organizational leaders were named more often than any other kind of person—more frequently than elected public officials, church and religious leaders, local business or professional people, or informal leaders who were not identified as occupants of any official positions.[5] Neighborhood associations, it appears, are the most widely recognized mechanisms for community mobilization. Not surprisingly, people who are affiliated with these institutions are also likely to report that they are acquainted with local leaders who can summon the neighborhood to collective action.

It is conceivable, of course, that ties to organizations and to community mobilizers may both be artifacts of some other personal characteristic. High-status people, for example, are more apt to report both kinds of connections than low-status people, and it may be that the two sorts of attachments go together only because they are both related to the respondents' social class positions, not because they are dependent upon one another. The evidence, however, shows that socioeconomic status is not responsible for the relationship between organizational involvement and acquaintance with community mobilizers. Controlling for social status hardly affects the strength of the association between these two kinds of neighborhood attachments.[6] The survey results, in other words, generally support the contention that ties to community organizations are important, independent elements in the political integration of neighborhoods. They place residents within the reach of political mobilization. Explaining the political integration of neighborhoods is partly a matter of understanding why people participate in community organizations.

They do not become participants, it appears, because they are already engaged in other forms of community participation. People who work, worship, or shop for groceries within their own residential areas are no more likely to report contacts with community organizations than residents who carry on these activities outside their neighborhoods.[7] The use of local facilities, in other words, has no more to do with participation in community groups than it does with other features of the neighborhood polity that we have already considered—like the sense of neighborhood identity or involvement in informal neighborhood discourse.

Some community ties, however, seem to make a greater difference for the organizational activities of residents. The simple duration of one's attachment to a residential area, for example, is related in a modest way to activity in neighborhood associations. Length of residence in a neighborhood has little to do with the sense of neighborhood identity or informal neighborhood discourse, but residential seniority is associated with being a member of a community group (gamma = .23), attending the group's meetings (.10), and contacting it about local problems (.22). Such ties to neighborhood groups may also reflect the respondents' friendship ties with their fellow residents. People who regarded most of the residents on the block as friends were more apt to belong to neighborhood associations than those who regarded them only as acquaintances, and these respondents in turn were much more likely to join community organizations than those who thought of their fellow block residents as strangers (gamma = .36).

Other signs of friendship among neighbors were less closely related to participation in community groups. Residents who reported that most of their friends lived inside the neighborhood were only a little more likely to be members of community associations than those who said that their friends were concentrated outside the neighborhood (gamma = .11), and it made scarcely any difference for organization membership whether a person's "really good friends" lived on the same block, somewhere else in the neighborhood, or outside the neighborhood. In these respects, local friendships seem to have no more influence on group membership than they do on the sense of neighborhood identity or informal neighborhood discourse. In this case, however, the evidence may not reveal all there is to know about the effects that residents' friendship ties have upon their organizational activities.

Previous research suggests that attachments to neighborhood associations may depend not simply on the existence of local friendship ties but also on the structure of these ties.[8] People who have close-knit networks of friends within their neighborhoods may actually have less chance to form attachments with community associations than people whose friendship networks are "loose-knit." A close-knit network is one in which most of a person's friends are acquainted with one another. In a loose-knit network, on the other hand, most of a person's friends do not know one another, and because they are not in contact they represent more diverse sources of information about goings-on in the neighborhood. A resident with a close-knit network of friends usually receives the local news and gossip from people who share the same set of informants. What can be learned from one friend is not likely to differ much from what another has to tell. In a close-knit network, after all, one speaks to friends who have probably been speaking with one another. But in a loose-knit friendship network, one draws the news from more disparate sources, and the probable result is more complete coverage of neighborhood happenings.

The findings reported in Table 5.1 may illustrate the effects of loose-knittedness. The two columns of the table distinguish the respondents who said that most of their friends lived inside the neighborhood from those who reported that their friends were concentrated outside the neighborhood. In the two rows of the table, residents who said that most of their friends knew one another have been separated from those who said that most of their friends were unacquainted. The responses of residents with loose-knit neighborhood friendship networks are reported in the lower right-hand corner of the table. These are people whose friends, though concentrated inside the neighborhood, were generally unacquainted with one another. The survey results show that the loose-knit respondents were more likely than any others to have attended meetings of community groups. They seem to have participated more actively in neighborhood organizations than either the close-knit respondents or the cosmopolitan residents who reported that most of their friends lived outside the neighborhood.

The disparate local contacts of residents with loose-knit neighborhood friendship networks may help to ensure that relatively high proportions of these people find out about the activities of community groups and contribute to those activities themselves. But the effects of loose-knittedness are rather modest—less impressive than

Table 5.1. Friendship networks and attendance at community organization meetings (Percentage of respondents in each category who reported attending at least one meeting)

Acquaintanceship among friends	Location of friends	
	Most live outside neighborhood	Most live inside neighborhood
Most know one another	24.8 (1,172)	24.9 (531)
Most do not know one another	26.9 (273)	38.0 (129)

previous research has found[9] — and the loose-knit respondents themselves are not numerous. The figures set off by parentheses in the table show that only a tiny minority of the respondents met the specifications for loose-knittedness. In only one neighborhood did they make up as much as 20 percent of the local population. The effects of loose-knittedness were also somewhat less pronounced for organization membership than for attendance at organization meetings. Even less affected was the likelihood that residents would contact neighborhood groups about local problems.

The evidence concerning residents' friendship networks shows that close-knit ties with neighbors do not necessarily constitute the most effective basis for organizational ties. In fact, friendships of a more disjointed kind tend to produce higher levels of participation in community organizations. But even these more loosely structured networks of neighborhood friendship do not make any striking difference for the organizational activities of neighborhood residents, and the difference becomes even less impressive when compared to the effects of two other factors. Socioeconomic status and homeownership have far greater influence on residents' participation in neighborhood groups than does the structure of friendship networks. The findings reported in Table 5.2, for example, show that high-status homeowners were about eleven times as likely to belong to community organizations as low-status renters. The results also indicate that the effects of homeownership and social status are at least partly independent of one another: Baltimoreans who owned their homes were more likely to belong to neighborhood groups than those who did not, no matter what their socioeconomic status was, and high-status residents were more apt to be organization members than low-status ones, whether they owned their homes or not.[10]

Table 5.2. Homeownership, socioeconomic status, and membership in community organizations (Percentage of respondents in each category who said they belonged to community groups)

Tenure	Socioeconomic status		
	High	Medium	Low
Own	78.4 (383)	40.0 (482)	22.0 (205)
Rent	15.6 (162)	12.9 (469)	7.4 (421)

The statistical evidence does not show just what it is about high status or homeownership that propels residents into community groups. In general, high-status people and homeowners tend to be more favorably disposed than other residents toward their neighbors and neighborhoods, and they are more likely than others to report both informal social contacts with fellow residents and unofficial public service activities. But none of the attitudes, contacts, or activities considered seems to contribute significantly to an explanation for the effects of social status and homeownership. Nor do the participatory inclinations of high-status homeowners appear to reflect, in any consistent way, the influence of neighborhood environment. Living in a high-status neighborhood, for example, is far less important for the organizational activities of high-status people than the simple fact that they enjoy high levels of individual income, education, and occupational prestige. Participation in neighborhood groups, unlike the sense of neighborhood identity, owes much more to the individual characteristics of the respondents than to the attributes of the neighborhoods where they live.

Homeownership represents a significant investment in a neighborhood — any neighborhood — and for that reason alone it probably stimulates participation in organized efforts to defend or enhance the value of one's share in the local community.[11] High levels of individual education, income, and occupational prestige supply the aptitudes and the wherewithal for such efforts. It is likely, in other words, that high-status homeowners are especially prone to participate in neighborhood groups simply because they have the means and the motive for doing so. Given these, they seem capable of making their own opportunities. The social environment of the neighborhood apparently does little to obstruct or facilitate the organizational activities of property owners who enjoy high status. Even in relatively disorganized communities, residents with such social advantages manage to generate levels of organized activity almost as high as they do in neighborhoods that are politically well integrated.

This does not mean that high-status residents are immune to the influence of neighborhood environment. But their susceptibility becomes fully evident only when their organizational activities can be compared with those residents who do not share the same social advantages. The findings in Table 5.3, for example, permit a comparison of group membership rates among high-, medium-, and low-status respondents who live in neighborhoods with varying levels of political integration. The index of neighborhood political integration in this case is the same as the one used previously — the proportion of respondents in a neighborhood who can name someone thought to be capable of mobilizing their fellow residents. The ability to name such a person is a sign of one's political connections in the neighborhood. The greater the proportion of residents who report such connections, the greater is the capacity of the neighborhood polity to mobilize its constituents — perhaps only to fight with one another, but at least to come into political contact with their neighbors.[12]

The evidence shows that high- and low-status residents respond differently to variations in the political connectedness of their neighbors. The less political integration there is in the neighborhood, the smaller the proportion of low-status residents who belong to community groups. Among high-status residents, however, the rate of organization membership at first drops sharply with declining levels of neighborhood political integration, but then rises almost as sharply again. The result is that the rate of group membership for high-status people in the least integrated neighborhoods approaches the rate in politically well-integrated neighborhoods. But between these two extremes in neighborhood political integration, there is sharp variation in the organizational participation of high-status respondents. Their group activities are in fact more sensitive to differences in political integration than to any other kind of variation in the local political or social context. But it is a peculiar kind of sensitivity. For the residents of low or medium social status, organizational membership seems to be stimulated by relatively high levels of neighborhood political integration. But respondents of high social status were moved to join community groups when they were ex-

Table 5.3. Neighborhood political integration and membership in community groups, controlling for respondents' socioeconomic status (Percentage of respondents in each category who said they belonged to community groups)

Proportion of politically connected residents in neighborhood	Socioeconomic status of individual respondents		
	High	Medium	Low
High	70.7 (375)	38.8 (268)	17.3 (139)
Medium	21.4 (103)	21.7 (418)	13.4 (194)
Low	58.8 (69)	21.8 (269)	9.0 (296)

posed either to well-integrated neighborhoods or to poorly integrated ones.

In politically well-integrated neighborhoods, the general tendency toward group participation can be understood rather easily. It is a matter of opportunity. Residents cannot join community organizations if their neighbors are not organized. In communities with high levels of political integration, neighbors will tend to be organized into groups. People who live in these communities — no matter what their motives or means — will have more opportunities to join neighborhood groups than people who live in neighborhoods with low levels of political integration.

This explanation, though useful as far as it goes, obviously fails to account for the organizational activism of high-status residents when they are exposed to low levels of neighborhood political integration. Their participatory inclinations in these circumstances cannot be attributed to the availability of opportunities for group membership; poorly integrated neighborhoods present few opportunities of this kind. Nor does it seem plausible in this case to suppose that high-status residents in poorly integrated neighborhoods enjoy a special preeminence that enhances their ability to participate in organizations — that their social and educational advantages, for example, become especially advantageous when they live in politically disjointed neighborhoods. Among other difficulties with this line of analysis, there is the inconvenience of explaining why the value of these supposed advantages should diminish so sharply in the neighborhoods that lie between the well-integrated and the poorly integrated ones, where high-status residents are not much more likely to be organization members than their low- or medium-status neighbors.[13]

What seems to stimulate the organizational activities of high-status residents is not an enhancement of the means or the opportunity for group participation, but an intensification of the motives for it. In a politically disorganized neighborhood, high-status residents may sense an unusually acute need to protect their stakes in the community from the disorder and unpredictability that surround them. Their investments in the neighborhood are likely to be threatened in particular by the presence of low-status neighbors, who happen to be especially numerous in the politically disjointed residential areas. The figures in parentheses in Table 5.3 show how many low-, medium-, and high-status respondents there were in neighborhoods with different levels of political integration. A comparison of the numbers across each row shows that in the least integrated neighborhoods, residents of high social status were outnumbered more than four to one by low-status neighbors. Politically disjointed neighborhoods also tend to be socially disadvantaged ones, although the association is less than perfect, and this means that high-status people who live in such neighborhoods will be surrounded by fellow residents who are less educated, less prosperous, and less prestigious than themselves — neighbors who may not share the same standards of neighborhood decorum or the willingness to uphold them. Along with these difficulties, there may also be problems that aggravate poor and prosperous residents alike — inconveniences of the kind that usually arise in neighborhoods where low-income people are concentrated. Confronted by an uncongenial and possibly hostile locale, therefore, the high-status residents of poorly integrated neighborhoods have especially powerful incentives to organize for the defense of their interests. Just as rich people in poor neighborhoods tend to perform informal public services, so they also become especially active in the organized political life of their neighborhoods.

Poor people respond differently. Instead of being moved to organized action by the conditions of life in politically disjointed neighborhoods, they seem relatively uninvolved in community groups — less active, in fact, than low-status people who live in more politically integrated residential areas. The likely explanation is that low-status people who live in poorly integrated neighborhoods have fewer opportunities for organizational activity than their counterparts in more integrated residential areas. It is not simply that organizations are scarce in these disjointed neighborhoods, but that many of the ones that exist are likely to have been created or captured by organizational activists from the neighborhood's high-status minority. These groups will have been established for defensive purposes, and one of the things that they are probably designed to defend against is the area's low-status majority. Poor people may not be excluded from these organizations, or even antagonized by them, but they are apt to find that such groups are hard put to accommodate their interests. Rates of organization membership among poor people in politically disjointed neighborhoods may therefore remain low, not because organizations are absent but because they are organizations of the wrong kind.

An alternative explanation, of course, is that low-status residents exhibit low rates of group membership in politically unintegrated neighborhoods because they lack the means or the motive for organized activity, not the opportunity. The means for organizational activism may be supplied by training or occupational experience that poor people are unlikely to have. The absence of these personal resources, and the organizational skills that arise from them, may help to explain why group membership rates for low-status residents are so much lower than the rates for high-status respondents. But it does not explain why low-status people are less apt to join community groups in politically disjointed neighborhoods than they are in politically integrated neighborhoods.

Variations in the motives of low-status residents cannot be dismissed from consideration so easily. We have already seen, for example, that living in a poor neighborhood tends to efface the sense of neighborhood identity, and that the failure to form a conception of one's neighborhood may also inhibit the perception of local problems. Perhaps low-status people are organizationally uninvolved in politically disjointed neighborhoods because they have stopped seeing local problems, become more "private-regarding," and therefore ceased to have strong reasons for political action. This explanation for their apparent political apathy would be more persuasive, however, if we could show that low-status residents become generally inactive in socially disadvantaged and politically unintegrated neighborhoods — withdrawing not just from organized political activity but also from informal efforts to deal with neighborhood problems. Evidence of this kind would help to support the contention that when low-status people live in poor and politically disjointed neighborhoods, they grow generally indifferent to local problems, unmoved or perhaps overwhelmed by them. But the evidence does not show this. The survey results concerning the informal political activities of neighborhood residents presented in Chapter 4, suggest that the unofficial activism of poor people is only slightly affected by exposure to life in poor neighborhoods. For most types of informal activity, low-status residents who live in poor neighborhoods are no less likely to engage in informal public service than low-status residents who happen to live in rich neighborhoods. In fact, there is one respect in which living in a poor neighborhood may actually stimulate informal efforts by poor people to cope with local problems. Informal direct action — the attempt to produce public goods oneself after consulting informally with neighbors — is clearly more widespread in poor neighborhoods than in rich neighborhoods, and this holds true no matter what the social status of the individual respondents.

The effects of living in politically disjointed neighborhoods are similar to those of living in poor neighborhoods. In Table 5.4 the survey results show that high-, medium, and low-status residents are all more likely to engage in informal direct action when they live in poorly integrated communities rather than well-integrated ones. In other words, low-status people who live in politically disjointed neighborhoods may participate in community organizations at a relatively low rate, but they engage in informal direct action at a relatively high rate—higher than the one that prevails among their counterparts who happen to live in more integrated neighborhoods. Their behavior is not what would be expected of people who have lost the impulse to take political action and have surrendered to apathy. The lack of neighborhood political integration seems to inhibit only their organized political activities; their involvement in informal neighborhood politics may actually grow more extensive under the influence of political disjointedness.

The experience of Reservoir Hill seems to suggest a similar relationship between political organization and political improvisation. In a factionalized and disorganized neighborhood, residents attempt to cope with local problems directly and informally, perhaps because they lack the organized institutions for dealing with them indirectly. The survey evidence, however, reveals some additional complexities in the relationship between political organization and informal public service. For residents of low and medium social status, political disjointedness does seem to stimulate informal indirect action but inhibits organized action. For high-status residents, on the other hand, it appears to encourage both types of participation in the neighborhood polity, and the organizational activism of the high-status residents could have something to do with the organizational withdrawal of their low- and medium-status

Table 5.4. Neighborhood political integration and informal direct action, controlling for respondents' socioeconomic status (Percentage of respondents in each category who reported unofficial efforts to deal with local problems)

Proportion of politically connected residents in neighborhood	Socioeconomic status of individual respondents		
	High	Medium	Low
High	14.4 (375)	7.5 (268)	4.3 (139)
Medium	19.9 (103)	12.6 (418)	4.4 (194)
Low	36.1 (69)	15.8 (269)	9.5 (296)

neighbors. In politically disjointed and socially disadvantaged neighborhoods, members of a high-status minority may be moved to organize against a hostile environment for the defense of their own interests. The organizations that high-status residents create under these circumstances are unlikely to be endowed with much capacity for accommodating the interests of their less fortunate neighbors. Community associations, in other words, can arise even in politically disjointed neighborhoods, but they are apt to be organizations poorly equipped to mobilize the community's low- and medium-status majority. That is probably one reason why these neighborhoods are politically disjointed in the first place. It may also help to explain why exposure to politically unintegrated and socially disadvantaged neighborhoods incites low- and medium-status residents to informal political action but not organized action.

What Attracts Members

In factionalized neighborhoods like Reservoir Hill, it is not simply a lack of political organization that forces residents to resort to informal direct action. The tendency toward improvisational politics is evident—and strong—even for the high-status minority who are active in community associations. In fact, residents who reported ties with neighborhood groups were consistently more likely than their detached neighbors to engage in informal public service activities, even when socioeconomic status was held constant.[14]

People do not take matters into their own hands because of an inability to place them in the hands of community organizations. The same residents who turn to neighborhood associations are also the ones who are most likely to resort to informal direct action. The heavy reliance on such improvised and unofficial expedients in politically disjointed neighborhoods probably reflects not the isolation of the residents from community groups but residents' exposure to aggravating, unpredictable, and unpleasant neighborhood conditions. Such immediate annoyances might be expected to incite them to direct action. What is striking about their political conduct is not this inclination toward impromptu measures but the unevenness of the tendency toward organized action. In politically unintegrated neighborhoods, high-status residents seem to be aroused to organized activity, but the organizational participation of low- and medium-status residents appears to be inhibited. If the social disadvantages and irritations of politically disjointed neighborhoods can move residents in general to informal political action, why do they not have the same general effect upon organized political activities?

One likely answer is that organizational participation depends not just on the characteristics of neighborhoods or of individual residents but on the attributes of the organizations themselves — the attributes that influence their ability to mobilize their constituents. Information about these organizational attributes came from a small handful of informants in each neighborhood. These informants were selected because they occupied positions in which they were likely to become knowledgeable about neighborhood affairs. Presidents and active members of all local community associations were interviewed, for example, along with members of the local clergy, owners and managers of neighborhood businessess, City Council members who represented the sample neighborhoods, and several others. The responses of the informants for each neighborhood were aggregated to produce average scores for various political and organizational characteristics of the sample communities. For example, the informants for each residential area were asked whether the handling of community issues and activities indicated that "the people who live in this area are very well organized." Neighborhoods were scored high or low according to the proportion of local informants who perceived a well-organized constituency.

The perceptions of informants closely paralleled information already collected from neighborhood residents in general. The extent to which the informants regarded the neighborhood as "well organized," for instance, seems to reflect the extent to which the residents at large reported that they were acquainted with people who could mobilize the neighborhood for concerted action (gamma = .65). The level of political connectedness among neighborhood residents was also associated — this time negatively — with the degree to which the informants perceived that "different factions of residents often seem to disagree with one another" ($-.68$), and with the prevalence of the belief that there were "too many different groups and organizations in this area all trying to get things done at the same time" ($-.55$). Not surprisingly, the informants' impressions about the organizational coherence of their communities tended to mirror the level of political integration that existed among the residents at large.

Information about the community organizations themselves came from those informants who were most active in them — the presidents of all formal neighborhood associations and (where possible) at least two active members of each group, selected from several suggested by each group's president.[15] The responses of these organizational informants were combined for each neighborhood to construct a profile of local community organizations. A disadvantage of this procedure is that in neighborhoods represented by more than one association, any sharp variations in the attributes of local organizations could be concealed behind the "average" characteristics. On the other hand, such averages do provide one convenient index of an entire neighborhood's organizational character, and in practice disparities among organizations in the same neighborhood were rarely sharp ones. One indication of the intraneighborhood similarities among community groups is that organizational informants from residential areas with multiple neighborhood organizations consistently tended to share certain impressions about the groups to which they belonged. The more plentiful the associations in a neighborhood, for example, the more likely the informants were to believe that the members of their particular organizations "don't really trust one another" (gamma = .61). The number of community groups was also associated with a tendency for informants to perceive that their organizations provided people with "a way of getting to know their neighbors" (.92).

Neighborhoods that generate several community associations seem to produce organizations that are similar in certain respects. At least their leaders and active members have similar perceptions of them, and the nature of these perceptions suggests something about the nature of the neighborhood polity. Residential areas with multiple community associations seem to be socially atomized. The fact that neighbors get to know one another through community associations suggests that they have not been able to find informal ways of becoming acquainted outside these organizations. Since organization members have not been previously acquainted with one another, perhaps, they also tend to mistrust one another. The division of residents among several different neighborhood groups, in fact, may help to accentuate mistrust in the neighborhood at large.

Inferences about causality, however, are complicated in this case by the fact that the proliferation of community associations may simply be a reflection of other neighborhood characteristics. The more community organizations there are in a neighborhood, the smaller the proportion of the residents who can identify a person capable of mobilizing their neighbors (gamma = −.57). Even more striking is the relationship between the number of neighborhood organizations and the socioeconomic status of the neighborhood. (−.88). Residential areas that are poor in other respects seem to be rich in community organizations, and perhaps it is poverty that accounts for the distinctive attributes associated with a multiplicity of neighborhood groups.

Socioeconomic status, as we have already seen, is a factor of critical importance for individual participation in neighborhood groups, and the evidence shows that the social standing of neighborhood residents can sometimes make a noticeable difference for the way that they respond to the characteristics of local organizations. High-status residents, for example, seemed much more sensitive than low-status respondents to the personal warmth that existed within community groups. The organizational informants were asked whether or not "a strong sense of personal friendship" existed among the members of the groups to which they belonged. Neighborhoods whose community organizations scored high on this reported sense of friendship were much more successful in mobilizing high-status residents than those that scored low. But the existence of a friendly atmosphere within community groups made scarcely any difference at all for the organizational participation of low-status respondents. The relevant survey data are reported in Table 5.5, where it is apparent that group friendliness makes its greatest difference for organizational membership among the high-status residents, a smaller difference for the medium-status respondents, and smaller difference still among those of low-status. One possible interpretation of the findings is simply that a friendly group atmosphere is more important to socially advantaged people than to the socially disadvantaged. Just as plausible, however, is the argument that the atmosphere within a community organization becomes more friendly as higher proportions of high-status residents are drawn into group

Table 5.5. Reported sense of friendship in community groups and group membership, controlling for respondents' socioeconomic status (Percentage of respondents in each category who said they belonged to community groups)

Proportion of informants reporting strong sense of friendship	Socioeconomic status of individual respondents		
	High	Medium	Low
High	78.7 (186)	32.8 (364)	12.9 (323)
Low	56.3 (319)	22.2 (537)	11.4 (290)

activities. The involvement of low-status activists may not have the same effect on the spirit of conviviality that exists within a community group.

Whatever the effects (or causes) of internal friendliness in community groups, its opposite—mistrust—seems to have much less to do with organizational participation. Membership rates for high- and medium-status respondents hardly varied at all with differences in the reported levels of mistrust among participants in neighborhood associations. In this case, it was the low-status residents whose organizational participation seemed most affected, and even then only slightly (gamma = − .24). Reports of contention among group members are similarly unrelated to the likelihood that residents would join community associations. Organizational informants were asked whether they thought that the members of their groups spent "an awful lot of time arguing with one another." Rates of group membership were just about the same in neighborhoods where reports of contention were frequent as they were in residential areas where such reports were uncommon.

In general, personal solidarity among the members of community associations did not have any consistent effects upon the organizational participation of community residents. A reported sense of friendship within neighborhood groups may have helped to attract high- and medium-status members, but internal contention and mutual suspicion did not seem to drive many of them away.[16] In fact, mistrust may actually have stimulated some types of organizational participation. Especially among the high-status respondents, for example, there were many residents who belonged to community organizations but did not attend their meetings, and these stay-at-homes were concentrated in neighborhoods where the members of local groups were reported to be highly trustful of one another. In other words, high-status residents were more likely to turn out for the meetings of community groups when the members were mutually suspicious, and less likely to attend when group members had confidence in one another. Among low-status respondents, on the other hand, intraorganizational mistrust made no difference for attendance rates. The evidence about meeting attendance is reported in Table 5.6. The findings here could show that meeting attendance by high-status residents helped to foster mutual suspicion in community groups, or they could show that mistrust prompted high-status residents to turn out for meetings—possibly because they trusted no one else to look out for their interests. The latter interpretation, of course, parallels Richard Sennett's line of argument about the sources of community involvement. Friction and mutual suspicion, he says, may drive neighborhood residents to take a hand in the management of local affairs.[17] In this case, the evidence seems consistent to his contention, but only in part. Mutual suspicion activates only high-status residents. It does not affect attendance rates among low-status respondents. This inconsistency in the findings is one to which we will soon return.

In any case, although the conduct of organizational business may have become rancorous and unpleasant in some community groups, the emergence of mutual suspicion and acrimony seems not to have discouraged many people from joining these organizations. The only exception was the of tendency low-status residents to withdraw from group membership in neighborhoods where organizational activists were reported to mistrust one another. Suspicion and conflict, of course, may have more indirect effects upon participation in community groups. They could undermine an organization's ability to conduct neighborhood business, and this loss of effectiveness could in turn reduce a community group's attractiveness to members and supporters. The willingness of local residents to work through neighborhood organizations for the achievement of collective benefits, as Richard Rich points out, "should vary directly with their estimates of the probability of success in securing collective goods."[18]

Friction in community organizations does in fact diminish the perceived probability of organizational success. When the organizational informants in a neighborhood reported frequent arguments among group members, they also tended to agree that one of their group's problems was that "it frequently has trouble finishing what

Table 5.6. Mutual trust in community groups and attendance at group meetings, controlling for respondents' socioeconomic status (Percentage of respondents in each category who said they had attended meetings of neighborhood groups)

Proportion of informants reporting that members of local groups mistrust one another	Socioeconomic status of individual respondents		
	High	Medium	Low
High	64.6 (216)	25.8 (400)	12.2 (349)
Low	42.3 (296)	19.7 (498)	12.5 (264)

it starts out to do" (gamma = .91). The same informants were also likely to indicate that their group had difficulty "figuring out the kinds of things to which it should devote its attention" (.56). This uncertainty about the composition of organizational agendas was not strongly associated with reports of mistrust among group members, but mutual suspicion did bear some relationship to the perceived inability of neighborhood associations to finish the tasks that they had started (.56).

Dissension and suspicion have predictable results for the reported effectiveness of community groups. But the lack of organizational efficacy does not have predictable consequences for the ability of community groups to mobilize their constituents. Neither the tendency to leave projects unfinished nor indecision about what projects to undertake significantly reduced rates of participation in community groups. For high- and medium-status respondents, in fact, levels of group membership were actually somewhat higher when organizations were uncertain about the matters to which they should devote their attention than they were when this uncertainty was not so prominent. Indecisiveness of this kind is almost certainly no attraction to high- and medium-status members. More probably, it is the presence of large numbers of medium- and high-status activists that increases the difficulty of arriving at a clear and agreed-upon conception of the issues that should concern a community organization.

If organizational effectiveness and group solidarity do not account for the drawing power of community organizations, perhaps their ability to attract members is based on more narrowly self-interested considerations. In community groups, as in other organizations, attracting members may be a matter of offering specific benefits to individual constituents, not collective benefits to the constituency in general. Neighborhood organizations with the resources to provide these inducements may also be the ones that are best able to mobilize the neighborhoods they claim to represent. The appropriate resources are most likely to come from government, whose grants and contracts make it possible for community groups to offer jobs and services to local residents — perhaps converting them into organization members in the process.

Presidents of all community organizations were asked whether any activities or programs of their groups had received government financial support during the preceding year. Table 5.7 distinguishes between respondents who lived in neighborhoods with government-supported organizations and those who did not. The findings show that government grants did not enhance the capacity of community groups to attract members. Being "funded" may even have reduced the drawing power of community organizations, though it is likely that factors other than government grants were responsible for the relatively low membership rates in the "funded" neighborhoods. Government agencies, after all, tend to concentrate their grants in troubled neighborhoods. It is probably the trouble, and not the money, that reduces participation rates in these neighborhoods.[19]

Just what sorts of trouble may impair the drawing power of community groups remains unclear. Neighborhoods with organizations that received government grants tended to be poor neighborhoods, and they were often communities where group members were reported to mistrust one another. But after the socioeconomic status of individual residents had been taken into account, neither of these factors seems to make a notable and consistent difference for membership rates in neighborhood groups. Perhaps the problem is precisely that these and other conditions tend to make *inconsistent* differences; they are related in different ways to the participation rates of people at different status levels. We have already seen, for example, that a reported sense of friendship in neighborhood organizations is associated with relatively high levels of group membership among high-status residents but makes no difference for membership rates among low-status residents. Mutual suspicion among activists, on the other hand, does not deter high- and medium-status residents from joining community groups, but it does seem to depress membership rates among low-status residents. A further piece of evidence shows even more clearly that the organizational participation of high- and low-status respondents was affected in contrary ways by the organizational characteristics of neighborhoods.

Every neighborhood informant was asked whether his or her

Table 5.7. Government grants and group membership, controlling for respondents' socioeconomic status (Percentage of respondents in each category who said they belonged to community groups)

Government-supported organizations in neighborhood	Socioeconomic status of individual respondents		
	High	Medium	Low
Yes	58.2 (163)	23.7 (473)	9.8 (412)
No	66.1 (350)	32.6 (427)	17.1 (201)

community was one in which "different factions of residents often seemed to disagree with one another about what's best for the area." In Table 5.8 residents of neighborhoods that scored high on factionalism have been distinguished from those who lived in neighborhoods that scored low. The percentage figures show how many of the high-, medium-, and low-status residents belonged to community organizations in factious neighborhoods and in those less agitated by conflict. High-status respondents were more likely to become members of community groups in the factionalized neighborhoods than in the more peaceful residential areas. For low-status residents, on the other hand, just the opposite was true. Their membership rate was lower in the contentious neighborhoods than it was in the more harmonious ones. The same patterns of behavior were clearly evident for forms of organizational participation other than membership — attendance at organization meetings and contacting community groups about neighborhood problems. In factious neighborhoods, the high-status residents tend to become active in community organizations, and the low-status residents tend to withdraw.

When high-status residents mobilize through neighborhood organizations for community conflict, it appears that low-status residents are inclined to give up their participation in local groups. The fact that the two kinds of respondents tend to move in opposite directions under these circumstances may help to explain why many of the same organizational attributes that seem to activate high-status residents have no effect or a negative effect upon the organizational activities of their low-status neighbors. The contrary inclinations of high- and low-status residents may also help us to understand why

Table 5.8. Reported factionalism in neighborhood and membership in community groups, controlling for respondents' socioeconomic status (Percentage of respondents in each category who said they belonged to community groups)

Proportion of informants reporting factionalism in neighborhood	Socioeconomic status of individual respondents		
	High	Medium	Low
High	68.0 (316)	25.7 (432)	9.0 (349)
Low	48.9 (232)	27.2 (523)	16.1 (280)

organizational attributes fail to provide a satisfactory and consistent explanation for the organizational participation of Baltimoreans. The organizational activities of high- and low-status respondents may represent a response not so much to the characteristics of community groups as to one another. Upper-class activism does not always diminish lower-class participation. But when the mobilization of high-status residents occurs in situations of conflict, it seems to be accompanied by a demobilization·of low-status residents. This is the same kind of process that was suggested earlier in order to explain the differing responses of high- and low-status residents to political disjointedness in neighborhoods. The present evidence helps to bolster that suggestion. Where high-status residents have organized to defend against threats to their interests, their organizations will often lack a capacity to accommodate the interests of low-status residents, perhaps because it is the low-status residents who constitute the threat. The result is that the organizational characteristics that seem to attract high-status residents to community groups do not appear to have the same attraction for their low-status neighbors. In fact, however, the organizational characteristics that we have considered may have little to do with the attractiveness of community groups. Organizations that have been successful in activating the high-status residents of strife-torn neighborhoods may simply offer little of interest to low-status residents.

Private interest has long been the central consideration in explaining the formation and survival of organizations. Groups attract members and supporters because they offer incentives that satisfy people's interests. Organizations created to produce collective benefits, for example, should enhance their attractiveness to prospective members if they can also offer individual benefits as side-payments for participation. Apart from these private inducements, an organization should improve its capacity to mobilize supporters when it demonstrates superior efficiency in producing collective goods, thereby reducing their cost to individual contributors. And aside from productivity and personal profit, the interest of group members in friendly socializing with other members should help to elicit their participation in organizations. These explanations for the ability of organizations to appeal to individual interests have all proven to be less effective than might be expected. More exhaustive testing might conceivably disclose hidden strengths in them, but in general the economic or incentive theory of organization has been a disappointing one where community groups are concerned.

The shortcoming of this approach does not lie in the basic proposition that people act on individual self-interest. The contention is difficult to dispute; under some definitions of self-interest, in fact, it is a tautology. The difficulty is that merely acknowledging the self-interest that stands behind organizational activity does not address the more fundamental issue of how people decide what their interests are in the first place. The issue seldom arises in connection with homogeneous and fungible commodities (like money) that can be used to serve almost any interests. It is reasonable to assume that most people will act as though they have an interest in maximizing their monetary incomes. But where nonmonetary and collective incentives are concerned, individual self-interest is not self-evident, and perhaps it is not so individual as we conceive it to be. The survey evidence implies that neighborhood residents' conceptions of their interests depend in part on what kinds of neighbors they have and on what these neighbors happen to be doing. Individual self-interest, in other words, is a product of social and political context. Similar kinds of people, presented with the same kinds of incentives for organizational participation, may respond in different ways because the organizations happen to be operating in different types of neighborhoods. Among high-status residents, for example, the interest in organizational participation seems to vary depending on whether the neighborhood is factious or peaceful, politically integrated or politically disjointed, prosperous or poor. For low-status residents, these interneighborhood variations grow even more complex because their organizational participation often seems to be contingent upon the participation of their high-status neighbors.

Under the circumstances, the drawing power of community groups may not bear any consistent relationship to the incentives that they offer. Incentives may be valued differently by different people in the same neighborhood, or by similar people in different neighborhoods. In fact, the incentives distributed by a community group may be related to the sorts of people who participate, not because the participants are attracted by the inducements, but because the people who participate determine what character the organization will have. Groups that mobilize high-status residents tend to exhibit high levels of internal friendship and low levels of certainty about the issues to which they should devote their attention. It is not the incentives that attract the members, perhaps, but the members who shape the inducements.

In any case, membership incentives do not seem sufficient to explain the participation of local residents in community groups. In addition to the private costs and inducements that are supposed to account for the mobilization of individual participants, there are also other interests that may have a far more important role in determining who joins a neighborhood association and who does not. An emphasis on the economy of individual incentives sometimes seems to obscure the obvious political interests that give rise to community groups in the first place. These broader group interests define the constituency from which participants may be drawn, and they probably explain why organizational activism among high-status residents sometimes deters the participation of their low-status neighbors. A community group formed to defend upper-class interests against lower-class neighbors is not likely to mobilize many low-status neighbors — even though it offers membership incentives that would otherwise appeal to low-status people.

Political Integration, Organization, and Representation

People of high social status may gain politically when their low-status neighbors fail to organize, but the resulting impairment of neighborhood political integration may also hamper their efforts to cope with local problems. The detachment of lower-class residents from community organizations increases the difficulty of mobilizing the local population for concerted action. Even the organizational activism of high-status residents themselves may fail to enhance the political integration of the neighborhood if the activists are divided among several different organizations. Mere affiliation with community groups does not necessarily represent political integration unless the organizational ties of local residents link them together in a single association. Respondents from the twenty-one sample neighborhoods were asked, therefore, not only to discuss the nature of their organizational attachments but also to identify the objects of those attachments, and each neighborhood was scored high or low according to the proportion of its residents who named the same community group as a place where neighbors gathered to work on local problems.

This index of organizational consolidation in neighborhoods is related to several other signs of political integration. It is associated with the extent to which residents could identify people whom they thought capable of mobilizing their neighbors (gamma = .54). It is even more strongly related to the likelihood that knowledgeable informants in a neighborhood would regard the residents as "very well organized" (.83), and there is a negative association between the degree of organizational consolidation in a neighborhood and the extent to which local informants thought there were too many groups and organizations in the area ($-.72$).

The proportion of neighborhood residents tied together by a single community group also diminished as the number of local organization increased ($-.67$), but other signs of community fragmentation were less clearly related to the emergence of one organization as a focus for neighborhood politics. Political harmony, for example, does not necessarily follow from the organizational unification of local residents. Reports of factionalism were just about as likely when residents were concentrated in one focal organizational as when they were not. Factional strife, it appears, is almost as common within the framework of a single community group as it is among a multiplicity of groups.

Some types of strife may even have become more probable when neighborhood residents congregated in one group. Organizational informants were more likely to report excessive arguing within their community groups when there was a single dominant community organization in the neighborhood than when there was not ($.56$), and this tendency toward disputation may have been responsible for the perceived failure to complete organizational tasks, which was also associated with the emergence of a dominant community group in neighborhood politics ($.56$). Whether or not one group had captured the attentions of local residents seems to have made little difference for other types of organizational infirmities—like the existence of mistrust among group members or their inability to decide just what subjects deserved the attention of the group. In general, neighborhoods where residents came together under the auspices of a single community group did not enjoy greatly enhanced capacities to conduct organizational business. Reports of controversy and organizational ineffectiveness were no less likely in these neighborhoods than in others. Their chief advantage seems to have been their ability to elicit participation in community groups. No matter what their social status, residents who lived in neighborhoods where a single group had emerged as the dominant one were much more likely to participate in community groups than people who lived elsewhere.

Neighborhood mobilization, however, may have been achieved at some cost to neighborhood representation. When the local population concentrated its attentions and activities in a single community group, the neighborhood gained an organized institution for the aggregation of community opinion, but it may have lost something in the articulation of those opinions. Organizations reflected the residents' concerns less accurately in neighborhoods that had developed focal community groups than they did in other neighborhoods.

All respondents in the sample survey of residents were presented with a list of ten common neighborhood problems ranging from crime to zoning to stray pets, and they were asked to indicate, for each type of problem on the list, whether or not it had been bothering them recently in their neighborhoods. The same list of neighborhood problems was also presented to organizational informants, and they were asked to indicate how much attention their community groups had devoted to each type of problem during the past year or two. The responses of the informants and the residents were used to construct two sets of scores for each neighborhood. Depending on the proportion of residents who complained about a problem, neighborhoods were scored either high or low in resident concern for each type of problem on the list. The responses of informants for each neighborhood were aggregated to produce a similar measure of organizational attention to the various types of problems. The two measures were then compared to see whether the concerns of organizations matched those of their constituents. If the scores for residents and organizations on a particular type of problem agreed with one another — both high or both low — local community groups were judged to have represented neighborhood opinion on that issue. The number of issues on which residents and organizations concurred serves as a rough measure of representativeness for the community groups in each neighborhood.

The measure suffers from several shortcomings. In the first place, although it may tell us whether residents and community groups were concerned about the same issues, it does not tell us whether they took the same positions on those issues. Second, in neighborhoods with more than one community organization, the measure reflects not the representativeness of any one group but rather the aggregated concerns of all local groups as they mirrored the worries of the entire neighborhood population. Finally, the index of representativeness does not distinguish more important issues from less important issues. Local residents may think it essential, for example, for community groups to voice residents' concern about a neighborhood elementary school, but they may care little whether or not community organizations share their indifference about parks and recreation. The index, however, would count both instances of representation equally.

The index of representativeness provides a highly imperfect measure of the extent to which community groups have been reflecting the concerns of their constituents. It cannot be regarded as a conclusive indication of organizational responsiveness to public opinion, but it can serve as a scale for assessing the general level of agreement between resident concerns and organizational agendas.[20]

Agreement was more frequent than divergence. For all ten of the neighborhood problems being considered, the agendas of community organizations reflected the expressed interests of their constituents 60.5 percent of the time. This is the percentage of instances in which individual residents' attitudes about the various neighborhood problems were matched by the amount of attention that local neighborhood associations had devoted to these problems. The degree of concurrence varied sharply from issue to issue. Community groups reflected the concerns of neighborhood residents least accurately when stray pets were at issue. The correspondence was closest in matters having to do with run-down buildings and houses. Neighborhood and organizational characteristics of the kind already considered were generally unrelated to the degree of concurrence between community groups and their constituents — with one notable exception. In neighborhoods where a single community group had captured the attentions of a high proportion of local residents, the representation of resident concerns tended to be least accurate (gamma $= -.52$). The result is all the more remarkable because the neighborhoods in which a single group had become dominant were also the ones in which rates of resident activism were relatively high. Citizen participation, it appears, does not ensure citizen representation.

When a single dominant organization emerges within a neighborhood, perhaps it becomes too vigorous for its constituents. Having mobilized large numbers of local residents, the organization finds itself blessed with plentiful volunteer labor but faced with the problem of keeping the laborers occupied. The organization might then multiply the projects, programs, and issues it handles in an effort to manufacture additional work for group participants. One possible result is that an organization might devote considerable attention to subjects in which its constituents have very little interest. This divergence between the concerns of local residents and the agenda of their community association would be reflected in a low score for the neighborhood on the index of representativeness. We can easily test this line of explanation. If it holds, we should find that in neighborhoods with dominant organizations, a disproportionate share of the mismatches between resident concerns and organizational agendas should be instances in which community groups evince high levels of interest in topics for which their constituents have shown low levels of concern. In other words, the dominant organizations in these communities are frequently paying attention to issues that the local residents do not care about.

This is not what the results show. If anything, they suggest that the opposite may be true. When a single focal organization has come to dominate the attentions of local residents, there is a slight tendency for the community group to ignore issues that bother its constituents.[21] The reason, perhaps, is that the emergence of a single dominant community group inhibits the political competition that would otherwise help to ensure the democratic responsiveness of a neighborhood group. Weighing against this explanation is the fact that the appearance of a focal organization in neighborhood politics, as we have already seen, is not associated with the diminution of factional contention or intraorganizational debate. Nor does the representativeness of neighborhood associations seem to be enhanced by electoral competition. Organizational informants were asked whether recent elections within their groups had included any contests in which two or more candidates had run for the same office. Neighborhoods that produced frequent reports of electoral competition were distinguished from those that did not. The neighborhoods' scores on the index of representativeness were related to the occurrence of electoral contests, but the relationship was negative (gamma = − .52). Mismatches between organizational agendas and resident concerns were more frequent in the more competitive neighborhoods than they were in communities where organizational leaders usually ran for office unopposed, perhaps because the absence of competion signified the presence of a strong consensus about the issues requiring attention.

In neighborhoods with focal organizations, neither a shortage of political competition nor an excess of organizational energy seems to account for the divergence of organizational agendas from residents' concerns. Perhaps the explanation is simply that it becomes difficult to tailor organizational agendas to constituent interests when most local residents are concentrated in a single community group. Where constituents are divided among several different neighborhood organizations, it may be possible for each group to specialize in the distinctive concerns of a different segment of the local population, and the aggregated agendas of the neighborhood's various organizations would therefore reflect community opinion with a relatively high degree of accuracy. Even conflicting interests can be represented simultaneously through different community groups. But with only one neighborhood association to speak for local constituents, such feats of democratic responsiveness may become inconvenient.

In general, the evidence suggests that political integration may not confer as many advantages on neighborhood polities as might be expected, and it could contribute to some significant disadvantages. Consolidating the conduct of neighborhood business in a single community group diminishes the representation of community opinion, and this political cost is not offset by any notable benefits. The reported ability of groups to define their tasks and to complete them is no greater in neighborhoods that have these focal organizations than in neighborhoods that do not. In fact, the emergence of a single dominant community group was accompanied by reports of frequent intraorganizational disputes and a tendency to leave projects unfinished.

Organizational consolidation, of course, is not the only mark of political integration in neighborhoods. Other signs of the same general phenomenon have to do with the capacity to mobilize local residents for political action, a capacity that presumably grows when residents belong to community associations (whether consolidated or not) or when they can identify local leaders capable of activating them and their neighbors. These two indicators of political integration are closely associated with one another but not with other signs of political life in urban neighborhoods. The larger the percentage of people in a neighborhood who report political connections with local organizations or leaders, the smaller the proportion who are likely to engage in various kinds of informal efforts to produce their own public services. It is conceivable that informal action is abandoned in these well-integrated neighborhoods simply because the opportunities for organized action are so plentiful. In politically disjointed neighborhoods, on the other hand, informal activities may be widespread precisely because formal organizations are so scarce. The problem with this plausible explanation is that circumstances in the politically disjointed neighborhoods seem to induce at least some of their inhabitants—the members of a high-status minority—to engage in both organized and informal activities. The evidence, in other words, is obviously inconsistent with the inference that people resort to informal direct action because they have no opportunity to deal with local issues through formal groups. In fact, the same high-status residents who are most likely to engage in informal direct action are also the ones who are most likely to have organizational ties.

Perhaps they turn to both sorts of activity simply because politically disjointed neighborhoods also tend to be troubled ones — full of the aggravations, inconveniences, and social disadvantages that drive city dwellers into politics. The puzzle is why these troubles should drive residents of all kinds into informal activism, but arouse only the high-status residents to organize against their shared misfortunes in formal groups. The organizational skills that go with high status may help to account for this. They could enable high-status residents to create formal community groups even when they live in politically disjointed neighborhoods. But when a beleaguered high-status minority organizes to protect its interests against the perils of a politically disjointed neighborhood, the organization that comes into being may be unable to mobilize low- and medium-status residents, because it cannot accommodate their interests. Stated simply, people of low and medium status tend to remain unorganized in these neighborhoods partly because their high-status neighbors *are* organized, and partly because of the interests that impelled this minority to become organized in the first place.

Once again, social inequalities among neighbors seem to acquire political significance. Privileged people living in underprivileged neighborhoods are the residents most likely to generate unofficial public services through informal direct action. They also exhibit a fairly pronounced tendency to participate in formal community organizations. But inequality plainly has different implications for formal neighborhood groups than it has for informal activism. So long as neighborhood governance remains informal and improvised, the political activities of socially disadvantaged residents are not much affected by the efforts of their more privileged neighbors. This does not mean that neighborhoods free of formal organizations would approximate streetcorner states of nature, with an idyllic equality of the kind that John Locke imagined to exist before the creation of government. Even in their informal political activities, high- and low-status residents are unequal. People of high social status are more likely to engage in informal public service efforts than people of low status, and they are most likely to undertake these efforts when they are surrounded by large numbers of low-status fellow residents. But their activism in these circumstances does not seem to deter the low-status neighbors from becoming informal activists themselves. Being surrounded by large numbers of low-status neighbors, after all, seems to provoke informal activism among low-status people too.

Organized activities are different from these informal ones because they represent an increase in political interdependence among neighbors. High-status residents are not only more active in community groups than low-status residents; under some circumstances, their activities may actually diminish the organizational involvement of their low-status neighbors. This is what seems to occur in poor and politically disjointed neighborhoods where privileged minorities organize to protect their interests against a threatening environment — one that happens to include large numbers of fellow residents less privileged than themselves.

Such circumstances give rise to politically handicapped neighborhoods, where large segments of the local population remain unorganized because existing community groups are unable to accommodate their interests, and because these unmobilized residents lack the skills or the self-confidence needed to create new organizations of their own. The result is that when rich people live in poor and politically disjointed neighborhoods, those neighborhoods are likely to stay disjointed. The same kind of neighborhood inequality that stimulates the production of unofficial public services also poses an obstacle to the creation of neighborhood-wide organizations that can claim to speak for residents in general.

In the construction of political societies, it appears, one political attainment does not lead naturally to another. The informal executive powers that are exercised among small handfuls of residents may not be consistent with the political integration of the neighborhood as a whole. It may be argued, of course, that this inconsistency represents no dilemma for neighborhood polities. Political integration, after all, does not seem politically advantageous. The evidence suggests that even when a single dominant organization arises to speak for a neighborhood, its claims to representativeness may be difficult to credit, and its effectiveness in the conduct of neighborhood business may not be impressive. But political organization and integration may have other benefits that are not reflected in the internal business of community organizations or the representation of community opinion. It is necessary, in particular, to consider how the political integration of a neighborhood may affect its dealings with external institutions and authorities like city government.

6.
Foreign
Entanglements

O'Donnell Square, Canton. Photograph by Charlotte Crenson.

W hen business is slow and the weather is pleasant, Marie Curry can step outside the laundromat that she manages on a street corner in Canton and look down Potomac Street at the tugboats churning up the harbor. Her vantage point also permits her to keep an eye on her more immediate surroundings in O'Donnell Square — an oblong park edged by brick paths that stretches for a city block between the two lanes of O'Donnell Street. At the far end of the square, Miss Curry can see the neighborhood firehouse and beyond it the gilt-tipped towers of St. Casimir's Church. Facing them from the opposite end of the park, Messiah Lutheran Church, backed by the neighborhood public library, marks the eastern limit of the square. In between, there is a bronze statue of John O'Donnell that seems to be carrying on a conversation with the occupants of the firehouse while gesturing in the direction of Canton Discount Liquors.

O'Donnell, the wealthy eighteenth-century sea captain whose memories of the Orient gave the neighborhood its name, is remembered as the founding father of Canton. Miss Curry is known as the "sidewalk mayor of Canton" and presides over a small fragment of the territory that was once O'Donnell's estate. In O'Donnell Square her presence is almost as constant as that of O'Donnell's statue. "There must be nothing that she misses," says one of her neighbors, "because she's either sitting over in the park or out front." Another resident of Canton, a professional community organizer, calls her "a natural neighborhood helper. People naturally go to Marie for advice and all . . . She's warm. People are just drawn to her. Believe it or not, the laundromat is one of the most important things in this neighborhood. People depend on that, and she'll help people."

Sometimes the need for help has been urgent. "They'd ask for food," explains Miss Curry. "So I'd stand up in the laundromat, and

I'd say, 'Anybody want to donate a can of vegetables or some pota-
toes or a loaf of bread? . . . They don't need it Christmas or Thanks-
giving, but now.' So they would all bring in food." But eventually
the requests for assistance became too numerous for Miss Curry to
handle by herself. Her neighborhood philanthropies required group
support. "It was so many people coming," she recalls, "asking for
[food] baskets, and I couldn't do it alone . . . So I did it with a couple of other friends of mine. They suggested getting together [as an
organization]. So we got together and after we got together, they
picked the name 'Curry's Crusaders.' So then we worked as a
group."

The work of the Crusaders soon expanded beyond the prepara-
tion of food baskets. The group raffled off hams and baskets of liquor
to pay rent and utility bills for needy neighbors; they donated radios
and television sets to a state institution for the retarded; and their attention began to shift toward neighborhood problems of a more
general character than the occasional family crises that created a
need for food baskets. On one occasion, for example, a growing concern about crime and narcotics in Canton led Miss Curry to arrange
a meeting between local residents and police officials. The neighborhood's resident community organizer remembers the occasion:
"I've tried to organize Canton and couldn't a couple of times. Marie
put just one sign in her laundromat for a week . . . and she got a
hundred people. I couldn't believe it."

By reputation, at least, Canton residents are not the sorts of people who aggressively make demands of outside authorities like the
police. Almost half of the institutional leaders who were interviewed
in Canton agreed completely with the statement, "People who live
in this area don't like to go to outsiders for help with neighborhood
problems." In no other sample neighborhood were the informants
more likely to perceive such insularity in their communities.
Canton's isolation from outsiders is probably reinforced by an unusually low rate of residential turnover. The median length of residence for adults interviewed in Canton was just under twenty years.
In only one of the sample neighborhoods did the inhabitants exhibit
greater staying power. Perhaps it is the very changelessness and insularity of Canton that makes the residents especially sensitive to
outside intrusions and disruptions. A neighborhood activist whose
four grown children all live within a few blocks of her home con-
cedes that "Canton is a little bit provincial." It resents foreign entanglements. But even a neighborhood as isolationist as Canton cannot
avoid external influences. If local residents do not take their prob-

lems to outsiders, the outsiders may still bring their own problems to the neighborhood.

In 1981, City Hall's fiscal problems came to roost in Canton. Like other municipalities, Baltimore had recently faced the need to economize, and one of its money-saving measures had been to close some of its neighborhood fire stations. Canton's firehouse had been marked for closing several years before, but a petition campaign saved it. The next effort by city authorities to shut down the station came with less warning, and it swept Marie Curry from the front steps of a Canton rowhouse to the televised evening news. Shortly after learning that Canton's firehouse was to be closed, Miss Curry remembers, "I was sitting on a lady's steps up here, and a man comes, and he says, 'You're the mayor of O'Donnell Street. Someone down on the lot wants to see you'[1] . . . So I went down. In fact, he took me by the hand and walked me down, and a couple of other ladies came along from the Crusaders. So when we got down there, there was Susan White [a local television news reporter] . . . And she says, 'Miss Curry, why are you against the firemen from this firehouse leaving?' I said, 'For the simple reason . . . what other protection do we have down here? We do have many fires down here.'"

But it was not only the loss of fire protection that concerned Miss Curry. She was especially incensed by the suddenness of the city's decision to order the station closed. It had taken the neighborhood by surprise: "If they wasn't to pull this trick on us like a Pearl Harbor attack, maybe we would feel a bit better about it. But no. They done it overnight. Maybe *they* knew about it, but they didn't leave none of *us* know." Though determined to protest what she regarded as a sneak attack upon her neighborhood, Miss Curry confessed herself uncertain about how to proceed. She was undecided, she told the television reporter, whether she would do anything about the firehouse closing. It was only when the newscaster, the lights, and the camera were gone that she began planning a course of action and mobilizing her Crusaders: "I said, 'Come on ladies. Let's get a petition up.' So we got a petition up. We got a thousand and some people's names on the petition. And one of the ladies spoke up, and she said, 'Let's picket the place.' I said, 'No, we're liable to get locked up.'" But a brief consultation with a neighborhood police officer helped to reassure the Crusaders that they could picket the fire station without necessarily breaking the law. "So the men made signs," Miss Curry recalls. "We went down here at night, and we picketed. Channel 2 came down again, and I got on television again [laughter] —twice in one day . . . We had a real ball that night. Even the firemen was signing our petition. They didn't want to go. [But] there was nothing we could do about it. It was too late . . . It's a heart-breaker. It really is a heartbreaker. I'm not just saying it. Everybody does. It was the friendliness . . . You look down there. You see the old fire engine house—not a fireman down there to wave at you or nothing."

The Crusaders had established their group to perform good works and unofficial public services within Canton, and perhaps they were unsuited to carry on the foreign relations of a neighborhood. Marie Curry's organization could run raffles, raise money, assemble food baskets, and turn out a hundred or more of their fellow residents for an important meeting. But the group was unable to get into the mayor's office to deliver its petition. Other Canton residents recognize the limitations of the Crusaders even while acknowledging their good works. "Fast-talkers from downtown," says one of Miss Curry's neighbors, "can talk them out of anything. They may have the best of intentions, but there's a lack of education." Another resident agrees. Recalling the Crusaders' meeting on neighborhood crime problems, he gives Miss Curry credit for achieving a respectable turnout of local residents. "But what she had there," he notes, "was a bunch of politicians and a bunch of political hopefuls, and a few police officers came in there, and it was a waste of time. Some nun came in and read a prayer that she wrote for policemen."

According to other local observers, the Crusaders' shortcomings arose from the same personalism, informality, and independence that helped to make the group an effective agency of mutual assistance and support within the neighborhood. Miss Curry's improvised and spontaneous style of operation was thought to undermine the political integration of Canton: "Instead of going in with an organization that was in the community, she formed her own little coalition . . . She does her own little things. I guess maybe she's not a person that can . . . work with an organized group of people." The past president of one organization in Canton expresses similar reservations about the Crusaders, because "it takes away from the strength of our organization when you have these smaller clusters forming."

The evidence has already shown that the tendency toward unofficial public service is strongest and most widespread in fragmented residential areas where the residents seem to lack political "connectedness." But the absence of this political integration may prove a serious inconvenience when a neighborhood attempts to conduct diplomatic relations with outside authorities like city government.

Residential areas where unofficial public servants are numerous and active, therefore, may fare poorly when they have to deal with official public servants. Since they generate some of their own public services, of course, such neighborhoods may be able to minimize their reliance upon municipal authorities. But encounters with city government are unavoidable. When Marie Curry occupies her vantage point in O'Donnell Square, she can see evidence of these encounters everywhere. The empty firehouse, the park, the neighborhood public library, the statue of Captain O'Donnell — all are monuments to past struggles and accommodations between Canton residents and City Hall. Even Miss Curry's view of the harbor calls attention to a City Hall presence in the neighborhood.

Fifteen years ago city officials decided to build a limited-access expressway, six to eight lanes wide, that would have passed roughly midway between Miss Curry's laundromat and the Canton waterfront, a few blocks away. In 1966, after the City Council passed a series of condemnation ordinances, more than two hundred Canton homes were taken for the highway. The displacement of residents and the subsequent demolition of the houses were traumatic for a neighborhood in which people commonly spent entire lifetimes, often living in the same houses that their parents or grandparents occupied. Fifteen years after the clearing of the highway corridor, a Canton activist could still observe that "the road and the torn-down houses are a very touchy subject in our neighborhood. The elderly people are very bitter, because a lot of people died. They were born and raised down there." The bitterness is intensified, perhaps, by the fact that there is still no highway along the Canton waterfront. Gasoline shortages, changes in transportation policy, financial difficulties, and political opposition all helped to curtail the city's plans for expressway construction, and the proposed highway has not yet come between Canton residents like Marie Curry and their view of the harbor.

Canton's invisible expressway nevertheless remains a constant presence in Southeast Baltimore, not only because of the houses it destroyed, but also because of the neighborhood organizations it helped to create, many of which continued to operate long after the threat of highway construction had receded. In Canton and in several surrounding neighborhoods, community associations originated as responses to an external challenge to the social and territorial integrity of residential areas. Few of them arose, like Curry's Crusaders, as agencies of domestic policy in neighborhoods — institutions through which residents might handle internal matters of mutual assistance or unofficial public service. Neighborhoods, as Gerald Suttles has pointed out, tend to develop their distinctive identities through "foreign relations" with outsiders, not merely as by-products of solidarity among insiders.[2] The same may often be true of political organization in neighborhoods. Even in Canton, where many residents are bound together by ties of kinship, friendship, and simple familiarity, the most powerful stimuli for community organization have recently come from outside the neighborhood.

Early opposition to the expressway was concentrated in Fells Point, a neighborhood west of Canton that also stood in the highway's path. But anti-expressway meetings in Fells Point frequently drew participants from Canton. One of them was Alex Tickner, a Methodist minister who headed the Canton Christian Council. His organization was a coalition of five Protestant churches that operated a storefront community center just across O'Donnell Street from Marie Curry's laundromat. One of the council's most energetic and voluble members was Gloria Aull, a lifelong resident of Canton. Tickner saw to it that she was invited to the Fells Point meetings, where both of them became acquainted with Barbara Mikulski. Miss Mikulski, who had grown up in Southeast Baltimore, had recently earned a degree in social work and was employed by Baltimore's Catholic Archdiocese. Her family owned a bakery on the northern fringe of Canton. Later she would become one of the area's representatives on the City Council and, later still, a member of Congress.[3]

In 1968 Barbara Mikulski, Alex Tickner, and several others began to discuss the creation of an areawide coalition of community groups for Southeast Baltimore, an organization sizable enough to cope with such large-scale threats as expressway construction whose disturbing impact might be felt across several neighborhoods. The purpose was not to create a new coalition to fight the expressway. But the struggle over the road had convinced them of the need for an areawide organization, and it provided an issue that could mobilize large numbers of area residents. For many of these people, the expressway issue seemed to expose the insufficiency of existing political arrangements in Southeast Baltimore. When the highway first threatened the neighborhood, says Gloria Aull, "people in Canton didn't get themselves together, didn't ask for help. They were dependent upon the city councilmen, who were going to take care of things for them, and you see how well they took care of things for them."

The neighborhood's access to outside authorities was monopolized by elected politicians, and managed through a network of precinct workers and Democratic clubs. "The way things were done in Southeast Baltimore," recalls one local resident "was through Democratic organizations. If you worked for the organization and you had a complaint, you went to your precinct captain, and he in turn would go to the president of the Democratic club, who would talk to the councilman." These were the arrangements whose efficacy had been called into question by the expressway issue. To Gloria Aull, the deficiencies of the standing order had become clear: "The thing of it was that the political organizations had become bureaucracies themselves . . . They had become entrenched, and they weren't changing their leadership, and they weren't listening. They were trying to serve people in the '50s and '60s the same way they had served them in the '30s. And we didn't need jobs on a garbage truck, and we didn't need a load of coal or a basket of food. We needed better schools. We needed our streets taken care of. We needed somebody to protect us from the negative decisions that were being made by the city administration and the federal administration."

When the expressway collided with Canton, it seemed to shake loose the animosities that many residents harbored toward their elected representatives. City Council members who dared to occupy the platform at neighborhood meetings were likely to become targets for the anger that boiled up from the audience. For one local resident, such a gathering seems to have marked the beginnings of neighborhood activism: "The first anti-road meeting that I attended, which was one of the big ones, took place in Canton . . . and it really turned into a raucous upheaval, and I had never been to a meeting like that in East Baltimore — anti-politician, anti-establishment, anti-everything — over the road. But it was not just the road. Everything was blasted out at those people [the local City Council representatives] . . . They were such an insult to your intelligence, and you looked around and saw all those people there — those good people in the neighborhood — and they were obviously being taken to the shower. And you really resented those politicians."

Such resentments supplied some of the energy that made possible the formation of the Southeast Community Organization (SECO), a coalition of neighborhood, ethnic, and church groups whose jurisdiction would eventually extend to more than half a dozen neighborhoods. But in 1969, when a small steering committee led initially by Alex Tickner was designing SECO, some of the constituent neighborhoods still lacked suitable organizations to represent them in the coalition. Canton was one of these until, in 1970, the Canton Improvement Association was formed. Gloria Aull was among its first members. Delores Canoles, another of the group's founders, was an active member of Alex Tickner's church, and it was he who invited her to join the organization for its first meeting. Others who helped to create the association had also been recruited by participants in the planning activities of the SECO steering committee. Kenneth Moore, for example, had met Barbara Mikulski when she addressed the parent-teacher association at the elementary school where he taught. "While she was there," he recalls, "she and I got into a conversation, and she felt that the local communities were really being taken advantage of by the politicians, and that the answer would be local neighborhood improvement associations." Mikulski brought him together with the other founders of the Canton Improvement Association for the group's inaugural meeting at Reverend Tickner's church.

In effect, the association was created to consolidate neighborhood support for an organization-to-be whose concerns extended well beyond Canton. "Canton Improvement Association," says Delores Canoles, "came about in order to be supportive of SECO." People like Barbara Mikulski might benefit indirectly from that support. "Being friendly with those [neighborhood] organizations," observes Kenneth Moore, "was of course a stepping stone for her politically, and she obviously used her connections within those organizations, and I think she did this all around the First District . . . She formed those improvement associations or got them started— just brought people together. And she talked the city up. She talked the First District up. She was very optimistic about the First District . . . and it was good to hear that for a change, after having been so downtrodden." Miss Mikulski's optimism was soon to be vindicated. Less than two years later, she would be elected to represent the district in the City Council, and SECO would be an operating organization with a small full-time staff, a $50,000 budget, and solid growth prospects.

The activities of the Canton Improvement Association expanded along with those of the organization that it was created to support. Beginning with a small handful of neighborhood activists like Gloria Aull, Delores Canoles, and Kenneth Moore, it was soon able to attract more than two hundred people to some of its more important meetings. It resisted changes in the expressway alignment that would have taken more Canton homes; it acted as spokesman for neighborhood interests in a revision of the city's comprehensive zoning ordinance; it provided much of the support for an effort to reduce truck traffic on the residential streets of the area. In time, it also grew more independent of SECO. By 1975 most of the association's founders had been replaced by a second generation of officers whose attachments to SECO had not been formed during the coalition's early struggle to assemble and organize its forces in Southeast Baltimore.

A number of the new leaders were relatively young and well-educated residents of Canton who had already experienced several neighborhood victories as members of the local improvement association. They had confidence in their ability to make further gains, and they did not believe that their organization's ties with SECO contributed substantially to Canton's political capabilities. In fact, they tended to regard their alliance with the southeastern coalition as a drain on their organization's political resources. A few were angry that SECO seemed to take credit for neighborhood triumphs that they regarded as their own. Others had tired of the demands that SECO made of their organization's leadership: "Sometimes you would get organizers from SECO that you weren't too fond of. They would work you coming and going . . . They'd just pound on you and pound on you and wear you out." Still others were disturbed that local energies that might have been devoted to the immediate problems of Canton were being scattered across the neighborhoods of Southeast Baltimore: "We didn't have the manpower that SECO required from us . . . They wanted us to stand behind them in issues that they were facing throughout the Southeast area, and we didn't have enough active members to stretch ourselves any thinner. So we had to make the decision either to be concerned strictly with the Canton area . . . as opposed to helping out Washington Hill or something."

Dissatisfaction with SECO mounted until, in the summer of 1975, the Canton Improvement Association reaffirmed the traditional separateness of its neighborhood by formally seceding from the confederation. One of the group's first projects as an independent organization was to create the park in O'Donnell Square that Marie Curry now keeps under surveillance. Part of the square was occupied by an asphalt-topped playground, which had to be relocated on a new site two blocks away. Part was covered by the corrugated metal roof of a onetime public market shed, where vendors had long ago sold fresh produce to Canton housewives. The roof was taken down and moved by truck with painstaking care through narrow Canton streets. Almost as delicate as this task was the job of negotiating with city officials to secure the desired improvements in the square. The discussions had culminated in a meeting with the mayor at City Hall. He began by reminding the Canton representatives of the inconveniences that their organization had created for his expressway construction efforts several years earlier, and he counseled a more cooperative approach to city government in the future. The Canton Improvement Association was ready to be accommodating. Its new leaders had not been so deeply embroiled as some of their predecessors in the bitter highway fights; they had developed a measure of confidence in their ability to bargain effectively with city agencies and officials. They were prepared, as one of them points out, to carry on diplomatic relations with external authorities in a somewhat different style: "I believe in the beginning, with the highway, they [the Canton leaders] were very aggressive. I remember at the City Fair, one of the reasons [the mayor] didn't like us was that they did a tombstone—'Canton Rest in Peace'—and he really got adamant about it. We started getting nothing—zilch . . . As that group sort of went out and our younger group came in, we decided that much as we didn't want to . . . we'd have to start playing political games, and we did, and we're getting a lot." The "political games" of compromise and accommodation brought Canton its statue of Captain O'Donnell, along with the park and other neighborhood improvements that surrounded it. But some blocks to the west of O'Donnell Square, the game was played differently.

The territory claimed by the Canton Improvement Association ended just beyond St. Casimir's Church. The region between this western frontier and Fells Point was still unclaimed by any formal community organization when SECO, less than a year after the secession of the Canton Improvement Association, dispatched one of the community organizers on its staff to mobilize the local residents. Joe Coffey, SECO's missionary to the western fringes of Canton, soon located a promising neighborhood leader in Bill Kelch, a former union organizer who had lived in the area as a boy, moved to the suburbs, and then came back to live in the neighborhood with his wife and children. Kelch was glad to return to the city: "One of the things I hated in the suburbs was that I had to cut grass on Saturdays. And my big thing here was that if I want grass, I can go over to Patterson Park and look at it and I don't have to cut it . . . I just kind of like the city. The excitement. Like every once in awhile, when there's nothing to do or you get bored with TV, we take a run downtown. Just take a ride downtown at night—Baltimore Street, check the Block out, and around the Inner Harbor. It's always something going on. In the county, after 8 o'clock, you got everything you want. You lock the house up, and you're inside." Kelch's restless energy would soon help to ensure that there was almost always something going on in his own neighborhood. "He had a big mouth," says Gloria Aull approvingly, "and was willing to stick his neck out and take a risk."

The quiet and inconspicuous "political games" of negotiation and compromise were not for Kelch — at least in his preliminary steps toward neighborhood organization. Instead, his approach to the task of mobilizing his neighbors seemed to draw some of its inspiration from the tradition of P. T. Barnum: "I always say [that] power is an illusion," Kelch announces, "and if you can build the illusion, you've got power . . . If people believe you have power, you have it." To create the belief, of course, it was first necessary to seize people's attention. Kelch and Coffey found their initial attention-getting opportunity on Bradford Street, a thoroughfare almost narrow enough for a medieval city, just around the corner from Kelch's home. One of the houses on Bradford Street was a neighborhood nuisance and eyesore of long standing. For Joe Coffey, however, it represented "an organizer's dream . . . because it was abandoned; it was a health hazard; there were rats; it was vacant for sixteen years. And the city owned it. So all we had to do was to beat up on the city."

The Bradford Street house provided a tangible focus for neighborhood dissatisfaction, an occasion for making demands of political authorities, and an opportunity for local residents to fight City Hall and win. It was not a long struggle. Four weeks after it began, city officials agreed to see that necessary repairs were made to the run-down house. In the process Kelch and Coffey had assembled a small nucleus of activists from the blocks surrounding the vacant row-house. They called themselves the Concerned Community of West Canton.

The West Canton group's next chance to "build the illusion" was supplied by Governor Marvin Mandel. In an effort to relieve over-crowding in the state's correctional system, Mandel had been trying to find an acceptable site for the construction of a new prison. No community regarded itself as an acceptable site. To sidestep this political inconvenience, the governor and his staff conceived a plan that would allow them to locate the new correctional facility outside the boundaries of any community. In mothballs at Norfolk was the U.S.N.S. *William O. Darby*, a World War II transport ship that the state might acquire from the federal government and convert into a six hundred–bed floating prison. In May 1976 the state made public a new plan to house its felons afloat, and announced that the vessel would be anchored off Clinton Street on the Canton waterfront.

The prison ship's mooring site would bring it closest to the residential area represented by the Canton Improvement Association, and the association's leaders met with state officials to discuss the ship shortly after the proposal became public. Their constituents were worried that the hundreds of work-release prisoners who were to be inmates of the ship would have to pass through Canton each day on their way to jobs around the city. Under state correctional regulations, many of these prisoners might not be employed but only looking for employment, and Canton residents feared that they might spend their leisure hours between job interviews committing criminal mischief in the neighborhood. Some were upset by reports that the ship's maintenance would be the responsibility of work crews composed of maximum-security prisoners from the Maryland State Penitentiary. The ship might also bring other troubles to the neighborhood. New sewer and water lines, for example, would have to be run through Canton's streets. Representatives of the Canton Improvement Association had no shortage of objections to raise in their meetings with state officials.

Some Canton residents, however, did not think the improvement association was sufficiently militant in the defense of neighborhood interests. One of them — not directly engaged in the attack on the prison ship — objected to the operating style of the association: "They were dealing one on one . . . They were meeting with [a state official] in their living rooms — saying, 'We're rational people. We don't picket or take to the streets.' And they were getting screwed." Meanwhile, Bill Kelch and Joe Coffey were collecting information about the prison ship themselves, and they decided to launch their own campaign against it. "I think Coffey had this prison ship thing planned anyway," Kelch reflects. "He found an issue to get you started — the house — and one just led to the other. It's an organizer's tactic." The Concerned Community of West Canton, fresh from its Bradford Street victory, now moved to challenge the governor's new nautical theme for the state prison system. Kelch's leadership in the fight was bolstered when SECO named him chairman of its areawide Prison Ship Coalition.

Through most of the summer that followed the announcement of the prison ship proposal, Kelch and his West Canton neighbors attempted to arouse their fellow residents to protest the governor's plan. Kelch went from one meeting to another carrying sheets of cardboard covered with newspaper clippings about the crimes committed by escaped prisoners. But the initial response was disappointing. The attempt to mobilize the neighborhood seemed to be making no more headway than the negotiating efforts of the Canton Improvement Association. But in midsummer Joe Coffey sensed that the West Canton leadership had reached a turning point in its campaign: "I remember in August, we had a rather slow meeting at St. Casimir's on the prison ship. Right after that meeting, we were a little despondent [that] we didn't get the turnout we wanted. But [Barbara] Mikulski was there. That was the first night Mikulski really got with those people . . . because the leadership from West Canton, who organized the meeting, felt real despondent that they didn't get hundreds of people . . . Barbara Mikulski sat down with them, and what she did to those people was really tremendous . . . I think that the jolt that she gave psychologically was like a shot in the arm to [the] leadership." Miss Mikulski, then campaigning for her second term in the House of Representatives, was a valuable ally, and she provided practical advice as well as encouragement. From her the West Canton activists received some suggestions about the profitable use of newspaper and television coverage.

Kelch and Coffey had already taken some steps to capture public attention. To raise money for their campaign, they and their supporters had begun to manufacture and sell T-shirts that advertised their cause. Beneath the message "No Prison Ship," each shirt carried a silk-screened representation of the U.S.N.S. *Darby*, and beneath that was a message for Governor Mandel, who was then standing trial for political corruption—"Float on it Marvin." The shirt was an immediate success in Southeast Baltimore. Kelch used the shirt, in a midsummer stunt, to reach a wider audience. In an attempt to capitalize on one of the many downtown promotional events sponsored by City Hall, Kelch recalls, "I went down to the Mayor's Hog-Calling Contest. I got my No Prison Ship T-shirt on with my shirt over top of it. So we registered and went through the whole thing. I felt like a real ass. But when they called my name, I got up there. I took off my shirt. Well, the press just turned around. The guy that won the contest didn't even get in the papers. But I was in every paper for two days with that shirt. One of the things I found out is that you got to be creative, bold, and crazy to get press. You got to be a show-off . . . So that's what they got."

Kelch's show-off tactics helped to give his followers a lift. "People began to feel good about it," says Joe Coffey, "They were sitting in hot little rooms till one o'clock in the morning, belting out T-shirts, making signs. It was incredible. It was the most fun issue we ever did. People worked. I've never seen so many people put in so much work in a short time to beat an issue." But hard work by itself might not be sufficient to persuade the state to abandon its plans for the prison ship. It was true that after designating Canton as the mooring site for the ship, state officials had begun to talk of alternative anchorages. The location of the prison ship, they said, would be definitely decided only after the state took possession of the vessel.[4] But Canton residents suspected that such talk was designed merely to quiet them. Once the state's ship came in, they feared, the neighborhood might not be able to resist the pressure to anchor it off Clinton Street. The state, after all, would have to put the *Darby* somewhere.

If Maryland failed to get its ship, of course, there would be no pressure to put it anywhere, and the state could not secure the *Darby* without the cooperation of several federal agencies. There was the requirement for an environmental impact statement, for example, which might require the state to reveal just where it intended to moor the prison ship.[5] Additional complications arose from the legal procedures for transferring the ship from the federal to the state government. The navy could not simply surrender the *Darby* to Maryland. After leaving the navy, the ship would first come under control of the Federal Maritime Administration, which could either sell the ship at auction or turn it over to another federal agency. The U.S. Department of Health, Education, and Welfare could then request the vessel and pass it on to the State of Maryland, but only if the *Darby* were approved by HEW as an "educational facility." In this extended series of administrative decisions, Canton activists saw several opportunities to keep the *Darby* from ever making port in Baltimore. They shifted their fire from the state government to the federal, where their ally Barbara Mikulski could supply them with strategic advice and intelligence information.

Kelch, Coffey, and their supporters quickly scrapped a plan to take busloads of Canton residents to Washington to lobby against the transfer of the *Darby*. Their reservations about such an approach, Coffey recalls, arose from a sense that "you get lost in Washington. You've got to have a million people before you make a splash." Within Canton, however, the opponents of the prison ship already had an attentive audience of partisans. Instead of taking their protest to the federal officials, the prison ship activists decided to bring the administrators to Canton, where they could meet with local leaders and take a tour of the neighborhood that would expose them to the feelings of the residents. With Barbara Mikulski's help, Kelch arranged for the federal expedition to Canton. Five officials — from the Federal Maritime Administration and the Department of

Health, Education, and Welfare—accepted his invitation to visit the neighborhood on October 14, 1976.

Canton's preparations to receive its guests began weeks before the visit. After deciding on a route for the neighborhood tour, Kelch and his adherents went door-to-door along the streets that the federal officials would travel and asked residents to put "No Prison Ship" signs in their windows. A few, including Kelch himself, draped bedsheets bearing the same message across the fronts of their houses. A mass meeting of neighborhood residents was scheduled for the week before the arrival of the federal administrators. Its purpose, says Joe Coffey, was to "get people all riled up to fight the prison ship . . . get them worked up and let that lead into the tour." Congresswoman Mikulski, then just one month away from election day, was the only elected public official invited to address the gathering. Still unsure of their ability to assemble a crowd, the prison ship opponents had decided to hold the meeting in one of Canton's smallest churches—the Canton Baptist Mission—where a small turnout might not look conspicuously small. The mission was also an appropriate meeting site because it stood only a short distance from the proposed mooring place of the *Darby*, and because its pastor had already lent support to the activists from West Canton.

There were no empty seats in the Baptist Mission on the night of the prison ship meeting. Standees filled the back of the meeting hall and spilled onto the steps outside. Each person attending received a pencil and a piece of paper, and instructions were given about how to write letters to federal officials concerning the prison ship. There was a pause in the proceedings so that letters could be drafted, and the meeting organizers mailed them in a batch immediately after the assembly broke up. Their constituents seemed well primed to meet the officials in person a week later.

The visitors' tour began at the offices of SECO near Fells Point. Then the government administrators were hustled into separate cars, each of them accompanied by a squad of prison ship opponents. As the caravan cruised through the streets of Canton, it passed streetcorner clusters of local residents who waved at the cars. A few people held banners aloft declaring their opposition to the plan for the prison ship. On some blocks, at least 80 percent of the houses had "No Prison Ship" signs in their windows. At St. Casimir's Church, the first stop on the tour, a group of about fifty prison ship opponents were waiting. The children from the church school happened to be at recess, playing in a closed-off street that doubled as a temporary playground. Curiosity about television cameras brought dozens of additional residents out onto the sidewalks. By prior arrangement, the television reporters were steered to a school crossing guard, who spoke her piece about the impact of the prison ship upon her neighborhood. "It worked out beautiful," recalls Bill Kelch, "with the church and the people and the kids playing in the street behind her there. It looked like a movie set." Then the tour proceeded to the Canton Baptist Mission, but by a roundabout route that "gave the people on the corner [at St. Casimir's] time to get in cars and beat us down there." When the recycled crowd arrived, it helped to swell a gathering of senior citizens who were assembling to eat lunch at the mission's center for the elderly. By the time the federal officials reached the mission, says Joe Coffey, "we had one hell of a crowd. They looked like hundreds of people there." After a further stop to discuss the impact of the prison ship with Canton businessmen, the caravan headed for a neighborhood restaurant where federal officials and prison ship opponents ate lunch, paid for in part by the proceeds of T-shirt sales.

Before lunch was over, at least some leaders of the campaign against the prison ship sensed that the federal officials had already decided not to release the *Darby* to Maryland. But the officials refused to commit themselves. It was not until a few weeks later that the Federal Maritime Administration announced that a legal technicality would prevent the government from donating the ship to Maryland without a special act of Congress. The Mandel administration made no effort to secure the necessary legislation. Not long afterward, a local City Council member who had scarcely participated in the prison ship campaign "announced" the neighborhood's victory through a community newspaper, and thanked several other local politicians and organizations for their efforts to prevent the *Darby* from docking at Canton. Bill Kelch, the Concerned Community of West Canton, Barbara Mikulski, and SECO were not mentioned.[6] Victory over the Mandel administration did not bring public recognition from the area's party politicians. But there were other rewards. Bill Kelch, for example, later served as president of SECO, until intraorganizational disputes drove him to resignation. There were also the satisfactions that came from the prison ship fight itself. "The thing we did with the issue," Kelch remembers, "was [that] we had a good time with it. We enjoyed it. We made fun of it."

Speaking through Leaders vs. Do-It-Yourself Diplomacy

The fun of neighborhood politics is often supplied by external enemies. Canton residents rarely seem to enjoy one another's company so much as when they are gathered together to wage a war against the outside world. Countless local inhabitants stand ready to tell their own war stories about the expressway fight or the prison ship battle or the truck traffic skirmish. The fact that serious matters may be at stake in these conflicts does not diminish the fun but only helps to justify it. Nor does the anger aroused by outside enemies interfere in a serious way with the pursuit of political recreation. The fact that this animosity can be discharged at targets outside the neighborhood may actually enhance the prospects for internal harmony and good feeling. Only when the hope of victory has vanished, it seems, does the fun go out of fighting City Hall, and even then it is sometimes possible to find diversion in defeat. Marie Curry and her Crusaders "had a real ball" picketing the neighborhood fire station on the very night that the firefighters were to be moved elsewhere, when it was already too late to compel municipal authorities to back down. The demonstration permitted local residents to express their outrage about the "Pearl Harbor attack" on their neighborhood.

Anger, animosity, and irritation, as we have already seen, frequently provide the foundations for neighborhood politics. People who produce unofficial public services in their neighborhoods tend to harbor unfriendly feelings toward their neighbors. Perhaps antagonism directed at outside authorities helps to stimulate neighborhood politics of a different kind — the creation and maintenance of local institutions for aggregating and expressing the sentiments of neighborhood residents. Such observations suggest a more general pattern of neighborhood politics in which different sorts of neighborhoods tend to specialize in different kinds of political functions.

In a diverse, fragmented, and unstable residential area like Reservoir Hill or Union Square, there are many occasions for friction among the local inhabitants, and these antagonisms drive them to acts of public service. It is not a sense of solidarity with fellow residents that stimulates these contributions to the general welfare, but rather the exposure to a disorderly neighborhood environment where public peace and civility cannot be taken for granted — at least not if the residents insist on their own heterogeneous standards of decorum. Public service activities are probably not much fun in these circumstances. They represent efforts to repair or prevent damage that local residents do to themselves or one another. The neighborhood polity therefore tends to become preoccupied with problems of domestic policy — matters of internal regulation and order maintenance. Attempts to organize the neighborhood for the conduct of foreign relations, on the other hand, are likely to be undermined by the same social diversity, antagonism, and political fragmentation that help to stimulate informal public services. The Reservoir Hill Community Association, for example, was often disabled by factional strife that diminished its capacity to represent the neighborhood abroad. An administrator in a municipal agency who has lived in Reservoir Hill and dealt with its community organization in an official capacity comments on the "tremendous turmoil" and "infighting" in the neighborhood, but notes that the residents' propensity to fight with one another does not seem to be translated into a readiness to fight City Hall: "They're militant in the community, not militant with city agencies. For instance, I could go to a meeting, and because they've known me for years, they will curse me out, do whatever they want. But if [the agency's Commissioner] comes out there, it's nothing . . . A lot of times, I would need some help to get a point across to the Commissioner, and I would say, 'All right, several of you can come down and have a meeting [with him] — Nothing."

In Canton, where racial and socioeconomic diversity are much less pronounced, informal public services are also less widespread than they are in Union Square or Reservoir Hill. In fact, reports of informal direct action were less widespread in Canton than in any other sample neighborhood; in Union Square and Reservoir Hill, on the other hand, reports were *more* widespread than in most other residential areas. Canton displays its political capabilities in pursuits of a different kind. It is a neighborhood polity that seems to specialize in the conduct of foreign relations with external authorities, not the informal production of internal order and amenities. In a neighborhood like Canton, perhaps, where a stable and socially homogeneous population is bound together by ties of friendship and kinship, residents may have such confidence in the public order of their community that they rarely feel driven to prop it up. They believe that the local order can stand by itself if left alone. Whatever threats they perceive tend to originate outside the neighborhood rather than inside, and the same social solidarity that gives them confidence in neighborhood order may also facilitate their mobilization against external menaces.

Canton and Reservoir Hill, in other words, may represent two different types of neighborhood polities. In one, internal heterogeneity and friction lead to an emphasis upon domestic policy — a preoccupation with informal efforts to create the internal order that the neighborhood lacks. But such neighborhoods are also likely to lack the social cement that make possible political integration and organization. This social solidarity is found in neighborhoods like Canton, where residents devote little attention to the maintenance of internal order but stand ready to meet external challenges, either through organizations that speak for them, or, if necessary, by mass mobilization.

Past studies, which have stressed the role of social solidarity in maintaining "strong" neighborhoods, may yet be reconciled with more recent views that find sources of neighborhood strength in weak social ties.[7] Perhaps one need only recognize that there are different sorts of strengths in neighborhoods. Efforts at internal regulation may be most pronounced in socially disjointed neighborhoods. Social homogeneity and solidarity, on the other hand, may contribute to the defensive capabilities of neighborhoods, and in fact it may take an external attack upon some of these homogeneous neighborhoods to activate the latent sense of fellow feeling among local residents. In any case, the distinction between internally active and externally active polities seems to provide a simple, convenient, and plausible way of interpreting variations in the pattern of neighborhood politics, one that may help to resolve some of the inconsistencies that have arisen in studies of residential areas. It certainly appears to make sense of the differences between Canton and Reservoir Hill. But some difficulties arise when the framework is applied more generally, and even where Canton is concerned the scheme may not be entirely satisfactory.

By reputation at least, Canton is an insular community whose residents do not like to deal with outsiders. The appearance of provincialism may seem inappropriate for a neighborhood polity that specializes in the conduct of foreign relations, but this insularity may be one of the factors that explains Canton's capacity to mobilize against outside threats. If local residents routinely took their individual problems and complaints to City Hall, they might be less easily attracted to collective arrangements for representing the demands of the neighborhood as a whole to outside authorities. In other words, Canton's ability to conduct diplomatic relations with these external authorities may depend less on the solidarity of the local population than on the residents' reluctance to speak for themselves downtown.

Some Canton residents attribute the diffidence of their neighbors to the local heritage of machine politics. Neighborhood politicians, they claim, convinced the local inhabitants that they needed intermediaries to represent them in dealings with city officials—"Look, you're not smart enough to do that, but I'll take care of it for you." "Politicians," says Joe Coffey, "don't do anything to teach people how to be citizens. They teach them how to be consumers. You want something, you go to the organization . . . But you're not a citizen. You don't know how to do it yourself." Neighborhood politicians, in this view, stifled the development of political life in Canton not only because they discouraged local residents from representing themselves at City Hall but because they undermined the self-reliance that might have led their constituents to manufacture their own unofficial public services. The tradition of dealing with City Hall through intermediaries, of course, may also have had political effects of a different kind. In particular, it may have primed Canton's inhabitants for the community organizations that would later speak on their behalf to outside authorities.

Political history, not neighborhood solidarity, may explain the ability of Canton to generate organizations that represent neighborhood interests to outsiders. More precisely, Canton's history suggests that in neighborhoods where local residents take their own requests and complaints directly to City Hall, it may be difficult to maintain community organizations that specialize in the conduct of foreign relations on behalf of their constituents. When almost all residents stand ready to serve as their own secretaries of state, they do not have much use for diplomatic representatives. But if the inhabitants are reluctant to speak for themselves at City Hall, as they are alleged to be in Canton, then their diffidence may provide a justification for community associations that do the talking for them.

Canton's experience, in other words, points to two different explanations for the diplomatic activism of local organizations. One holds that neighborhood homogeneity and solidarity supply a firm foundation for political organization and integration; these political assets enable the neighborhood to present a united and imposing front to the outside world. The second version says that a neighborhood's prowess in foreign policy depends on the reluctance of its individual residents to conduct foreign relations on their own.

Each of these explanations needs to be considered — along with the possibilites that neither or both of them may be correct. Neither may account for the diplomatic activism of neighborhoods simply because the sources of this activism cannot be found in neighborhoods themselves. The vigor that communities exhibit in dealing with external institutions, after all, depends at least in part on the actions of those outside institutions, and not on the characteristics of the local residents or the organizations that represent them. On the other hand, both explanations could help to account for neighborhood foreign policy if solidarity among neighbors reduced their willingness to contact outside authorities on their own, and therefore created a need for organizations to make these contacts on their behalf. Close personal ties among residents could discourage individual inhabitants from acting on their own to make contacts of a more impersonal kind with city agencies or officials.

Residents in each of the twenty-one sample communities were asked whether they themselves had ever contacted anyone in city government about problems that had arisen in their neighborhoods. The survey findings suggest that neighborhood solidarity does not account for the kind of insularity that prevents local residents from speaking for themselves at City Hall. Respondents who said that most of their friends were concentrated inside the neighborhood were no less likely to contact city officials than people who had more cosmopolitan friendship ties (gamma = .02). Whether a person's "really good" friends lived on the same block, somewhere else in the neighborhood, or outside the neighborhood also made no difference for the propensity to take one's complaints directly to city government (− .01). Other signs of strong neighborhood attachments — shopping, working, or worshiping inside the neighborhood rather than outside — were similarly unrelated to the occurrence of direct contacts with municipal authorities.[8] Length of residence in a community was the only sign of neighborhood attachment that bore some relationship to the likelihood that people would take their complaints directly to City Hall, and in this case the evidence indicates that direct contacts with municipal officials were more likely for long-time residents than they were for newcomers (.24). The explanation, perhaps, is simply that residents of long standing have had more opportunity to register neighborhood complaints with city government than have recent arrivals.

In general, the existence of strong neighborhood attachments does not deter individual residents from operating on their own in dealings with city officials. People who have been absorbed into cohesive neighborhoods do not become reluctant to speak for themselves at City Hall.[9]

Social class rather than close-knittedness seems to account for the propensity of neighborhood residents to contact city officials directly. High-status Baltimoreans were more likely to report these contacts than either medium- or low-status residents, but they were most likely to have communicated with city government when they lived in low-status neighborhoods. The survey findings in Table 6.1 show the varying effects of individual status and neighborhood sta-

Table 6.1. Individual socioeconomic status, neighborhood status, and respondents' contacts with city government (Percentage of respondents in each category who say they have contacted city government about problems in the neighborhood)

Socioeconomic status of neighborhood	Socioeconomic status of individual respondents		
	High	Medium	Low
High	40.0 (410)	21.5 (295)	17.5 (57)
Medium	53.9 (84)	35.7 (398)	19.7 (239)
Low	59.5 (51)	30.7 (258)	17.7 (330)

tus on people's direct dealings with municipal authorities. A comparison of the percentage figures across each row shows that high-status residents, no matter what kind of neighborhood they lived in, were more likely than low- or medium-status respondents to say that they had contacted city officials about neighborhood problems. Comparing the figures within the first column, however, shows that high-status residents were most likely to have made these contacts when they lived in low-status residential areas. The contacting behavior of medium-status respondents was less strongly affected by the kinds of neighborhoods in which they lived, and low-status residents were hardly affected at all.

The pattern of responses is similar to others we have seen, and it seems to call for a similar line of explanation. The training, occupational experience, and financial resources of high-status residents give them political advantages over their less favored neighbors. They are most apt to put these advantages to use when they face unpleasant local conditions that seem to demand political action, the kinds of conditions that are most common in low-status residential areas. In other words, individual residents of high status have the political means to take their dissatisfactions straight to City Hall. When they are exposed to the conditions of life in poor neighborhoods, they develop strong motives for doing so.[10]

Other evidence concerning the high-status respondents suggests that it is not only their motive to complain that grows stronger in low-status neighborhoods, but also their reported ability to command the favorable attention of city officials. High-, medium-, and low-status residents were all asked whether they thought that "peo-

Table 6.2. Individual socioeconomic status, neighborhood status, and respondents' perceptions of their influence in government decisions (Percentage of respondents in each category who said that people like themselves could have a lot of influence in local government decisions)

Socioeconomic status of neighborhood	Socioeconomic status of individual respondents		
	High	Medium	Low
High	19.0 (400)	11.9 (294)	13.4 (57)
Medium	21.1 (84)	16.8 (391)	14.4 (215)
Low	30.7 ((51)	20.1 (252)	14.7 (296)

ple like yourself" could have a lot of influence over local government decisions, a moderate amount of influence, or none at all. The findings presented in Table 6.2 show how individual status and neighborhood status were related to the proportion of respondents who believed that they could have a lot of influence in local government. Not surprisingly, high-status respondents tended to be more confident of their influence upon municipal decisions than either low- or medium-status residents. But a comparison of the percentage figures within the first column of the table shows that the high-status residents were most likely to believe in the political clout of people like themselves when they lived in low-status neighborhoods, surrounded by people who were unlike themselves.

Rich people who live in poor neighborhoods not only exhibit the most pronounced tendency to take their complaints directly to City Hall, they also seem the most confident of their ability to secure a favorable response from city officials. The political confidence of medium-status respondents also appears to become somewhat more pronounced as their low-status neighbors become more numerous. Only the political self-assurance of the low-status residents themselves is unaffected by variations in the social-class composition of the neighborhoods where they lived.

Just why the presence of many low-status neighbors should enhance the feeling of political efficacy among high- and medium-status respondents cannot be determined from the survey evidence alone. But two kinds of explanations seem plausible. In the first place, living in a low-status neighborhood supplies high- and medium-status residents with many occasions to complain to City Hall about local conditions. Perhaps the simple experience of actually making these complaints and having them listened to bolsters confidence in one's ability to influence city government. Since complaints are made most frequently by rich people who live in poor neighborhoods, these are also the residents who tend to develop the most impressive estimates of their own potential impact upon municipal decisions. Their perceptions reflect past political actions and events. They could also reflect the interests and practices of city government. The municipal determination to attract and retain prosperous, tax-paying residents and to upgrade inner-city residential areas may in fact lead city officials to be especially responsive to the expressed dissatisfactions of high-status people who live in low-status neighborhoods. The chief difficulty with this explanation is that actual contact with city officials is not very powerfully related to confidence in one's ability to influence them (gamma = .17). Past dealings with city government, therefore, do not go far toward accounting for people's impressions of the impact they can have in municipal decisions.

Another possibility is that people's estimates of the weight they carry in city government are formed not as a result of dealings with city officials but as a by-product of relationships with neighbors. High-status people who live in low-status neighborhoods are surrounded by fellow residents less fortunate than themselves. Perhaps they are struck by the significance of their own political advantages because they can so often compare what they have with what their neighbors lack. Under the circumstances, "people like themselves" might seem highly influential indeed. When high-status people live surrounded by neighbors of similar status, on the other hand, they may reasonably conclude that they command no more respect or deference than anyone else in the neighborhood. "People like themselves" may not seem especially influential at all when high-status people are actually surrounded by people like themselves.

The political advantages of relatively rich people seem to acquire enhanced importance when rich people live in poor neighborhoods. The phenomenon is one that we have encountered before. The tendency to engage in unofficial public service activities was generally found to be stronger for high-status than for low-status people, and was strongest of all for high-status residents in low-status neighborhoods. It was in these poor neighborhoods that the gap between the unofficial activism of high- and low-status respondents usually became widest. A similar pattern is evident in the respondents' dealings with City Hall. High-status residents in all sorts of neighborhoods were more likely than their low-status neighbors to contact city officials directly, but the margin was widest in poor neighborhoods. The same thing was true when the respondents assessed their political influence downtown. The estimates of high- and low-status respondents tended to diverge most sharply when they lived together in socially disadvantaged neighborhoods. In dealings with officials of city government, as in the production of most unofficial public services, the political advantages of relatively rich people tend to become most pronounced when they live in relatively poor neighborhoods.

This is one of several parallels between two different approaches to the solution of neighborhood problems — taking them to City Hall and taking matters into one's own hands. The same people who pursue one of these strategies also tend to pursue the other. Residents who said that they had contacted city government about problems in the neighborhood, for example, were also likely to report instances of informal direct action — efforts to cope with local problems directly and unofficially after informal consultations among neighbors. The association between these two forms of neighborhood political action, of course, could be a mere reflection of the fact that both of them are related to the respondents' socioeconomic status. But even after the political effects of individual status have been taken into account, there is still a strong and positive relationship between reported contacts with city government and informal direct action (partial gamma = .56). Informal direct action is more closely related to reports of City Hall contacts than it is to other kinds of neighborhood political action like membership in community associations,[11] and the parallel between informal action in the neighborhood and individual action aimed at City Hall is further strengthened by the fact that similar predispositions seem to lie behind both forms of political involvement. Residents who engaged in informal direct action, for example, tended to be people whose relationships with their neighbors had been marred by annoyance and argument. The same thing is true of people who reported direct contacts with city officials. Like the informal public servants, respondents who complained to municipal authorities about neighborhood problems also tended to report that they had been annoyed at their fellow residents' behavior (gamma = .46) and that they had argued with neighbors (.31). Of course, the same local problems that prompt the complaints may also account for the annoyance and the arguing, which would explain away the relationship between neighborly antagonism and the propensity to take grievances to City Hall. But even among residents who had similar impressions about the severity of neighborhood problems, those who reported aggravation and contention with their neighbors were more likely to take their complaints to City Hall than those who had more harmonious relationships.[12]

Taking grievances to municipal authorities and dealing with them unofficially inside the neighborhood are forms of political behavior that seem to have something in common with one another. Two circumstances may help to account for their kinship. In the first place, both kinds of activities are responses to disorders, inconveniences, and irritations that originate inside the neighborhood. Informal direct action represents an attempt to cope with these domestic disturbances oneself. Complaining to municipal authorities could be a way of bringing the resources of city government to bear on the same sorts of problems. Previous research, in fact, suggests that this is just what many city residents have in mind when they register complaints with municipal officials. They have been bothered by some disturbance within their neighborhoods, and they expect city authorities to step in and set things right.[13] Taking matters into one's own hands and taking them directly to City Hall are both likely to be actions aimed at creating or restoring the internal order of the neighborhood, not measures to defend it against external threats. One seldom enlists city officials in the defense of the neighborhood because the external threats that imperil neighborhood order so frequently originate in municipal government itself. To meet these foreign menaces, it is probably more common for people to rely on formal community organizations than on their own individual efforts to produce unofficial public services or to influence the official public servants.

Complaining to city officials and improvising one's own public services are both forms of neighborhood political action that can be carried on outside the framework of formal community organizations; this is a second point of similarity between them that probably helps to explain why they are found so often in one another's company. They are both species of neighborhood politics that can be pursued in politically unorganized or disjointed neighborhoods. We have already seen, for example, that informal direct action occurs with greater frequency in neighborhoods where residents are politically disconnected from one another than in residential areas where they are tied together in political mobilization networks. The lack of political integration by itself may not drive local residents to take matters into their own hands, but the friction, factionalism, and inconveniences that accompany political disjointedness seem to stimulate acts of unofficial public service among citizens of all social classes.

The same sorts of conditions may also explain complaints directed at city officials. When political fragmentation and divisiveness cause residents to despair of solving local problems within their neighborhood polities, they may turn instead to the authorities at City Hall. The residents' propensity to take their own grievances downtown will vary inversely with their neighborhood's political integration — especially its capacity to produce organizations that speak to city government on behalf of local interests. Canton is a case in point. The reported reluctance of its inhabitants to speak for themselves to municipal authorities may help to explain the emergence of community organizations that do the talking for them. At the same time, the existence of these organizations may reinforce their constituents' tendency to refrain from making their own complaints directly to city officials. If Canton lacked the capacity to generate these organizations, its inhabitants might be more inclined to overcome their insularity and speak for themselves at City Hall. Neighborhood political disorganization, in other words, could compel local residents to take their own individual grievances and complaints directly to municipal authorities. We should therefore expect the evidence to show that individual contacts with city government are more common in politically fragmented neighborhoods than they are in politically integrated ones.

But the evidence does not live up to these expectations in a consistent way. Differing degrees of political connectedness within neighborhoods do not seem to affect the likelihood that residents will take their individual complaints directly to City Hall. The frequency of direct contacts between residents and city officials hardly varies at all with differences in the extent to which local inhabitants could name people capable of mobilizing the entire neighborhood. Nor did it make much difference whether or not a single dominant community organization had emerged in a neighborhood. The degree to which local residents had congregated in one neighborhood association was unrelated to their reports of contacts with city government. Such signs of neighborhood political integration had almost nothing to do with the likelihood that individual residents would take their troubles to municipal authorities.

In other respects, however, the political fragmentation of neigh-

Table 6.3. Reported factionalism in neighborhood and respondents' contacts with city government, controlling for individual socioeconomic status (Percentage of respondents in each category who said they have contacted city government about problems in neighborhood)

Proportion of informants reporting factionalism in neighborhood	Socioeconomic status of individual respondents		
	High	Medium	Low
High	51.2 (314)	31.1 (430)	20.5 (347)
Low	34.2 (231)	28.9 (521)	15.9 (280)

borhoods does seem to encourage people to seek assistance from city government. Factional strife, for example, may create some tendency for neighborhood residents to turn toward municipal authorities. Where knowledgeable informants from a residential area reported high levels of factionalism, local inhabitants tended to contact city government about neighborhood problems. The relevant findings are presented in Table 6.3, where the survey results show that people who lived in factionalized neighborhoods, no matter what their individual status, were somewhat more likely to report direct contacts with city government than people in neighborhoods that scored low on factionalism. The effects of factionalism are more evident for high-status respondents than for either low- or medium-status residents, but in no case does factional strife seem to make a very large difference for the likelihood of citizen complaints aimed at city authorities.

Perhaps the political inconveniences of factionalism lead residents to bypass the internal processes of the neighborhood polity and seek the help of city officials in dealing with local problems. Unfortunately, the evidence does not permit us to rule out completely some alternative explanations for the tendency of people in factionalized neighborhoods to take their problems straight to City Hall. One possibility, for example, is that neighborhood factionalism usually occurs in residential areas that suffer from other problems such as run-down housing or crime. These problems, it might be argued, and not the political disabilities arising from factionalism, are the things that stimulate citizen complaints to city government. The plausibility of this argument is bolstered by the fact that neighborhoods suffering from factional strife also tend to be low-status residential areas that probably face disadvantages other than factionalism itself. But the connection between factionalism and neighborhood socioeconomic status is not a strong one (gamma = .44), and other evidence indicates that the apparent effects of factionalism may not be explained away as mere by-products of neighborhood troubles associated with low status.[14]

The absence of factionalism in a neighborhood is one form of political integration that seems to dampen slightly the propensity of citizens to take their dissatisfactions directly to City Hall. There is another sign of political cohesion that may have the same effect. The political connectedness of local residents — their acquaintance with leaders capable of mobilizing the neighborhood's population — has already been dismissed as a factor influencing the frequency of citizen complaints to municipal authorities. But in addition to their political connections with local leaders, neighborhood residents may also develop political connections with one another — "lateral" rather than "vertical" relationships. Participation in informal political discourse with fellow residents is one sort of lateral political relationship that we have already considered. Not surprisingly, it is related to the likelihood that individual residents will make complaints directly to municipal authorities. Those who engage in neighborhood political discourse are much more likely to report direct contacts with city officials than those who do not (gamma = .55), and their propensity to register complaints at City Hall cannot be explained away as a by-product of irritation about the same neighborhood problems that prompted their discussions with fellow residents. Controlling for people's perceptions of the severity of local problems hardly makes any difference for the relationship between participation in neighborhood discourse and contacts with city government (partial gamma = .53).

There is certainly nothing unusual about the fact that people who discuss neighborhood affairs with their fellow residents also tend to talk to city officials about these matters. What is more striking, perhaps, is that residential areas where participation in neighborhood discourse is *most* widespread generate proportionately *fewer* complaints for municipal authorities than neighborhoods where involvement in informal political discussion is less extensive. In other words, individual contacts with City Hall are most common among people who engage in neighborhood discourse but who live in neighborhoods where few of their fellow residents are similarly talkative. The findings reported in Table 6.4 show that the effects of local political discourse cannot be explained away by referring to

Table 6.4. Level of informal political discourse in neighborhood and respondents' contacts with city government, controlling for individual socioeconomic status (Percentage of respondents in each category who say they have contacted city government about problems in neighborhood)

Proportion of residents in neighborhood who discussed local issues with neighbors	Socioeconomic status of individual respondents		
	High	Medium	Low
High	38.4 (294)	22.4 (268)	18.4 (103)
Medium	48.4 (71)	31.1 (375)	17.9 (277)
Low	51.5 (178)	35.2 (308)	19.0 (247)

the socioeconomic status of individual respondents. Nor does it seem likely that its influence is an artifact of neighborhood status.[15] In general, it appears that neighborhoods with the highest levels of informal political discussion are the ones where residents tend to refrain from taking their complaints to City Hall — even though individual participation in these discussions seems to stimulate contacts with city government. The extensiveness of local political discourse does not have the same influence for all respondents. Among low-status residents, the volume of neighborhood political discussion has no effect on the frequency of complaints to city government. But the high- and medium-status residents tend to refrain from taking their neighborhood troubles to city authorities when they live in residential areas where the level of informal political discourse is relatively high.

Perhaps neighborhood discourse creates opportunities to resolve local problems locally — without taking them to city officials. When fellow residents are talking with each other about neighborhood needs and problems, the inconveniences that neighbors create for one another may often be resolved through discussion. But when people do not speak with one another about local affairs, the chances for resolving these matters through mutual adjustment are diminished, and outside authorities must be called upon to mediate between neighbors. The effectiveness of informal discussion as a mechanism for problem solving naturally depends on the extensiveness of involvement in the conversation. Discussants, no matter how loquacious, cannot resolve their differences with nondiscussants. That is why a high level of political deliberation in a neighborhood at large, not individual participation in discussions, is the factor that seems to obviate the need to contact City Hall about local problems.

It does not reduce this need very sharply. Complaints to municipal officials are only slightly less frequent in neighborhoods with widespread political discussion than they are in residential areas with low levels of discourse. The effects of factionalism on City Hall contacts are no more pronounced than this, and other signs of political disjointedness and cohesiveness are unrelated to the likelihood that residents will look outside the neighborhood for municipal solutions to local problems. In general, the connection between neighborhood political integration and City Hall contacts is neither so consistent nor so strong as might have been expected. There is only uncertain support here for the contention that neighborhoods achieve the cohesiveness to carry on diplomatic activities when their individual residents lack the inclination to engage in these activities on their own behalf.

Perhaps contacting city government differs from other kinds of neighborhood political actions because the opportunity to complain to municipal officials does not depend in a significant way on neighborhood conditions. No matter what political variations there may be among Baltimore's neighborhoods, they all fall within the jurisdiction of the same city government. The local residents' motives to complain may vary in strength from one place to another; their means for reaching city officials may be more or less effective in different neighborhoods; but City Hall is always present for those who wish to call upon its services, whether their neighborhoods are politically integrated or not. Because this opportunity is available to the residents of all neighborhoods, variations in local political conditions may not go far toward explaining the frequency of individual contacts with city government.

There is also the possibility that the local political conditions we have considered are not the appropriate ones. In the first place, the occasions that stimulate individual complaints to city officials may not be the same as the ones that lead entire neighborhoods to mobilize through organizations that speak for them downtown. The political organization of the neighborhood as a whole may serve to defend the community against external threats. Individual complaints to city officials, as we have already seen, may have more to do with disturbances that are internal to the neighborhood itself. The achievement of neighborhood political integration, therefore, may not reduce the need for individual complaints to city officials about the inconveniences that arise inside the neighborhood.

The fact that neighborhood political integration comes in more than one variety is a source of further difficulty. We have already referred to several different indicators of the phenomenon. The evidence shows that they are not always associated with one another in a sensible and coherent way. But they all have one attribute in common. The emergence of a dominant community organization, the occurrence of neighborhood factionalism or political discourse, the development of political connectedness in a residential area — all refer to the political relationships that exist among neighborhood residents themselves, not to the neighborhood's relationships with city government. Perhaps these external realtionships are the ones that should receive attention.

Domestic Tranquillity and the Common Defense

Some neighborhoods have leaders who are almost always engaged in diplomatic missions to city government. Others have no leaders at all to speak on their behalf — political disjointedness and incoherence deprive them of the means to conduct orderly foreign relations. Still other neighborhood polities, though well organized, may exhibit isolationist tendencies, and city officials will rarely hear from their leaders. Indicators of political cohesion and organization, in other words, do not always measure the extent to which a neighborhood's political integration has actually been put to the test in dealings with city government. Even in well-integrated and organized neighborhoods, leaders may not be on speaking terms with city officials, or they may restrict their diplomatic efforts to a few salient issues and congenial municipal agencies. As a result, the residents of these politically integrated neighborhoods may persist in taking their own complaints directly to City Hall, because the leaders who might serve them as ambassadors have proven to be stay-at-homes, or because the matters in which they desire City Hall action are not the ones in which their ambassadors represent them. We obviously need to know more about the relationship between neighborhood political integration and the diplomatic activism of neighborhood leaders, and we need to find out how these diplomatic activities are related in turn to the local residents' individual contacts with city officials.

Diplomacy is conducted not by individual citizens acting on their own but by representatives who can claim to act on behalf of the polity as a whole. It is the leaders of neighborhood institutions and organizations who transact the neighborhood's business with City

Hall. The institutional leaders and activists who served as informants in each sample neighborhood were all asked to identify the "specific issue or problem" they had discussed most with people living in the neighborhood. Next, they were asked if they had ever personally taken up this issue with any of several kinds of municipal officials — the mayor or a member of his staff, administrative officials working for city agencies, City Council members who represented the area, and members of city boards or commissions. All twenty-one sample neighborhoods were then ranked according to the proportion of local informants who reported each of the four types of City Hall contacts. Neighborhoods that stood relatively high in all four rankings received the highest scores for the extensiveness of their diplomatic relations with city government. Next came the neighborhoods that ranked high on three types of municipal contacts, and so on.

In Table 6.5 the sample neighborhoods have been divided into three catagories according to the scores they received for the extensiveness of their diplomatic relations with municipal government. The percentage figures in the table show what proportion of the residents in each category of neighborhoods had made individual complaints directly to City Hall. The influence of the neighborhood's diplomatic relationships appears to vary with the socioeconomic status of the individual respondents. High-status residents tended to take their individual complaints directly to city government when they lived in neighborhoods that scored low on the index of diplomatic communications with municipal authorities.

Table 6.5. Neighborhood diplomatic relations with city government and respondents' individual contacts with city government, controlling for individual socioeconomic status (Percentage of respondents in each category who say they have contacted city government about problems in neighborhood)

Neighborhood score on index of diplomatic relations with city government	Socioeconomic status of individual respondents		
	High	Medium	Low
High	35.6 (172)	30.4 (312)	23.7 (196)
Medium	35.1 (88)	32.1 (335)	18.9 (180)
Low	51.8 (284)	27.1 (304)	14.0 (250)

In neighborhoods that had more extensive diplomatic relations with city government, the high-status respondents were less apt to go directly to City Hall with their individual dissatisfactions. Such behavior is understandable. Where representatives of the neighborhood carry on extensive communications with city officials, the need for individual residents to contact City Hall on their own can be expected to diminish. But when they live in neighborhood polities that have only limited relations with municipal authorities, individual residents may find more frequent occasions on which they have to contact city officials themselves. For high-status respondents, therefore, the more neighborhood contacts there are with City Hall, the less frequent the individual contacts with municipal government.

Among the low-status respondents the situation is different. Their tendency to complain directly to city government seems stronger in residential areas that carry on extensive diplomatic relations with City Hall than it is in more isolationist neighborhood polities. In this case high- and low-status residents respond in opposite ways to the same political conditions. The reason for their divergence is not clear, but two possible explanations seem at least plausible. In the first place, low-status residents are more likely than their high-status neighbors to lack the personal political advantages that allow them to establish direct contacts with City Hall. They may be uninformed, for example, about the appropriate municipal offices to which they can take their individual complaints, or timid about speaking for themselves to city officials. But when they live in neighborhoods that carry on extensive diplomatic relations with city government, they gain access to channels of communication that would otherwise lie beyond their reach. Exposure to the local political environment may help them to overcome obstacles that would normally prevent them from taking their personal dissatisfactions directly to municipal authorities. They may acquire information about the availability of particular city services, for example, or about the agencies to which they should address their complaints. High-status residents, no matter where they live, are more apt to possess the political confidence and information necessary to initiate their own direct contacts with municipal authorities. When their neighborhood does not carry on extensive diplomatic relations with city government, they can communicate with City Hall on their own — and that is what they seem to do. But low-status respondents may be more dependent on the political cues and encouragements provided by the neighborhood environment. When the neighhood as a whole is not actively represented at City Hall, low-status residents may lose the inclination or the means to represent themselves as individuals. Perhaps that is why their direct contacts with city government are less frequent in neighborhoods that lack extensive diplomatic relations with city government than in communities that dispatch frequent diplomatic missions to City Hall.

An alternative explanation for their behavior is that these neighborhood diplomatic missions represent the interests of some residents better than others. High-status residents, perhaps, can be confident that their own interests are being represented when emissaries of the neighborhood as a whole speak for the community at City Hall. In neighborhoods with active diplomatic spokesmen, therefore, high-status residents can afford to slacken their individual efforts to speak for their own interests. But the interests of high-status neighbors may be inconsistent with those of their low-status neighbors, and if these high-status interests are the ones being represented at City Hall, low-status residents may feel compelled to defend themselves by initiating their own contacts with municipal government. The more active the neighborhood's representatives are in communicating with city officials, the more active the low-status residents must be in looking out for their own interests at City Hall.

Whatever the explanation, it is at least evident that the relationship between individual contacts and neighborhood contacts with city government is more complex than might be suggested by the case of Canton. The representation of the neighborhood as a whole at City Hall is not necessarily undermined when individual residents represent themselves. Conversely, when individual residents refrain from taking their own complaints directly to municipal government, their diffidence does not consistently result in the emergence of active diplomatic representatives who speak to city officials on behalf of the neighborhood at large. The evidence does suggest that individual contacts and neighborhood contacts with city government are related to one another — but in different ways for residents of different social classes.

Roughly similar terms might be used to describe the connection between the political integration of neighborhoods and their diplomatic activism. In this case, however, it is not social class that complicates the relationship, but the fact that political integration has been measured in several different ways, and these various indicators are not uniformly associated with the extensiveness of diplomatic communications between neighborhoods and city officials. In fact, the only sign of political integration that bears any relationship to the diplomatic activism of a neighborhood is the absence of factionalism (gamma = .48). The emergence of a single dominant community organization, by contrast, has little to do with the pursuit of an active foreign policy. Neither does residents' political connectedness — the extent to which people are acquainted with neighborhood mobilizers.

Being politically disconnected or organizationally unconsolidated apparently constitutes no hindrance to the conduct of neighborhood diplomacy with outside authorities. But diplomatic contacts with City Hall do seem to be inhibited when fellow residents choose sides and fight with one another. Such factionalism may divert the attentions of local activists from the task of dealing with city officials to the difficulty of dealing with their own neighbors. Or perhaps city officials are inclined to shun neighborhoods where amicable contacts with one faction are apt to incur the hostility of another. In either case, factional conflict might reduce the extensiveness of contacts between neighborhood leaders and City Hall.

It is also worth considering whether the reverse might be true. Extensive contacts with outside authorities could conceivably reduce neighborhood factionalism. In Canton, after all, combat with outside authorities seemed to elicit a degree of neighborhood unity and harmony that was not always evident in more tranquil times, and sometimes even nonhostile relations with government officials seemed to contribute to the unity of the neighborhood. In her role as the area's legislative representative, for example, Barbara Mikulski more than once attempted to enhance the political integration and organization of Canton. Jeffrey Davidson reports similar occurrences in a study of relationships between neighborhoods and City Council representatives in Ann Arbor, Michigan.[16] These fragments of evidence give us some reason to believe that extensive diplomatic contacts with external authorities may foster neighborhood integration, and not just that political integration encourages diplomatic contacts.

There is a further reason to adopt this alternative view of the relationship between neighborhood diplomacy and political integration: it helps to make better sense of political integration itself. The various indicators of neighborhood political integration are not consistently related to one another, a fact that is reflected in the inconsistency of their relationships to diplomatic activism. Only some measures of integration seem to fit together in a sensible way. The absence of factionalism is associated with political connectedness of local residents (gamma = .66), and political connectedness is related in turn to the emergence of a single dominant community organization (.54). One might also expect that the emergence of a dominant neighborhood organization would be associated with the absence of factionalism, but this is not the case. There is no apparent connection between these two signs of political integration. Neighborhood foreign relations, however, may account for this unanticipated discontinuity.

Among neighborhoods that carry on extensive diplomatic relations with city government, the evidence shows that the presence of a dominant community organization *is* related to the absence of factionalism. Reports of factional conflict are less frequent for neighborhoods that have achieved organizational unity than for those that remain unconsolidated. But among the neighborhoods that seldom send diplomatic missions to City Hall, this relationship disappears. Almost all of the "isolationist" neighborhoods scored high on factionalism, whether they had achieved organizational unity or not.

Table 6.6 illustrates how reports of factionalism varied in different kinds of neighborhoods. The names marked with asterisks are the sample communities that scored high on factionalism, not in any absolute sense but in comparison to other sample neighborhoods.

Table 6.6. Organizational consolidation, diplomatic relations with city government, and factionalism in neighborhood (Asterisk indicates that the neighborhood scored high on factionalism)

High or medium score on index of diplomatic relations with city government		Low score on index of diplomatic relations with city government
High proportion of residents naming same community organization	Low proportion of residents naming same community organization	
Canton	Gardenville	Cedarcroft*
Hunting Ridge	Highlandtown	Coldstream-Homestead-
Raspeburg	Johnston Square*	Montebello*
Roland Park	Little Lithuania*	Dickeyville*
Ten Hills	Oliver	Easterwood*
Waverly	West Arlington*	Reservoir Hill*
	Walbrook*	Union Square*
		Upton
		Wakefield*

Relatively large proportions of the informants in these starred neighborhoods concurred completely with the statement that "different factions of residents often seem to disagree with one another about what's best for the area." The frequency of these reports of strife varies sharply among the three categories of neighborhoods identified in the table, and the variations suggest that the actions of city government—not just the internal attributes of the neighborhood itself—may help to determine whether residential areas will be politically unified or divided. Extensive dealings with city government seem to banish factional strife from neighborhoods where the attentions of local residents are concentrated on the same community organization. Among the six neighborhoods that combined organizational unity and active diplomacy, none scored high on factionalism. In these communities, perhaps, the need to face outside authorities increases the importance of internal harmony, and the existence of a single dominant community organization provides the mechanism for achieving this unity.

In neighborhoods where such organizational mechanisms are absent, dealings with city government may produce occasional factionalism. Of the seven neighborhoods that carried on active diplomatic relations with City Hall but lacked a single dominant community organization, four scored high on factionalism. In these cases, the involvement of city authorities in neighborhood politics may generate issues on which local residents can disagree, but there is no common organizational forum in which to adjust these factional differences.

Finally, eight neighborhoods did not conduct extensive dealings with municipal authorities. Seven of the eight scored high on factionalism. When there are few occasions to confront outside authorities, it seems, neighborhood unity dissolves. The existence of a single dominant community organization makes no difference for the likelihood of factionalism within these isolationist neighborhoods. Without the opportunity to focus their collective attentions on outside authorities, perhaps, neighborhood residents tend to concentrate on their disagreements with one another.

Neighborhood diplomatic activities supply the missing ingredient necessary to make sense of the relationship between neighborhood factionalism and organizational unity. The emergence of a single dominant community organization is associated with the resolution of factional differences for neighborhoods that conduct extensive foreign relations with city government. Where active diplomacy is absent, the relationship is also absent.

A consideration of neighborhood diplomatic activities therefore helps to clarify the character of political integration in neighborhoods. Some additional pieces of evidence help to clarify the nature of the diplomatic activities themselves. In the first place, neighborhoods appear to differ not only in the extensiveness of their contacts with city government but also in the kinds of contacts that they make. Some communities seem to gravitate toward administrative officials while others are drawn to elected officeholders, and political integration is one of the factors that seems related to the types of governmental ties that neighborhoods form. In particular, although the degree of organizational unity in neighborhoods does not predict the overall volume of their diplomatic communications with City Hall, it does have something to do with the kinds of city officials who hear from neighborhood leaders. Residential areas in which a single community organization has become dominant do exhibit a special propensity for dealing with officials of administrative agencies (gamma = .72). The emergence of one dominant organization to speak for a neighborhood may represent a significant administrative convenience that facilitates relationships between community representatives and bureaucratic officials. When neighborhoods are represented by several organizations (or by none at all) dealing with them threatens to become a controversial "political" matter that city administrators may prefer to avoid or to leave to elected officials.

Other conditions seem to be responsible for drawing neighborhoods into communication with elected officials. The most important determinant of frequent neighborhood contacts with City Council members, for example, is whether or not activists in local neighborhood organizations have ever run for elective office in state or local government (gamma = .88). Where community organizations have provided way stations in the political careers of elected officials or would-be elected officials, the neighborhood tends to concentrate its diplomatic activities among these same sorts of officials. The production of political candidates, however, is not accompanied by any tendency to carry on diplomatic relations with officials of administrative agencies. The evidence, in other words, suggests that a distinction between "political" and "administrative" neighborhoods might be added to the one that we have already made between diplomatically active and inactive neighborhoods.

The example of Canton suggests another kind of distinction that could be significant: whether relations with city officials are hostile. Conflicts with outside authorities appeared to trigger political cohesion and mobilization in Canton, and such hostility is an aspect of diplomatic relations with city government that could prove to be similarly important for neighborhood polities in general. But hostility of this kind seems infrequent — at least in Baltimore — and its significance for neighborhood polities is therefore limited. Informants from all the sample neighborhoods, after identifying the issue that they had discussed most with local residents, were asked whether people in the area had disagreed with city government about the matter. In no neighborhood did a majority of the informants say that residents had "disagreed a lot" with municipal authorities about the issue in question. Reports of friction with city government did tend to be concentrated in certain neighborhoods, but these neighborhoods were not grouped together in any particular political category. Amicable relations with city authorities were somewhat more common for neighborhoods where a single dominant community organization had emerged than for areas that lacked such organizations (gamma = .45), but the extensiveness of a neighborhood's diplomatic communications with municipal authorities did not have much to do with reports of friction or friendliness between the neighborhood and City Hall.

Hostilities with city government may have more to do with the internal communications of a neighborhood than with its external diplomacy. Each informant was asked not only about contacts with city officials but about communications with leaders of other institutions and organizations in the neighborhood — other community organizations, parent-teacher associations, church groups, and business people. Neighborhoods were graded for the extensiveness of their internal communications in the same way that they were scored for their diplomatic relations with municipal authorities. The evidence suggests that these internal communications among local groups and institutions tended to proliferate in residential areas where there were reports of disagreement with city government (gamma = .56). Internal contacts among neighborhood activists and institutions may reflect attempts to mobilize residential areas for fights with City Hall. These mobilization efforts may also influence membership rates in community organizations, which were consistently higher where there was antagonism toward city government than for neighborhoods that were not engaged in such hostilities.[17]

Canton's experience does seem to be mirrored in the political activities of other neighborhoods. Conflict with external authorities supplies an occasion for the internal mobilization of the neighborhood, but it is not associated with organizational unity or the resolution of intramural strife. In fact, there is some tendency for neighborhoods that fight with City Hall to experience internal fighting among factions of residents (gamma = .51). Political unity and integration are explained less by the occurrence of hostile relations with city government than by the mere extensiveness of any relations at all.

Carrying on extensive diplomatic contacts with outside authorities may of course diminish other political capabilities of neighborhoods. A preoccupation with external affairs could reduce the attention devoted to the management of internal affairs. Like Canton and Reservoir Hill, neighborhoods may specialize in either domestic or foreign policy. The conditions that lead to an emphasis on one may prevent the other from becoming prominent.

Some of the survey evidence seems to support this distinction between internally oriented and externally oriented neighborhoods. Informal direct action, for example, is least common in those residential areas that appear to conduct the most vigorous foreign policies—the ones that score high on both organizational unity and diplomatic contacts with city government. In these externally oriented neighborhoods, the residents—no matter what their social status—exhibited a slight disinclination to produce their own unofficial public services after informal discussions with their neighbors. But it was not the isolationist neighborhoods, as one might predict, where people became most active in these domestic affairs. Reports of informal direct action were most frequent in the neighborhoods that conducted active diplomatic relations with City Hall but had failed to achieve a high degree of organizational unity.[18]

Informal direct action is not related in a strong or straightforward way to the extensiveness of neighborhood diplomatic relations with city government. Neither is the occurrence of more formal efforts to generate unofficial public services in neighborhoods. All informants were asked whether they knew of any organizations in their communities (other than government organizations) that provided any of several different kinds of services—trash cleanups, recreational programs for young people, crime prevention, or services for the elderly. Neighborhoods were ranked according to the proportion of informants who could name local organizations that supplied each of the four types of services, and each neighborhood was assigned a score from 0 to 4 that corresponded to the number of these rankings in which it stood relatively high. A comparison of these scores with the ones for diplomatic activism shows that foreign entanglements do not diminish the capacity of a neighborhood to generate its own domestic services through local organizations. In fact, there is a slight but statistically insignificant tendency for neighborhoods with extensive contacts at City Hall to score high on the index of domestic services (gamma = .33). The explanation may be that diplomatic relations with city government are a necessary step toward receiving government grants, and neighborhoods where organizational informants reported that their groups had received public grants also tended to be neighborhoods where local groups generated extensive domestic services (.62). Homegrown public services appear to be sustained in many cases by foreign aid.

The Appearance of Power

The shape of the neighborhood polity is not fixed within the neighborhood itself. In several important respects it is formed through interactions with outside authorities, and the neighborhood by itself does not determine whether these external contacts will occur. City government is often responsible for initiating the foreign involvements of neighborhoods. This probably explains why some of the important organizational features of neighborhood polities have little to do with the internal lives of neighborhoods, with their social solidarity or homogeneity or stability. A neighborhood's organizational arrangements are its chief means for conducting foreign relations; thus, these arrangements may be especially sensitive to the influence of external factors, even when they are being used to generate domestic services.

The susceptibility of neighborhood organizations to the effects of outside circumstances is apt to create a constitutional division within the neighborhood polity. Some neighborhood political capabilities — the tendency to produce informal public services, for example — have much to do with the internal lives of residential areas. These internally oriented endowments of the neighborhood polity may be largely disconnected from the political capacities that neighborhoods display through formal community organizations, because the organizational capacities are developed and evoked by events that originate outside the community. The prevalence of informal direct action, for instance, is not systematically related to many of the activities that occur within formal community organizations. The propensity of local residents to manufacture their own informal public services after impromptu deliberations with one another has nothing to do with the manufacture of public services by formal organizations in the neighborhood. It also has little to do with the diplomatic activism of the neighborhood's institutional leaders. It is unrelated to overall membership rates in local community organizations, and virtually unrelated to reports of neighborhood factionalism, degrees of organizational unity, and most other organizational characteristics.

Briefly stated, the informal political interactions of neighbors do not represent a foundation for the development of formal political institutions. The same individual residents who engage in the informal activities are also likely to participate in the formal ones, but there is no strong and consistent relationship between the level of informal activity in the neighborhood as a whole and its pattern of organizational activity. This means that formal and informal activities do not depend heavily on one another, but it also means that they are not alternatives to one another. Neighborhoods are not neatly divided into those that specialize in carrying on foreign relations through formal community organizations and those that specialize in producing unofficial public services through informal arrangements among neighbors. Some neighborhoods do seem to concentrate on one or the other of these specialties, but they do not significantly outnumber the neighborhoods that engage in both patterns of activity or in neither.

Patterns of formal and informal activity, of course, cannot be translated directly into political power, and even though the internal life of the neighborhood may not be clearly reflected in local organizational arrangements, it may be responsible for investing these arrangements with the power to influence or resist municipal authorities. Measuring the power of neighborhoods with respect to outside authorities would require a careful assessment of the outcomes of those encounters in which the interests of city government collided with the interests of particular residential areas — as well as the nonencounters in which one or the other protagonist sidestepped a confrontation. No attempt has been made to gauge the power of neighborhoods in this way, but neighborhood informants were asked to offer their own assessments of their community's political standing in relation to city government. After examining a list of neighborhood groups and organizations, they were asked whether they thought that "city government agencies and administrators" were more important in the handling of neighborhood affairs than any of the local groups on the list, more important than most of them, or less important than most of them. Their responses to these inquiries certainly provide no adequate index of the power of the neighborhood, but they do reveal the prevailing perceptions of the political importance of neighborhood institutions as opposed to municipal institutions.

Local perceptions of neighborhood importance are related in a predictable way to several neighborhood characteristics — socio-economic status, for example. In high-status neighborhoods the political reputations of local institutions tend to outweigh the reputations of city agencies, but in low-status neighborhoods the political balance shifts toward the municipal institutions (gamma = .54). Neighborhood political reputations were also associated with certain signs of political integration. Where many residents were acquainted with people capable of mobilizing the neighborhood, the perceived power of local institutions was likely to be substantial. It was less substantial in neighborhoods where smaller fractions of residents were included in these political mobilization networks (.68). Surprisingly, the perceived influence of neighborhood polities was not related in a significant way to the organizational unity of neighborhoods or to the extensiveness of their relations with city government. But the classification scheme formed by combining both of these variables does seem to make sense of variations in the power reputations of neighborhoods. Residential areas that scored high on both organizational unity and diplomatic activism also tended to enjoy substantial political reputations. In only two of these six neighborhoods was the political importance of city officials seen to outweigh the importance of neighborhood institutions. At the other extreme, perceptions of neighborhood influence were least evident in residential areas that carried on extensive diplomatic relations with city government but lacked organizational unity. Municipal institutions were seen to dominate the neighborhood ones in five of the seven neighborhoods — including all those that suffered from high levels of factionalism. Between these two extremes were the neighborhoods that did not have extensive contacts with City Hall and whose ability to influence city government may not have been severely tested. They were evenly divided between those where municipal government was accorded political superiority and those where neighborhood institutions were perceived to have greater political importance.

Perceived neighborhood influence seems to depend on a combination of circumstances. It is most pronounced in neighborhoods that have achieved organizational unity and where active diplomacy has supplied plentiful opportunities to demonstrate the organizational capabilities of the neighborhood in dealings with city government. It is least pronounced where organizational unity has not been achieved and where extensive foreign relations with municipal authorities are likely to have disclosed the community's organizational and political deficiencies. In other words, the evidence suggests that the political reputation of a neighborhood may rest on its actual record of performance in dealing with external authorities.

But perceived neighborhood influence may also reflect the internal performance of the neighborhood — in particular, the kinds of political relationships that exist among its individual residents. Two different kinds of political connections are represented in Table 6.7. We have already considered them separately from one another. They had to do with "lateral" and "vertical" political integration. A neighborhood is vertically integrated when a relatively high proportion of its residents are acquainted with people who seem capable of mobilizing the entire neighborhood. Vertical integration therefore refers to the extent to which local inhabitants are "politically connected" with local leaders. Lateral integration, on the other hand, has to do with the extensiveness of political relationships among residents at large — the proportion of local inhabitants who discuss neighborhood affairs with their fellow residents.

The distribution of sample neighborhoods in the table shows that

Table 6.7. Lateral and vertical political integration of neighborhoods and their perceived influence in relation to city government (Asterisk indicates that neighborhood residents thought city agencies and administrators were more important than neighborhood groups and organizations)

Proportion of politically connected residents in neighborhood (vertical integration)	Proportion of residents who discussed local issues with neighbors (lateral integration)	
	High	Low
High	Dickeyville Gardenville Roland Park* Ten Hills Wakefield* Waverly*	Cedarcroft Highlandtown Hunting Ridge Raspeburg Upton
Low	Coldstream-Homestead- Montebello Little Lithuania* Union Square* West Arlington*	Canton Easterwood* Johnston Square* Oliver* Reservoir Hill Walbrook*

284 / Neighborhood Politics

some residential areas exhibited one form of political integration but not much of the other. In Union Square and Coldstream-Home-stead-Montebello, for example, relatively high proportions of residents reported that they had discussed neighborhood affairs with their neighbors (lateral integration), but relatively low proportions were politically connected with leaders who were thought capable of mobilizing the neighborhood to deal with important local issues (vertical integration). The neighborhoods marked by asterisks are the ones in which municipal authorities enjoyed relatively substantial political reputations. The most striking feature of the evidence is that starred neighborhoods are completely absent from one cell of the table. All the residential areas grouped in the upper right-hand corner of the table are places where the perceived influence of municipal institutions tended to be overshadowed by the perceived influence of neighborhood institutions. The neighborhoods that so consistently enjoy these favorable political reputations are not the ones that are most fully integrated—both vertically and laterally. Instead, they are residential areas where relatively high proportions of people are politically connected with local leaders but where relatively low proportions of the inhabitants are linked to one another by political discussion. A belief in the political importance of the neighborhood is found most consistently in residential areas that exhibit vertical but not lateral political integration.

Perhaps these neighborhoods enjoy their reputations for political importance in relation to city government because they are places where local leaders can command the attention of their constituents and do not have to contend with much talking in the ranks. Political discussion among local residents, as we have already seen, is associated with interpersonal friction. Such animosity may help to make neighborhoods politically unmanageable and reduce the effectiveness of local leaders as they attempt to represent the neighborhood in dealings with outside authorities. The absence of extensive political relationships among neighborhood residents may also contribute in other ways to the power of local leaders. Residents who do not discuss local matters with their neighbors may depend instead on the leaders that they recognize in the neighborhood for information about community issues, and they may rely heavily on these same leaders to resolve the problems that neighbors create for one another. Residents cannot resolve these problems among themselves, after all, if they seldom talk with one another. In general, the absence of lateral integration in neighborhood polities may enhance the position of neighborhood leaders in relation to their constituents, and for that reason it may also strengthen the position of these leaders when they speak for their neighborhoods at City Hall.

Once again the evidence implies that cohesiveness among neighbors does not necessarily enhance the neighborhood's political strength. But the findings also show more than this. They consistently suggest that neighborhood activism in the handling of internal affairs does not lead in any direct way to activism or strength in the conduct of foreign relations. It is true that individual residents who discuss local matters informally with their neighbors also tend to bring these matters to the attention of City Hall. But widespread informal discourse in a neighborhood does not mean widespread complaints for city officials. Nor does this sort of lateral integration provide a basis for formal community organizations that pursue active diplomatic relations with municipal authorities on behalf of neighborhood constituencies.

What is true of informal political discourse is also true of formal political action. Neighborhoods that are notable for generating unofficial public services do not exhibit any notable tendency to generate either individual or leadership contacts with municipal authorities. An active domestic policy, in other words, is not necessarily accompanied by a vigorous foreign policy. But this does not mean that domestic activism is associated with the avoidance of foreign entanglements. Neighborhoods that appear to be preoccupied with matters of internal regulation and order maintenance do not seem to be deterred from conducting extensive relations with external authorities. Although the political contrasts between Canton and Reservoir Hill suggest that neighborhoods may specialize in either domestic or foreign affairs, this pattern of specialization does not extend to the sample neighborhoods in general. Instead, the general pattern is one in which the internal functioning of neighborhood polities is largely disconnected from their external activism.

The likely explanation for this detachment is that neighborhood contacts with City Hall result not merely from the initiatives and inclinations of neighborhoods themselves but from the actions and policies of city government. In some respects, therefore, the character of a neighborhood polity may be shaped downtown. Municipal authorities may influence both the external affairs of neighborhoods and the neighborhood political activities that follow from these external linkages. The creation of diplomatic channels between city government and neighborhood spokesmen, for example, seems to be reflected in the frequency of contacts between individual residents and municipal authorities. The availability of these channels appears to increase the frequency of contacts for low-status residents but reduces it for high-status residents.

Diplomatic communications may also have something to do with the occurrence of factionalism in neighborhoods. They do not cause factional strife—at least not directly—but diplomatic dealings with city government may activate a neighborhood's potential for either unity or divisiveness. When a neighborhood is represented by a single dominant community organization, active foreign relations with city government seem to accentuate the tendency toward harmony. Factionalism is absent. But where no single organization has become prominent, diplomatic relations with municipal authorities appear to stimulate the neighborhood's propensity for strife.

Activism in foreign affairs does not necessarily mean strength. In fact, the perceived strength of a neighborhood's institutions in relation to city government has almost nothing to do with the extensiveness of its dealings with municipal officials. Such strength is one aspect of the neighborhood's relationship to external authorities that seems to be closely connected with the internal political characteristics of the residential area itself—specifically, its political integration. Reports of neighborhood strength were most widespread where political relationships among residents indicated a high degree of vertical integration and a relatively low degree of lateral integration. Stated simply, these are neighborhoods in which people are politically connected to local leaders, but not to one another. In such circumstances, leaders are likely to enjoy a special and relatively uncontested influence over their followers. Power relationships between neighborhoods and City Hall, in other words, may reflect the power relations and political inequalities that exist within neighborhoods themselves.

Conclusion

Hollins Street, Union Square. Photograph by Charlotte Crenson.

The Twelfth Annual Baltimore City Fair is held on three piers—now parking lots—that once stretched out to meet the world's shipping. The fair is a strenuously promoted celebration of the city's neighborhoods, and about seventy of them are on hand to be celebrated. Parallel rows of identical wood and canvas booths have been provided for the participating communities. Delegations from each of the seventy-odd neighborhood associations have been busy decorating and furnishing their assigned cubicles according to their own tastes and capabilities. When the three-day fair opens, a million visitors are expected to stroll past a miscellaneous assortment of neighborhood exhibits. Neighborhood representatives armed with pamphlets and leaflets look out at the passing crowd from the interior of each booth, waiting to explain themselves to strangers.

At the Canton exhibit a local artist's view of O'Donnell Square serves as a backdrop. The green-and-white flag of the Canton Improvement Association hangs from a table at the front of the booth. Other organizations from the neighborhood—Curry's Crusaders and Bill Kelch's Concerned Community of West Canton—have demobilized, and for the present, at least, the Improvement Association stands alone as the organizational representative of Canton. Some of its members are answering visitors' questions about a collection of neighborhood photographs displayed on either side of the booth. No more than twenty feet away, a delegation from Union Square is also surrounded by neighborhood snapshots, before-and-after pictures of nineteenth-century townhouses that have undergone rehabilitation. Representatives from the Union Square Association are busy selling homemade cookies, candies, and preserves to passers-by. In another row of exhibits, Willie Mae Davis presides over the Reservoir Hill booth, handing out pamphlets that explain the neighborhood's homeownership program and selling items that have been donated by her fellow residents. The booth carries a large stock of T-shirts and houseplants. The T-shirts carry a legend that advertises community aspirations: "Reservoir Hill — Climbing to the Top."

Not far away from the temporary stall where Mrs. Davis does business, there are shops where people who have already reached the top can buy designer T-shirts. The stores are housed in a new waterfront commercial development called Harborplace that now occupies the site of several previous city fairs. Even closer to Reservoir Hill's booth is the new Baltimore National Aquarium, where an indoor tropical rain forest, complete with animals, vies for attention with the neighborhood's houseplants.

Baltimore's celebration of neighborhood vitality goes on against a background of grander enterprises that have grown up in vigorous profusion, competing for space in an economically exuberant central business district. In addition to the Aquarium and Harborplace, a World Trade Center, a convention center, the Maryland Science Center, and a futuristic glass hotel have all recently been constructed on the harbor's fringe. Further from the waterfront, there are more hotels, office towers, theaters, luxury apartments, and stores soon to rise or already in place. Beneath the ground the tunnel for a new subway system edges foward under downtown streets, and under the water near the entrance to the Inner Harbor another tunnel is invisibly making a path for a new expressway.

By comparison with these great works downtown, the provincial enterprises of the city's neighborhoods seem merely charming. The big money and the big decisions are both being made at the center of the city, not in the residential communities that stretch out from the harbor along the stream valleys and over the hills to suburbia. In fact, it seems difficult to credit the commonplace claim that Baltimore is a city of strong neighborhoods when so much of the city's strength appears to be concentrated at its center. The resurrection of the central business distict reflects a resurgence of central power, and Baltimoreans generally acknowledge that the lines of local political authority, both legal and informal, converge at the City Hall office of the mayor.

Mayor William Donald Schaefer is an admirer of his late Chicago counterpart, Richard J. Daley: "I've always sort of suggested that I liked Mayor Daley . . . because [if] you went out to Chicago, [you saw] the city was alive, moving. He was a dynamic individual and he knew how to move a city . . . He had temporary employees for 18 years. When he wanted something done, they didn't have to monkey around. It was just done."[1] Like Mayor Daley, Mayor Schaefer denies that he himself is powerful: "The press says that I hold the power. I don't hold the power. There's an awful lot of people . . . that I get information from, listen to, am advised by . . . There is a tremendous amount of input. So this power is not there. The power is a conglomeration of a whole lot of things. Power, where's the great power? . . . I never really thought of it as being a powerful person. Let me put it another way: The mayor's office . . . is a powerful office, but I've got more constraints on me than you know . . . I make a move and the City Council moves."[2]

It is true that the mayor has had differences with individual members of the City Council, but when the council moves, it is almost always at the behest of the city's chief executive. It is also true that an "awful lot of people" supply a "tremendous amount of input" to the mayor, but they would hardly bother to do so if they thought the mayor lacked the power to act on their advice.

This power, as the mayor says, is a conglomeration of many things. One ingredient is state and federal grants, which now make up more than half of the city's annual budget; the mayor is widely credited with winning Baltimore's outsized share of money from Washington. A second important foundation for the mayor's authority has been the unwavering support of the local business community, organized for the purpose of civic action into the Greater Baltimore Committee. Finally, there is the compliance of the city's bureaucratic agencies, bent to the mayor's will and temper during his ten years in office. When put together, this conglomeration of things adds up to an executive-centered coalition — a pattern of mayoral influence and policy making first identified in Robert Dahl's study of New Haven and later elaborated by Robert Salisbury.[3] The pattern became fully developed in Baltimore only during the late 1970s, but in other cities it has usually been associated with the downtown urban renewal efforts of the 1950s and early 1960s. In this as in other things, Baltimore seems to have caught up with national trends only as they were passing.

This time, however, the city may have come out ahead by lagging behind. It achieved its centralization of power just as the apparent signs of political fragmentation, deterioration, and ungovernability were being recognized in cities elsewhere.[4] While other northeastern municipalities seemed to be losing control of themselves, Baltimore was gaining it. Its recent good fortune at the hands of the federal government and private investors probably reflects the fact that it acquired a reputation for political efficacy at a time when such reputations had become rare among urban governments.

It is uncertain whether Baltimore's competitive edge will survive the budget cuts of the Reagan adminstration, but the political centralization that helped to make the city a contender may outlast the present prosperity of the central business district. The current enhancement of mayoral authority has been written into the structure of local government. This institutionalization of central power is symbolized by the so-called Shadow Government of Baltimore — a complex network of quasi-public corporations financed by the city through two trustees appointed by the mayor. The corporations perform management and economic development functions that might normally be assigned to municipal agencies. But since they operate outside the legal limitations of the City Hall bureaucracy, they are also liberated from many of the inconveniences that might be imposed by civil service regulations, the city charter, and the City Council.[5] The accountability of this corporate system is defended by the mayor, who points out that all loans made to the corporations by the trustees must be approved at public meetings by the city's Board of Estimates. He does not point out that he controls three of the board's five votes.

As authority takes root downtown, the political prospects for neighborhoods seem to wither away. If the political vitality of Baltimore's residential communities has depended on the political limitations of its central institutions, then how can the neighborhoods be expected to fare when the center overcomes these limits? The current political doctrine in Baltimore holds that they fare very well. A local newspaper editorial announces that "Schaefer has made believers of those who once thought a city could not have *both* a Harborplace and strong neighborhoods where people are working and content."[6] The Mayor himself consistently expresses the belief that strong neighborhoods are essential to his ambitions for the city. When asked what he regards as the principal accomplishment of his ten years in office, there is no uncertainty in his response: "Neighborhoods. Neighborhoods and people . . . I'm positive that without neighborhoods, without people, and the word 'pride' in the city, we would not have moved as far as we have. Neighborhoods have improved themselves. Neighborhoods have developed a sense of pride. Neighborhoods are working."[7]

Neighborhood is next to motherhood is the political liturgy that accompanies Baltimore's ribbon cuttings and playground dedications. But the important place accorded to the city's residential communities is not merely an honorary one. The mayor, for example, has been known to spend many of his weekends cruising Baltimore's neighborhoods in his 1975 Pontiac, on the lookout for such things as unrepaired potholes and uncollected garbage. On Monday morning the appropriate city administrators receive mayoral memoranda informing them of what needs to be done. Budget allocations for neighborhood projects and housing rehabilitation add substance to the concern that is exhibited in the mayor's inspection visits.

Perhaps the mayor's professed devotion to neighborhoods reflects his own political origins. The dogged boosterism that he brings to City Hall seems to have taken shape when he was not yet a powerful presence in the central business district. Before it became a mayoral political style, it was a neighborhood style:

> I'd been working for years in improvement associations and I knew what positive improvement associations could do against negative improvement associations. I was in the [Allendale-Lyndhurst] Improvement Association years ago, and one of the things I remember talking about [was that] improvement associations shouldn't always be anti.
>
> We ought to be for something. We were against the gas station, we were against the zoning, we were against this. What are we for? We started to talk about the positive side and that was a long, long time ago.[8]

More than a hundred years ago Walter Bagehot pointed out how national temperament might originate in local convention. "A national character," he wrote, "is but the successful parish character; just as the national speech is but the successful parish dialect, the dialect, that is, of the district which came to be more — in many cases but a little more — influential than the other districts, and so it set its yoke on books and on society."[9] In a similar way, perhaps, the political culture of "successful" neighborhoods may tinge the political atmosphere of the city as a whole. Neighborhoods with "positive improvement associations," for example, may propel their leaders into citywide politics more frequently than those with "negative improvement associations," and the result is that the political attitudes and practices nurtured in certain neighborhoods begin to dominate the conduct of public business downtown.

This is one way to understand the Baltimorean belief that strong neighborhoods somehow stand behind the concentration of activity and power now evident at their city's center. But it is not an entirely adequate understanding. When Walter Bagehot wrote about parishes and nations, he had in mind a Darwinian process of natural selection in which the competition was among localities rather than species. But in a city—or a society—there is reason to wonder just how natural this selection process can be. It is not the law of the jungle that determines which neighborhoods will be the "successful" ones, but the established political and economic arrangements of the city itself. The survival of the fittest may serve as a metaphor for the struggle through which neighborhood polities eventually influence the character of the urban political system at large. But the struggle is one in which fitness may be defined by the very institutions that are supposed to be influenced. The neighborhood whose predispositions and capabilities are favored by citywide institutions will probably enjoy a competitive edge over the ones that are not so favored.

Neighborhoods, of course, may sometimes have it within their power to compel favor. They represent pressure groups as well as political cultures, and the model of pressure group politics provides another framework that may help to make sense of the supposed symbiosis between central authority and neighborhood strength in Baltimore. Although interest group politics is not normally regarded as a basis for political centralization, its contribution to central power becomes evident when one imagines politics without interest groups. In a study of Oakland, for example, Jeffrey Pressman found that the absence of such organized groups was one of the factors that added to the disjointedness of local politics and undermined the authority of the mayor.[10] Pressure groups help to structure political activity, and their existence facilitates the processes of bargaining, compromise, and coalition formation. Without them, urban executives may find it impossible to construct the political alliances that are essential preconditions for political authority.

The conception of neighborhood as interest group catches another facet of the political situation that has helped to solidify political power in the city. But it can make only limited sense of the relationship between neighborhood polities and central authority. The chief problem with this perspective is that neighborhoods seldom provide sufficiently sturdy foundations for organized interest groups. In fact, a number of community organizations whose leaders were interviewed for the present study had ceased to be active by the time the research was completed. Stable mayoral authority requires stable alliances, and mayors cannot form such alliances with organizations that threaten to fade away before the next election.

Not all neighborhood associations are ephemeral, but transience is common enough so that it raises questions about the status of neighborhoods as organized interest groups. This does not necessarily mean that neighborhood ties themselves are weak or transient. It signifies instead that these neighborly relationships do not have much to do with the character of community organizations or the extensiveness of their lobbying activities at City Hall. It usually takes some immediate threat to provoke the mobilization of a neighborhood as an organized interest group, and when the threat is seen to recede, the organization of the community often declines as well. This episodic ebb and flow of interest group activity is one of the things that has led Norman and Susan Fainstein to suggest that community groups are more properly regarded as political movements than as political organizations.[11]

Such neighborhood movements, according to the Fainsteins, can influence public authorities only under special conditions. In particular, they are apt to be politically successful only when they have been able to cultivate allies among the public officials themselves. A city agency is not likely to give way to the demands of a community group, for example, unless the group has an administrative advocate to speak for its interests in internal deliberations among bureaucratic decision makers — someone to overcome official resistance to proposed policy changes.[12] Looked at from the perspective of the administrators, the situation is one in which a temporary, neighborhood-based constituency can provide some bureaucrats with the political leverage that they need to overcome the opposition of other bureaucrats in intramural fights about the conduct of agency business.

The bureaucratic infighting that helps to enhance the political status of neighborhood groups cannot be expected to occur frequently or to last very long in a city where the mayor has established firm central control of municipal administration. This may not prevent neighborhood groups from forming alliances with bureaucratic officials, but it will transform the nature of those alliances. Instead of contributing to the resolution of conflicts within bureaucratic agencies, neighborhood groups may help bureaucracies to avoid conflicts with their external constituencies. Agencies can attempt to sidestep trouble by coopting the groups that exhibit troublemaking capabilities or inclinations. The mismatch in political resources between a cohesive city bureaucracy and a neighborhood-based coalition of part-time amateurs makes cooptation a likely outcome whenever the two confront one another.[13] Government grants, public services, personal favors, special attention to neighborhood problems, or even the prestige that comes from associating with high government officials may all help to turn neighborhood leaders into allies of officialdom.

The frequency of these occurrences does not show that neighborhoods are powerless as organized interest groups. The benefits of being cooperative, after all, are sometimes substantial, and they can provide the resources needed to overcome the organizational instability that is characteristic of neighborhood groups. Moreover, public officials would hardly go to the trouble of coopting interest groups if they thought them powerless. But it is not as coopted interest groups that Baltimore's neighborhoods seem to make their principal contributions to the consolidation of political authority in the city at large. Many neighborhoods, as we have seen, do not have close or extensive contacts with municipal officials; many of the communities that do maintain these relationships are so factionalized or politically incoherent that it is unclear just who should be coopted. In general, neighborhood interest groups can provide only a limited and uncertain footing for the development of central power, and in any case, a wide variety of studies suggest that interest group politics is not especially prominent in cities.[14]

Baltimore's neighborhood polities enhance the authority of the city's leadership not so much because of the organized backing that they provide but because they help to ensure that the task of leadership itself remains a manageable one. Governing cities has become a frenetic business in which policy makers are likely to be confronted with such a disparate variety of urgent and disconnected problems that they rarely have the opportunity to make policy. A hundred street-level crises converge on City Hall from different directions. In the process of dealing with them, the attentions and energies of government officials disintegrate. The ability to pursue large enterprises or to move city government toward some coherent purpose is likely to disappear in the face of numerous and immediate distractions. As Douglas Yates points out, "it is precisely because urban policy makers must deal with so many different, fragmented problem and policy contexts that urban policy making as a whole is so fragmented, unstable, and reactive." In an ordinary week, central decision makers may have to cope in succession with problems of violence in the schools, arson in abandoned buildings, vandalism in a public park, complaints about broken street lights or uncollected garbage or a new X-rated movie theater, a threatened strike by public employees, possible budget overruns in a city housing program, and more. Because so many of these disjointed matters demand the immediate attention of urban executives, says Yates, cities become increasingly ungovernable.[15]

The operations of neighborhood polities can help to protect municipal officials from the cities that they are attempting to govern. Some portion — we cannot say how large — of the discordant business that would normally fracture the energies of urban policy makers is disposed of instead through the extemporaneous assemblies and the informal executive powers of residential communities. Where these unheralded political institutions operate vigorously, the official decision makers at City Hall may enjoy sufficient breathing space to plan for large-scale undertakings that extend beyond the end of the week. The centrifugal tendencies in city government, arising in part from the need to deal with an infinity of disconnected problems, are likely to grow less pronounced. Municipal executives like Mayor Schaefer might then find it easier to consolidate their authority over City Hall than they would if their subordinates were continually being drawn in different directions by a proliferation of urgent distractions. It is in this way that Baltimore's neighborhoods have probably made their most significant contributions to the growth of central authority in their city. By handling a multiplicity of small matters, they help to create a political environment in which it is possible for government decision makers to be important.

They perform other functions too. Some neighborhoods have undoubtedly emerged as powerful, organized interest groups whose cooperation and support are sought by politicians and administrators. Others may have served as training grounds for citywide political leaders. But more fundamental than either of these functions is the service that the neighborhood does as a Lockean "political society," preparing and preserving a site for the exercise of government authority. It is not quite the political society that Locke himself had in mind. It does not embrace the society as a whole; it does not necessarily preexist government; it does not cease work when government begins. Perhaps most important, it does not exhibit the unity or equality that Locke imagined to exist in his political society. Diversity and friction, in fact, sometimes make it function more vigorously than social uniformity and friendship. The results of other recent research efforts seem to point in the same general direction. Inequality, according to Jane Mansbridge, is not necessarily inimical to democracy; in some political circumstances it may actually be appropriate. As for friendship ties, Claude Fischer acknowledges that personal bonds may develop only occasionally in urban neighborhoods, but this does not mean that local residents are unengaged or socially subnormal. It may simply signify that they have chosen to exercise their "freedom from proximity" by seeking sociability further from home, while forming more utilitarian relationships with their neighbors.[16]

The general implication is that social groups do not need internal solidarity or homogeneity in order to function. Neither does political society. In cities, not surprisingly, it tends to exhibit the impersonality and internal diversity associated with urbanism itself. The appearance of these urbane attributes does not indicate that city residents have lost the capacity for social intimacy but rather that they have gained a capacity to deal with non-intimates or strangers who may be sharply different from themselves.[17] The "political society" of the urban neighborhood depends heavily on the exercise of such cosmopolitan talents, and for this reason it may seem far removed form Locke's vision of the political arrangements that were supposed to have been made by primitives in a state of nature.

In fact, the urbane version of political society has much in common with Locke's way of thinking. His strenuous effort to distinguish political relationships from the intimate web of family and kinship ties endowed his political society with an impersonality that anticipates life in the big city. A commonwealth, Locke conceded, might sometimes grow out of a single family, but it could just as easily have its beginnings in a variety of families, "whom Chance, Neighborhood, or Business brought together." Social intimacy could not be a prerequisite for Locke's political society. It had to accommodate the featureless strangers who happened to wander in from the state of nature. They might be drawn together, of course, by the desire for social solidarity — "the love, and want of Society" — but Locke noted that they were also prompted to incorporate by the "inconveniencies" of their prepolitical state, and the most significant of these was the enmity that repeatedly caused open conflict among them.[18]

Locke seems to have recognized that a measure of diversity and contention were essential ingredients for political society. If human beings were all pretty much alike, and united by bonds of personal friendship, there would be little occasion for politics. Impersonality and diversity, in other words, are not merely consistent with the functioning of Locke's political society, they may actually provide reasons for its formation. There may be similar reasons for the "political society" of the urban neighborhood. The inconveniences that arise from impersonality and diversity in big cities can inhibit the formation of close personal relationships among neighbors but also contribute to a tendency for neighborhoods to become political units. The work done by these units is consistent with the kind that Locke imagined. His political society was supposed to rise up from an ungovernable state of nature to create the possibility of government. In less primordial circumstances, the political societies of neighborhoods may do the same sort of thing. In cities that are alleged to be ungovernable, neighborhood polities can help to make government possible.

City government may be expected to have a complementary interest in making neighborhood polities possible. Support for policies of decentralization among municipal officials is probably one reflection of this interest. In some instances, central authorities have exhibited a remarkable readiness to delegate decision-making powers to neighborhood institutions. Their willingness to do so does not signify that urban executives are so indifferent to the importance of their own powers that they would casually surrender them to amateurs in the provinces. Instead, they seem to regard decentralization as a means for avoiding some of the localized troubles that incessantly interrupt the orderly conduct of business at headquarters and hamper the exercise of central authority. They delegate authority to a host of small-time operators in the hope that they will have more opportunities to behave like big-time operators themselves.

There is certainly some basis for these hopes. Analysts like Douglas Yates, in fact, have recommended decentralization as a way of providing relief to overburdened city governments.[19] Neighborhood organizations can serve as vehicles for the delivery of public services, and simplify the work of some public agencies in the process. City officials may find it easier to learn about neighborhood problems through discussions with a recognized community group than to hear about them through angry and disjointed telephone calls from a hundred unorganized residents. These are the kinds of administrative conveniences that may sometimes be realized through neighborhood-based organizations. Other objectives of decentralization seem much less certain of achievement—the hope, for example, that disadvantaged people and neighborhoods will be better represented in a politically decentralized than in a politically centralized city. Any such claims for neighborhood-based organizations must contend with evidence that high-status people are more likely to participate in neighborhood groups than low-status people, that the institutions of high-status neighborhoods are generally reputed to be more powerful than those of low-status neighborhoods, and that high-status neighborhoods are more likely to achieve organizational unity than low-status neighborhoods. Decentralization achieved through community organizations would probably accentuate existing political inequalities between rich neighborhoods and poor neighborhoods.[20]

Moreover, this loss in political equality might not be offset by any compensating gain in the governability of the city. It is a mistake to assume that the strengthening of neighborhood organizations amounts to the same thing as the strengthening of neighborhoods. The operations of neighborhood associations have little to do with the more widespread, informal efforts of neighborhood residents at large to resolve local differences among themselves or to generate their own unofficial public services. These activities — essential to the governability of a city — do not seem to be distinctive of well-organized neighborhoods. In fact, such informal governance is occasionally associated with signs of disorganization in neighborhoods. This does not mean that city government should seek to sow dissension in neighborhoods as a way of stimulating the public service activities of their residents. But city government is not powerless to encourage these activities, either. Official attempts to foster unofficial public service activities need not bother with the impossible task of making neighbors love one another. Nor does it seem important, for this purpose, to mobilize residents through community organizations. Nurturing social bonds and social groups may seem a necessary step toward overcoming the loss of community that is supposed to be characteristic of big cities, but the evidence suggests that such measures would not significantly strengthen the informal governance of neighborhoods.[21] In the first place, a number of studies have shown that communitarian social ties persist even in cities; community has not been lost, only underestimated.[22] In the second place, these communitarian social ties are largely unrelated to the public service efforts of neighborhood residents. To encourage people to look after public order, public sanitation, and public safety within their residential areas, it is not necessary to convert urban neighborhoods into villagelike fellowships.

Students of urban society have been making similar observations for some time now. Neighborhood vitality, according to Jane Jacobs, was engendered by the diversity, not the unity, of a residential area. In a study of the community press, Morris Janowitz showed how the maintenance of community identity might be achieved by a handful of local "specialists," without the organized support of the local population at large.[23] Both lines of investigation suggested that the urban neighborhood was not held together by communalism of the traditional sort, and both seemed to express vaguely similar notions about the kinds of forces that actually did help to sustain neighborhoods. Diversity and specialization could very well be different manifestations of the same phenomenon. Specialization, after all, is a form of diversity, and both of these things could also be reflections of a third aspect of neighborhood structure — inequality. This is the correlate of specialization and diversity that has emerged in the present investigation as a critical feature of neighborhood polities.

The residents who seem most frequently to become "specialists" in informal governance are relatively rich people who live in relatively poor neighborhoods. They are exposed to the aggravations of life in disadvantaged communities; their own educational, economic, and occupational advantages may increase their ability to respond to these inconveniences through informal political action; the value of their political advantages is not diluted by the presence of many other people who possess the same advantages. In short, they have the makings of power, and they seem inclined to exercise it, in an informal way, to support the public order, health, and safety of the neighborhoods where they live.

It may be argued, of course, that such people are also inclined to exercise power over their less fortunate neighbors — as they unquestionably do when they complain successfully to fellow residents about unruly children or an unsanitary backyard. Informal governance of this kind might simply add another indignity to the burdens already suffered by disadvantaged people living in disadvantaged neighborhoods. What needs to be added to such arguments, however, is the recognition that the economically disadvantaged residents of cities are not simply people with loud children and messy backyards. Probably far more numerous than these are low-income people who express serious concern about the order, cleanliness, and safety of their neighborhoods but lack the political wherewithal to do much about these matters.

Objections to inequality *within* neighborhood polities should also be weighed against the more serious inequalities that exist *between* residential areas. Achieving equality among people in a disadvantaged community does not diminish the disadvantages of living there. It may very well aggravate them. The income restrictions imposed on residents of public housing projects inadvertently produce a similar sort of neighborly equality. But it does not seem to make public housing more livable.[24] Equality of condition among the residents of a poor neighborhood creates an illusory sort of democracy. It contributes nothing to the self-governing capabilities of the neighborhood. It therefore does nothing to narrow the disparity in living conditions between poor neighborhoods and more prosperous ones; in fact, these differences probably grow wider.

The inequalities that result when relatively rich people live in relatively poor neighborhoods may be preferable to the ones that occur when rich people live only in rich neighborhoods. Having prosperous neighbors does not increase the incomes or educations of poor people; inequality close at hand is still inequality. But inequality close at hand is more useful than inequality at a distance, because it can enhance the political capabilities of the neighborhood as a whole — perhaps those of the city itself. Efforts at informal governance are most extensive among high-status people who are surrounded by low-status neighbors. The examples of Union Square and Reservoir Hill suggest that the informal public service activities of the low-status neighbors themselves may also be stimulated under these circumstances. These activities may be prompted in part by the annoyances that come from living in poor neighborhoods, but the evidence indicates that the awareness of these problems, by itself, is not sufficient to explain why people become unofficial public servants. The tendency toward informal governance also seems to depend on the possession of informal power — the kind of power, for example, that is available to rich people who live in poor neighborhoods. Power is just as essential to the development of a neighborhood polity as to the construction of an executive-centered coalition at City Hall.

In neighborhoods the exercise of informal power often seems to create a commotion, even though its aim may be to create order. The unofficial production of public goods tends to occur against a background of personal friction, not personal solidarity, and the result may be that the same neighborhoods that produce widespread efforts at unofficial governance may also generate disputes requiring the intervention of city officials. Rich people who live in poor neighborhoods, after all, are not only most inclined toward informal public service but also most inclined to contact municipal government about local problems. Residents who take matters into their own hands may therefore be people who increase the burdens of City Hall instead of reducing them. But they are also people who tend to engage in informal political discourse with their neighbors, and the evidence shows that the more widespread these neighborhood discussions become, the less likely it is that local residents will take neighborhood problems to City Hall.

Municipal government and disadvantaged neighborhoods may both gain something when relatively rich people move into relatively poor neighborhoods. The problem, of course, is that most rich people apparently do not perceive that they have anything to gain by living in these neighborhoods, and it is therefore useless to recommend that they should do so. The answer to such objections is that there are already relatively prosperous people living in relatively poor neighborhoods, and even more significant is the fact that many of them have taken up residence in decaying inner-city neighborhoods as a result of deliberate government policies. The inducement of low-cost housing or low-interest loans has been sufficient to convince some people of relatively high status to move into neighborhoods where high-status residents were — and still are — a minority. Government tax, housing, and zoning policies could contribute further to this movement.[25] Public policies of this kind can hardly be expected to reverse or counterbalance the flow of middle-class city residents to suburbia. But "gentrification" is not the object in any case. To enhance the informal capabilities of neighborhood polities, is is not necessary that all rich people move to poor neighborhoods, or that poor neighborhoods be converted into rich ones. Relatively modest changes in the social composition of urban neighborhoods can be expected to make a difference.

Just how much difference remains uncertain. We know, for example, that variations in neighborhood political culture cannot be completely determined by variations in the social composition of residential areas. The political strengths and weaknesses of some neighborhoods may not change significantly with changes in population characteristics. It is also difficult to say just what benefits can be expected to result from increases in the unofficial public service efforts of neighborhood residents. Informal governance should certainly enhance the public order, safety, and cleanliness of neighborhoods, but the available evidence does not tell us how much improvement occurs when neighbors attempt to produce their own informal public services. What the evidence does suggest is that public authorities who are seriously interested in increasing "voluntarism" and self-help among city residents, and the governability of cities themselves, should also be seriously interested in increasing the social and racial integration of city neighborhoods.

Certain kinds of social diversity help to create public order rather than disorder. It is not the kind of order that we have traditionally associated with the intimate society of the small village. It does not rest on bonds of sentiment and friendship, it does not depend on mutual affection and harmony, and it does not require equality. It is remarkably like the kind of order that existed in the various wards of Baltimore more than a hundred years ago, when the presence of neighborhood notables contributed to development of vigorously functioning systems of unofficial governance in each residential area. "Each ward," says Joseph Arnold, "was virtually a separate little town having almost the full range of income, ethnic, and racial groups to be found in the entire city."[26] From this urban diversity came the spirited public life of the neighborhood of the Civil War era. The conditions that converted neighborhoods into polities, and residents into citizens, are the same today as they were then.

Notes
Index

Notes

1. The Neighborhood as a Polity

1. Baltimore *Sun*, February 20, 1979.

2. Ibid., February 21, 1979.

3. Ibid., February 20, 1979; Baltimore *Evening Sun*, February 22, 1979.

4. Norton Long, *The Unwalled City* (New York: Basic Books, 1972), pp. 51-52.

5. See Richard Rich, "Equity and Institutional Design in Urban Service Delivery," *Urban Affairs Quarterly*, 12 (1977), 390.

6. Milton Kotler, *Neighborhood Government: The Local Foundations of Political Life* (Indianapolis: Bobbs-Merrill, 1969), p. 8.

7. Alexis de Tocqueville, *Democracy in America*, trans. Henry Reeve, 2 vols. (New York: Vintage Books, 1954), I, 198.

8. See Gabriel Almond and G. Bingham Powell, *Comparative Politics: A Developmental Approach* (Boston: Little, Brown, 1966).

9. Lucy Mair, *Primitive Government*, (Baltimore: Penguin Books, 1962), chap. 3.

10. Kotler, *Neighborhood Government*, pp. 3-5.

11. H. H. Gerth and C. Wright Mills, *From Max Weber: Essays in Sociology* (New York: Oxford University Press, 1958), p. 78.

12. Isaac Schapera, *Government and Politics in Tribal Societies* (London: Watts, 1963), p. 119.

13. Gerald Suttles, *The Social Construction of Communities* (Chicago: University of Chicago Press, 1972), p. 190.

14. See Alfred Radcliffe-Brown, *Structure and Function in Primitive Society* (New York: Free Press of Glencoe, 1963); Almond and Powell, *Comparative Politics;* Robert MacIver, *The Web of Government* (New York: Macmillan, 1947).

15. Almond and Powell, *Comparative Politics*, p. 18.

16. David Easton, *A Framework for Political Analysis* (Englewood Cliffs, N.J.: Prentice-Hall, 1965), pp. 50-54.

17. Ibid., p. 52.

18. See Peter Rossi and William Dentler, *The Politics of Urban Renewal: The Chicago Findings* (New York: Free Press of Glencoe, 1961); J. Clarence Davies III, *Neighborhood Groups and Urban Renewal* (New York: Columbia University Press, 1966); Richard Cole, *Citizen Participation and the Urban Policy Process* (Lexington, Mass.: Lexington Books, 1974); Matthew Crenson, "Organizational Factors in Citizen Participation," *Journal of Politics*, 36 (1974), 356-378.

19. See J. David Greenstone and Paul Peterson, *Race and Authority in Urban Politics: Community Participation and the War on Poverty* (New York: Russell Sage Foundation, 1973); Theodore Lowi, *The End of Liberalism*, 2d ed. (New York: W. W. Norton, 1979); Curt Lamb, *Political Power in Poor Neighborhoods* (New York: Schenkman, 1976), chap. 8.

20. Mary Parker Follett, *The New State* (New York: Longmans, 1918); Alan Altshuler, *Community Control: The Black Demand for Participation in Large American Cities* (New York: Pegasus, 1970); Douglas Yates, *Neighborhood Democracy: The Political Impacts of Decentralization* (Lexington, Mass.: Lexington Books, 1973); Kotler, *Neighborhood Government*.

21. Tocqueville, *Democracy in America*, II, 123-125.

22. See Max Weber, *Theory of Social and Economic Organization*, trans. A. M. Henderson and Talcott Parsons (New York: Free Press of Glencoe, 1964); Robert H. Lowie, *The Origin of the State* (New York: Russell and Russell, 1964); Sir Henry Maine, *Ancient Society*, ed. Leslie A. White (Cambridge, Mass.: Belknap Press of Harvard University Press, 1964).

23. Georges Balandier, *Political Anthropology*, trans. A. M. Sheridan Smith (New York: Pantheon Books, 1970), pp. 133-134.

24. Mair, *Primitive Government*, p. 11.

25. Easton, *A Framework for Political Analysis*, p. 52; Siegfried Nadel, *The Foundations of Social Anthropology* (New York: Free Press of Glencoe, 1958), p. 187.

26. See, for example, Charles M. Tiebout, "A Pure Theory of Local Expenditures," *Journal of Political Economy*, 64 (1956), 416-424.

27. John Locke, *Second Treatise of Government*, ed. Thomas P. Peardon (Indianapolis: Bobbs-Merrill, 1952), p. 54.

28. Ibid., p. 44.

29. Ibid., pp. 73-74.

30. Ibid., p. 122.

31. Ibid., p. 126.

32. Jeffrey Pressman and Aaron Wildavsky, *Implementation* (Berkeley: University of California Press, 1973).

33. Robert Alford, *Health Care Politics: Ideological and Interest Group Barriers to Reform* (Chicago: University of Chicago Press, 1975).

34. James S. Coleman et al., *Equality of Educational Opportunity*, 2 vols. (New York: Arno Press, 1979); Christopher Jencks, *Inequality: A Reassessment of the Effect of Family and Schooling in America* (New York: Basic Books, 1972).

35. James Q. Wilson, *Thinking about Crime* (New York: Basic Books, 1975); George L. Kelling et al. *The Kansas City Preventive Patrol Experiment* (Washington: Police Foundation, 1975).

36. See Matthew Holden, "The Politics of Urbanization," in Harlan Hahn (ed.), *People and Politics in Urban Society* (Beverly Hills, Cal.: Sage Publications, 1972), pp. 557-578; Norton Long, "The City as Reservation," *Public Interest*, no. 25 (Fall 1971), 22-38; George Sternlieb, "The City as Sandbox," *Public Interest*, no. 25 (Fall 1971), 14-21.

37. Edward C. Banfield, *The Unheavenly City Revisited* (Boston: Little, Brown, 1974); Jay W. Forrester, *Urban Dynamics* (Cambridge, Mass.: MIT Press, 1969).

38. Banfield, *The Unheavenly City Revisited*, pp. 1-2.

39. Sheldon Wolin, *Politics and Vision* (Boston: Little, Brown, 1961), pp. 307-308; see also C. B. McPherson, *The Political Theory of Possessive Individualism: Hobbes to Locke* (Oxford: Clarendon Press, 1962).

40. William C. Baer, "On the Death of Cities," *Public Interest*, no. 45 (Fall 1976), pp. 3-19.

41. William F. Whyte, *Streetcorner Society*, 2d ed. (Chicago: University of Chicago Press, 1955); Herbert Gans, *The Urban Villagers* (New York: Free Press of Glencoe, 1962); Elliott Liebow, *Tally's Corner* (Boston: Little, Brown, 1967); Gerald Suttles, *The Social Order of the Slum* (Chicago: University of Chicago Press, 1968).

42. Joel Smith, William H. Form, and Gregory P. Stone, "Local Intimacy in a Middle-Sized City," *American Journal of Sociology*, 60 (1954), 276-284; Aida K. Tomah, "Informal Group Participation and Residential Patterns," *American Journal of Sociology*, 70 (1964), 28-35; Phillip Fellin and Eugene Litwak, "Neighborhood Cohesion under Conditions of Mobility," *American Sociological Review*, 29 (1963), 365-376, Scott Greer and Peter Orleans, "The Mass Society and the Parapolitical Structure," *American Sociological Review*, 27 (1962), 634-646.

43. Anne Tyler, *The Clock Winder* (New York: Knopf, 1974).

44. Sherry Olson, *Baltimore* (Cambridge, Mass.: Ballinger, 1976), p. 11.

45. Suzanne Keller, *The Urban Neighborhood* (New York: Random House, 1968), p. 99.

46. Joseph L. Arnold, "The Neighborhood and City Hall: The Origin of Neighborhood Associations in Baltimore," *Journal of Urban History*, 6 (1979), 3-4.

47. Council on Municipal Performance, "City Hall Ears," *COMP News*, no. 3 (April 19, 1976).

48. Keller, *The Urban Neighborhood*, pp. 98-99.

49. H. L. Ross, "The Local Community: A Survey Approach," *American Sociological Review*, 27 (1962), 77.

50. Albert Hunter, *Symbolic Communities: Persistence and Change in Chicago's Residential Communities* (Chicago: University of Chicago Press, 1974), p. 77.

51. Council on Municipal Performance, "City Hall Ears."

52. Olson, *Baltimore*, p. 11.

53. Joseph Arnold, "The Neighborhood and City Hall"; Joseph Garonzik, "The Racial and Ethnic Make-up of Baltimore Neighborhoods, 1850-1870," *Maryland Historical Magazine*, 71 (1976), 392-402.

54. Joseph L. Arnold, "The History of Urban Development in Baltimore," paper presented at Baltimore Neighborhood Expo Conference, Baltimore Neighborhood Design Center, October 10, 1975.

55. Samuel P. Hays, "The Changing Political Structure of the City," *Journal of Urban History*, 1 (1974), 16.

56. William J. Evitts, *A Matter of Allegiances — Maryland from 1850 to 1861* (Baltimore: Johns Hopkins University Press, 1974), chap. 4.

57. James Crooks, "The Baltimore Fire and Baltimore Reform," *Maryland Historical Magazine*, 65 (1970), 11; see also Eleanor Bruchey, "The Industrialization of Maryland, 1860-1914," in Richard Walsh and William Lloyd Fox, eds., *Maryland: A History, 1632-1974* (Baltimore: Maryland Historical Society, 1974), pp. 406-407.

58. Eleanor Bruchey, "The Development of Baltimore Business, 1880-1914," *Maryland Historical Magazine*, 64 (1969), 32.

59. Charles Hirschfeld, *Baltimore, 1870-1900 — Studies in Social History* (Baltimore: Johns Hopkins University Press, 1941), pp. 45, 53.

60. Jean Baker, *The Politics of Community: Maryland Political Parties from 1858 to 1870* (Baltimore: Johns Hopkins University Press, 1973), p. 12n. One family of the period did have combined assets of more than a million dollars, but no individual Baltimorean is known to have accumulated so much wealth.

61. Bruchey, "The Development of Baltimore Business," p. 155; see also Alan Anderson, *The Origin and Resolution of an Urban Crisis: Baltimore, 1890-1930* (Baltimore: Johns Hopkins University Press, 1977).

62. See Hays, "The Changing Political Structure of the City"; Robert Wiebe, *The Search for Order, 1877-1920* (New York: Hill and Wang, 1967).

63. James B. Crooks, *Politics and Progress: The Rise of Urban Progressivism in Baltimore, 1895-1911* (Baton Rouge: Louisiana State University Press, 1968); Joseph Arnold, "The Last of the Good Old Days: Politics in Baltimore, 1920-1950," *Maryland Historical Magazine*, 71 (1976), 443-448.

64. Arnold, "The Neighborhood and City Hall," p. 6.

65. On the political effects of absentee ownership, see Robert O. Schulze, "The Bifurcation of Power in a Satellite City," in Morris Janowitz, ed., *Community Political Systems* (New York: Free Press of Glencoe, 1961), pp. 19-80.

66. Russell Baker, "The Biggest Baltimore Loser of All Time," *New York Times Magazine*, October 21, 1973, p. 35.

67. Quoted in Olson, *Baltimore*, pp. 89-90.

68. Baker, "The Biggest Baltimore Loser of All Time," p. 34.

69. Keller, *The Urban Neighborhood*, p. 12.

70. Suttles, *The Social Construction of Communities*, p. 12.

71. Ibid.; see also Lee Rainwater, *Behind Ghetto Walls* (Chicago: Aldine Press, 1970); Hunter, *Symbolic Communities*.

72. Suttles, *The Social Construction of Communities*, pp. 13, 51-52, 54.

73. Ibid., p. 50.

74. David Easton, *A Systems Analysis of Political Life* (New York: John Wiley, 1965), p. 176.

2. Local Political Climates

1. Norman G. Rukert, *Historic Canton* (Baltimore: Bodine and Associates, 1978), p. 18.

2. D. Randall Beirne, "Residential Growth and Stability in the Baltimore Industrial Community of Canton During the Late Nineteenth Century," *Maryland Historical Magazine*, 74 (1979), 39-51.

3. Ibid.; Rukert, *Historic Canton*, pp. 45-46.

4. Baltimore *Sun*, September 7, 1923; May 11, 1924; Rukert, *Historic Canton*, p. 85.

5. Baltimore *News-American*, September 26, 1971.

6. Hunter, *Symbolic Communities*, pp. 72ff.

7. On compositional (or contextual) effects, see Peter Blau, "Structural Effects," *American Sociological Review*, 25 (1960), 178-193; James A. Davis, Joe L. Spaeth, and Carolyn Huson, "A Technique for Analyzing the Effects of Group Composition," *American Sociological Review*, 26 (1961), 215-226; Robert M. Hauser, "Context and Consex: A Cautionary Tale," *American Journal of Sociology*, 75 (1970), 645-664; George Farkas, "Specification, Residuals, and Contextual Effects," *Sociological Methods and Research*, 2 (1974), 333-363.

8. Leonard Cottrell, Jr., Albert Hunter, and James F. Short, Jr., eds., *Ernest Burgess on Community, Family, and Delinquency* (Chicago: University of Chicago Press, 1973), pp. 42-44.

9. Eshref Shevky and Wendell Bell, *Social Area Analysis* (Stanford, Cal.: Stanford University Press, 1955); see also Scott Greer, *The Emerging City* (New York: Free Press of Glencoe, 1962), pp. 41ff.

10. Harvey Molotch, "Capital and Neighborhood in the United States: Some Conceptual Links," *Urban Affairs Quarterly*, 14 (March, 1979), 289-312.

11. Albert Hunter, "The Urban Neighborhood: Its Analytical and Social Context," *Urban Affairs Quarterly*, 14 (1979), 274; see also David Harvey, *Social Justice and the City* (Baltimore: Johns Hopkins University Press, 1973), pp. 281-282.

12. Shevky and Bell, *Social Area Analysis*, pp. 18-19.

13. Ibid., p. 20.

14. Ibid.

15. Amos H. Hawley and Otis D. Duncan, "Social Area Analysis: A Critical Appraisal," *Land Economics*, 33 (1957), 227-245; J. R. Udry, "Increasing Scale and Spatial Differentiation: New Tests of Two Theories from Shevky and Bell," *Social Forces*, 42 (1964), 404-413.

16. R. J. Johnston, "Residential Area Characteristics: Research Methods for Identifying Urban Sub-areas — Social Area Analysis and Factorial Ecology," in D. T. Herbert and R. J. Johnston, eds., *Social Areas in Cities*, 2 vols. (London: John Wiley, 1976), I, 217; Brian J. L. Berry and Philip H. Rees, "The Factorial Ecology of Calcutta," *American Journal of Sociology*, 74 (1969), 445-491; Maurice D. Van Arsdol, Jr., Santo F. Camilleri, and Calvin F. Schmid, "The Generality of Social Area Indexes," *American Sociological Review*, 23 (1958), 277-284.

17. The index of socioeconomic status was constructed by computing, for each respondent, standardized scores for income, years of schooling, and occupational status. These three standarized scores were then added together to produce a general index of socioeconomic status.

18. Respondents were asked whether they thought of themselves as belonging to any particular ethnic or nationality group. White respondents who identified themselves as members of a non-American ethnic group were counted as "ethnics." Although respondents were also asked to identify the particular ethnic group to which they belonged, this information was not used to make further distinctions among various kinds of "ethnics." The number of respondents identifying with any specific ethnic group was usually so small that there was little to be gained by making these distinctions.

19. The sex of the respondents was not taken into account because the ratio of males to females in each neighborhood sample was fixed in advance so as to ensure that females, who are more often home to respond to interviewers, would not be overrepresented in the sample.

20. Howard Schuman and Barry Gruenberg, "The Impact of City on Racial Attitudes," *American Journal of Sociology*, 76 (1970), 213-261.

21. The neighborhood's "official" name was the one recognized by city government.

3. Neighborhood Identity

1. Hunter, *Symbolic Communities*, p. 165.

2. Greer, *The Emerging City*, pp. 111 ff.

3. See Suttles, *The Social Construction of Communities*.

4. James Beshers, *Urban Social Structure* (New York: Free Press, 1962), pp. 105-106; Richard P. Coleman and Bernice L. Neugarten, *Social Status in the City* (San Francisco: Jossey-Bass, 1971), pp. 30-38.

5. See Easton, *A Systems Analysis of Political Life*, p. 176.

6. J. Gilman Paul, "Montebello, Home of General Samuel Smith," *Maryland Historical Magazine*, 42 (1947), 253-260.

7. Baltimore *Sun*, May 27, 1951.

8. See J. Thomas Scharf, *History of Baltimore City and County* (Philadelphia: L. H. Everts, 1881), p. 890.

9. Arnold, "The Neighborhood and City Hall."

10. Baltimore *Sun*, December 28, 1969.

11. Ibid.

12. I am grateful to Mr. Philip Johnson, whose undergraduate research papers provided detailed information about the development of political rivalries in Coldstream-Homestead-Montebello.

13. *CHM Charette Booklet* [xerox, n.d.], p. 14.

14. Hunter, *Symbolic Communities*, p. 68.

15. For an excellent critical discussion of this view, see Suttles, *The Social Construction of Communities*, pp. 7-16; for expressions of the view itself, see Louis Wirth, "Urbanism as a Way of Life," *American Journal of Sociology*, 44 (1938), 1-24; Maurice R. Stein, *The Eclipse of Community: An Interpretation of American Studies* (Princeton, N.J.: Princeton University Press, 1960); Robert A. Nisbet, *The Quest for Community* (New York: Oxford University Press, 1953); Norton Long, *The Unwalled City*.

16. See Richard Sennett, *Families against the City* (Cambridge, Mass.: Harvard University Press, 1970), pp. 36-43.

17. Keller, *The Urban Neighborhood*, pp. 103-106.

18. Ibid.

19. All five of the neighborhoods where "standard" names did not prevail were places where most residents were not aware of *any* neighborhood name.

20. Whether most of one's friends lived inside or outside the neighborhood made no difference for one's ability to give the standard name of the residential area (gamma = .00). The location of "really good friends" was only slightly related to the likelihood that respondents would offer the standard neighborhood name (.14). People who regarded most of the residents on their blocks as strangers were somewhat less likely to volunteer the standard neighborhood name than those who regarded other people on the block as either acquaintances or friends (.19). As for the use of local facilities, neither church attendance in the neighborhood (−.02) nor grocery shopping in the neighborhood (.05) seemed to enhance the likelihood that respondents would give the accepted names of their residential areas.

21. See Peter H. Mann, "The Neighborhood," in Robert Gutman and David Popenoe, eds., *Neighborhood, City and Metropolis* (New York: Random House, 1970), pp. 568-582.

22. Greer, *The Emerging City*, pp. 49-50.

23. Albert Hunter, "The Loss of Community: An Empirical Test through Replication," *American Sociological Review*, 40 (1975), 537-552.

24. Barry Wellman and Barry Leighton, "Networks, Neighborhoods, and Communities: Approaches to the Study of the Community Question," *Urban Affairs Quarterly*, 14 (1979), 363-390.

25. See Hunter, "The Loss of Community," pp. 549-550.

26. Morris Janowitz, *The Community Press in an Urban Setting*

(Chicago: University of Chicago Press, 1967); Greer, *The Emerging City*.

27. Hunter, *Symbolic Communities*; Suttles, *The Social Construction of Communities*.

28. William W. Philliber, "Prior Training, Opportunity, and Vested Interest as Factors Influencing Neighborhood Integration," *Pacific Sociological Review*, 19 (1976), 231-244; Kevin R. Cox, "Housing Tenure and Neighborhood Activism," *Urban Affairs Quarterly*, 18 (1982), 107-129.

29. Controlling for homeownership reduces the relationship between socioeconomic status and the sense of neighborhood identity only slightly, from a gamma coefficient of .65 to one of .60. The relationship between race and neighborhood identity is similarly unaffected by controlling for homeownership. The gamma coefficient is reduced from .75 to .70.

30. Donald I. Warren, *Black Neighborhoods* (Ann Arbor: University of Michigan Press, 1975), p. 32.

31. The socioeconomic heterogeneity of neighborhoods was measured by using the standard deviations of socioeconomic status scores for all respondents living in each of the residential areas under study. For neighborhoods where more than 90 percent of the respondents were black, the mean standard deviation was 1.91; for predominantly white neighborhoods, it was 1.77. But for racially mixed areas (those in which neither race made up as much as 90 percent of the population) it was 2.29. To examine the relationship between socioeconomic diversity and the sense of neighborhood identity, sample neighborhoods were divided among high, medium, and low categories according to the socioeconomic heterogeneity of their populations. The association between neighborhood heterogeneity and the sense of neighborhood identity is negative but weak (gamma $= -.17$).

32. Warren, *Black Neighborhoods*, p. 38.

33. Suttles, *The Social Construction of Communities*, p. 33; see also Suttles, *The Social Order of the Slum*, pp. 227-229.

34. Suttles, *The Social Construction of Communities*, p. 57.

35. Ibid., pp. 57-58.

36. W. G. Haney and Eric Knowles, "Perception of Neighborhood by City and Suburban Residents," *Human Ecology*, 16 (1978), 201-214.

37. Suttles, *The Social Construction of Communities*, pp. 27, 33-34.

38. The gamma coefficient of association between the socioeconomic status of the respondents and their ability to specify at least one boundary for their neighborhoods was .45. Black respondents were less likely to identify boundaries than whites (gamma $= .35$).

39. The gamma coefficient of association between feeling safe on the local streets after dark and assigning a name to the neighborhood is only .17. For the relationship between perceived safety and the specification of neighborhood boundaries, the coefficient is .09.

40. The socioeconomic status of the neighborhood was associated with the likelihood that its inhabitants would regard their fellow residents as good neighbors (gamma $= .41$), and with the likelihood that they would favorably evaluate the physical appearance of the neighborhood (.69). The predomi-

nance of blacks in residential areas was also related both to the evaluation of fellow residents (− .41) and the evaluation of physical appearance (− .63). Both kinds of evaluations are related to indications of neighborhood identity. The assignment of a name to one's neighborhood, for example, was positively associated with favorable impressions of fellow residents (.27) and physical surroundings (.56).

41. Albert O. Hirschman, *Exit, Voice, and Loyalty* (Cambridge, Mass.: Harvard University Press, 1970).

42. John M. Orbell and Toru Uno, "A Theory of Neighborhood Problem Solving: Political Action vs. Residential Mobility," *American Political Science Review*, 66 (1972), 471-489.

43. Philip H. Ennis, *Criminal Victimization in the United States, A Report of a National Survey* (Washington, D.C.: Government Printing Office, 1967), pp. 41-43; see also Wesley G. Skogan, "Crime and Crime Rates," in Wesley Skogan, ed., *Sample Surveys of the Victims of Crime* (Cambridge, Mass.: Ballinger, 1976), pp. 105-120.

44. There was a positive relationship between living in a high-theft neighborhood and being bothered by the problem of crime in the neighborhood (gamma = .33).

45. George Sternlieb, *The Tenement Landlord* (New Brunswick, N.J.: Center for Urban Policy Research, 1969).

46. Residents of neighborhoods with relatively high proportions of abandoned housing units were more likely than others to complain that "run-down houses and buildings" were a problem in the area (gamma = .75).

47. Banfield, *The Unheavenly City Revisited*, pp. 72.

48. On public-regardingness, see Edward C. Banfield and James Q. Wilson, "Public-Regardingness as a Value Premise in Voting Behavior," *American Political Science Review*, 58 (1964), 876-887.

49. Wolin, *Politics and Vision*, pp. 16-17.

50. A similar observation has been made by Donald I. Warren, *Black Neighborhoods*, pp. 59-60.

51. Where high proportions of neighborhood informants perceived effective local leadership, high proportions of neighborhood residents at large tended to share the same impression (gamma = .36).

52. When high proportions of residents perceived that there were "real leaders" in the neighborhood, local informants tended to believe that the neighborhood was well organized (gamma = .54).

53. For additional evidence concerning the relationship between neighborhood identity and political action, see Jeffrey L. Davidson, *Political Partnerships: Neighborhood Residents and Their Council Members* (Beverly Hills, Cal.: Sage, 1979), pp. 56, 89.

4. Informal Governance

1. Baltimore *Sun*, August 10, 1967.
2. Ibid.

3. Ibid., June 27, 1977.

4. City of Baltimore, Department of Housing and Community Development, Research and Analysis Section, "Impact of Expanding the Boundaries of Union Square Historic and Preservation District" (unpublished report, July 7, 1977), p. 3.

5. Henry L. Mencken, *Happy Days* (New York: Knopf, 1940), p. 8.

6. Communities Organized to Improve Life, "Memorandum to Members" (n.d.).

7. Baltimore *Sun*, May 26, 1977.

8. Bernard R. Berelson, Paul F. Lazarfeld, and William N. McPhee, *Voting: A Study of Opinion Formation in a Presidential Campaign* (Chicago: University of Chicago Press, 1954), p. 106.

9. Nor did such evidence turn up elsewhere. There is no relationship, for example, between talking to neighbors about local problems and the perception that the neighborhood is "very friendly" (gamma = .01). In fact, people who discuss neighborhood affairs with fellow residents may not even like their neighbors. There is a slight negative association between participation in such discussions and the belief that most people who live in the area are "good neighbors" (−.14).

10. Controlling for socioeconomic status does, however, reduce the strength of the association between neighborhood identity and neighborhood discourse (from .44 to a partial gamma of .28).

11. After controlling for participation in neighborhood discussions, the partial coefficient of association between personal discussions and annoyance is only .18. But when controlling for participation in personal discussions, the partial gamma for the relationship between neighborhood discourse and neighborly annoyance is .46. Discussions about neighborhood matters are more closely related to annoyance with neighbors than is participation in conversations about personal matters.

12. The relationship between annoyance and argument was examined in order to find out whether it was stronger among those who had discussed personal problems with neighbors than among those who had not. A stronger relationship would reflect a greater propensity for annoyed residents to express their annoyance in arguments. The results show that annoyance and argument were more closely associated for those who engaged in personal discussions (gamma = .81) than for those who did not (.57). The findings suggest that annoyance is either a more potent source or a more probable consequence of arguing for people who discuss personal matters than for others. Discussion of neighborhood matters, on the other hand, made hardly any difference for the relationship between annoyance and argument. The coefficient of association among those who talked about neighborhood problems was .68; for those who did not, it was .71.

13. Norton Long, "The City as a Local Political Economy,"*Administration and Society*, 12 (1980), 18-20, 31.

14. Easton, *A Framework for Political Analysis*, p. 50.

15. Ibid.

16. Robert L. Bish and Hugh O. Nourse, *Urban Economics and Policy Analysis* (New York: McGraw-Hill, 1975), pp. 20n, 116.

17. Bish and Nourse, *Urban Economics and Policy Analysis*, pp. 116-119; see also Mancur Olson, *The Logic of Collective Action* (Cambridge, Mass.: Harvard University Press, 1965).

18. Controlling for problem perceptions reduces the gamma coefficient for the relationship between direct action and evaluations of one's neighbors from − .23 to − .09.

19. Controlling for problem perceptions reduced the strength of the association between arguing and informal direct action from .33 to a partial gamma of .23.

20. The gamma coefficient for the association between annoyance and informal direct action was originally .42. After controlling for the respondents' problem perceptions, it was reduced to .35.

21. Locke, *Second Treatise of Government*, p. 57.

22. Jane Jacobs, *The Death and Life of Great American Cities* (New York: Random House, 1961).

23. Ibid., p. 14.

24. Ibid., p. 36.

25. Ibid., pp. 30-32, 37.

26. Ibid., pp. 50, 222.

27. Ibid., p. 114.

28. Ibid., p. 57.

29. Richard Sennett, *The Uses of Disorder: Personal Identity and City Life* (New York: Knopf, 1970).

30. Ibid., pp. 32-34.

31. Ibid., pp. 138-139.

32. Ibid., pp. 144-145.

33. The gamma coefficient for the association between informal direct action and keeping an eye on a neighbor's home was .46. For the relationship with joint efforts to improve the appearance of the street, the coefficient was .42, and for the association with child-policing activities, it was .25.

34. Findings similar to these were reported in a study of the determinants of neighborhood stability. Although measures of the diversity of land use were associated with residential stability, the association was largely explained by referring to the social composition and structural characteristics of residential areas. See W. L. Yancey and E. P. Ericksen, "The Antecedents of Community: The Economic and Institutional Structure of Urban Neighborhoods,"*American Sociological Review*, 44 (1979), 253-261.

35. The only exception occurs in connection with child-policing activities (in part B of the table). Renters may be more likely to discipline neighborhood children than owners because they are more likely to have young children themselves.

36. Olson, *Baltimore*, p. 3.

37. It may also be significant that surveillance activities have been found, in previous research, to be associated with social integration into

neighborhood networks—the extent to which residents are linked to other people in the neighborhood. This is not what we have found for other forms of neighborhood public service. See Wesley G. Skogan and Michael G. Maxfield, *Coping with Crime: Individual and Neighborhood Reactions* (Beverly Hills, Cal.: Sage, 1981).

38. For the twenty-one sample neighborhoods, the Spearman rank-order correlation for the relationship between the proportion of respondents who said that they had policed local children and the proportion who perceived that local residents were engaged in these activities was − .50.

39. People who say that they have kept an eye on the homes of their neighbors are also likely to believe that their neighbors do the same sort of thing (gamma = .50). Similarly, residents who say that they worked with others to improve the appearance of their street are likely to think that their neighbors voluntarily cleaned up trash in public places (.35). There is a weaker connection between reported child-policing activity and the perception that fellow residents are also trying to control the behavior of local children (.18).

40. There is a strong relationship between the percentage of people in a neighborhood who say that they have tried to police the local children and the neighborhood's median number of children per household (Spearman's $r = .72$). Child-policing activities are also associated with the proportion of local residents who say that children play in large groups rather than in small ones (Spearman's $r = .64$) and with the percentage of residents who report that children play in public places rather than private ones (Spearman's $r = .64$).

41. A more complex explanation for the survey results holds that beliefs about the child-policing activities of neighbors are not only a source but also a result of one's own activities in this direction. The opportunity to police children, according to this argument, is greatest where children are most plentiful, but it is also in these neighborhoods that the experience of policing children is likely to be most frustrating. In such communities, a resident who deals with one group of unruly children may soon find them replaced with another just as obstreperous. Under these circumstances, people who supervise neighborhood children may find it more and more difficult to believe that their fellow residents are making similar efforts. The result is that beliefs about the child-supervision efforts of fellow residents will eventually become less prevalent in these neighborhoods than in other communities where children are not so numerous and where actual child-policing efforts are in fact not so extensive. Neighborhoods that generate high levels of child policing activity will therefore exhibit low levels of belief in the prevalence of these activities. But within these neighborhoods individual residents who believe that child-supervision activities are common will still be more likely to make such efforts themselves than those who do not hold this belief.

There is one serious problem with this line of explanation. If it is correct, then it follows that individual beliefs and activities should be less closely associated in neighborhoods where children are plentiful than in neighborhoods where children are scarce. This is so because, in neighborhoods where children are numerous, people who act on the belief that there is local support for child supervision will probably face repeated instances of juvenile misbehavior, and such experiences will tend to undermine their confidence in the child-policing efforts of their neighbors. Where the juvenile population is large, therefore, we should also find large numbers of adults who have tried to police neighborhood children but who have come to believe that their neighbors do not make similar attempts — in other words, a weakened relationship between personal child-policing activities and beliefs in the child-policing activities of others. In fact, however, the evidence shows that just the opposite is true. The relationship between child-policing activities and beliefs is actually stronger in neighborhoods where children are numerous than in neighborhoods where they are scarce.

5. Community Organizations

1. Baltimore *Sun*, February 5, 1977.

2. Ibid., October 5, 1977.

3. In Coldstream-Homestead-Montebello, 87 percent of the residents interviewed said that they were bothered by trash and sanitation problems; In Reservoir Hill, the proportion was 77 percent. Among the sample neighborhoods, the two areas ranked first and third respectively in the frequency of complaints about such problems.

4. See David J. O'Brien, *Neighborhood Organization and Interest-Group Processes* (Princeton, N.J.: Princeton University Press, 1975).

5. Almost three-fourths of the respondents named someone capable of getting "the whole neighborhood active." Of these, 37.6 percent identified the mobilizers as leaders of community or block associations. The next most frequently mentioned category of community mobilizers — at 30.1 percent — was made up of people who were not identified as occupants of any formal positions.

6. When socioeconomic status is held constant, the gamma coefficient for the relationship between neighborhood group membership and acquaintance with community mobilizers is reduced from .77 to .71.

7. Reported membership in community associations is scarcely associated with attending religious services inside the neighborhood (gamma = .08), and there is a modest negative association between belonging to community groups and doing one's grocery shopping in the neighborhood (−.24). Other forms of participation in neighborhood groups — attending their meetings and contacting them about local problems — were related in a similar way to the use of local facilities.

8. Mark Granovetter, "The Strength of Weak Ties," *American Journal of Sociology*, 78 (1973), 1360-80; Matthew A. Crenson, "Social Networks and Political Processes in Urban Neighborhoods," *American Journal of Political Science*, 22 (1978), 578-594.

9. Crenson, "Social Networks and Political Processes in Urban Neighborhoods."

10. Other forms of organizational participation were similarly related to socioeconomic status and homeownership. High socioeconomic status encouraged both attendance at organization meetings (gamma = .55) and contacting of community groups about local problems (.46). Homeownership was also associated both with attendance at meetings (.54) and with contacting organizations about local problems (.63).

11. Philliber, "Prior Training, Opportunity, and Vested Interest as Factors Influencing Neighborhood Integration."

12. See Lewis Coser, *The Functions of Social Conflict* (New York: Free Press of Glencoe, 1956).

13. An additional piece of evidence casts further doubt upon the hypothesis that the political advantages of high-status people become especially advantageous when they live in politically disjointed neighborhoods. If this were the case, we would expect to find that the difference in organizational activism between high- and low-status residents was greater in politically disjointed neighborhoods than in politically integrated ones. A comparison of the percentage figures in the top and bottom rows of Table 5.3 shows that this is not the case.

14. Informal direct action, for example, was positively associated with membership in community associations (gamma = .40). Since both types of political participation are related to the respondents' socioeconomic status, however, it is conceivable that the relationship between them may be an artifact of status. But controlling for the socioeconomic status of the respondents did not explain away this relationship (partial gamma = .31).

15. One neighborhood with no formal community associations could not be included in this analysis. In addition, a few of the associations identified were so marginal that it was not possible to find two active members beside the president. Of the forty organizations included in the survey, fewer than half a dozen presented this problem. In no sample neighborhood were more than five active organization members interviewed in addition to organization presidents.

16. The reason for this curious asymmetry, perhaps, is that the members of some organizations were reported to be friendly and contentious and mistrustful all at the same time. Friendship, in fact, may have been related to contention and mistrust. Community groups scored high on both friendship and contention in five neighborhoods. In four of these five cases, organizational informants also reported high levels of mistrust among group members. Contention by itself, unaccompanied by high levels of friendship, was never associated with frequent reports of mistrust. When arguments occur among friends, it appears, they tend to be accompanied by mutual suspicion. But disagreements among mere acquaintances were not associated with mistrust, possibly because there was little chance for these controversies to become personalized. See Matthew A. Crenson, "Organizational Factors in Citizen Participation," *Journal of Politics*, 36 (1974), 356-378.

17. Sennett, *The Uses of Disorder*, pp. 144-145.

18. Richard Rich, "A Political-Economy Approach to the Study of Neighborhood Organizations," *American Journal of Political Science*, 24 (1980), 563.

19. The association between government financial support and the socioeconomic status of the neighborhood was strong and negative (gamma = -.79). There was also a somewhat weaker relationship between receiving government grants and reports of mistrust among group members (.56).

20. Neighborhood scores on the index of representativeness ranged from 2 to 9.

21. Where focal organizations had emerged, only 38.0 percent of the mismatches between resident concerns and group agendas were cases in which the organizations raised issues that their constituents did not care about. The comparable figure for neighborhoods without focal organizations was 53.3 percent.

6. Foreign Entanglements

1. "The lot" is a local designation for O'Donnell Square, which was once a children's playlot.

2. Suttles, *The Social Construction of Communities*, p. 13.

3. Lee Truelove, *SECO History* (Baltimore: Southeast Community Organization, 1977).

4. Baltimore *Sun*, August 1, 1976.

5. Ibid., October 4, 1976.

6. Baltimore *Guide*, November 4, 1976.

7. On the utility of weak ties, see Granovetter, "The Strength of Weak Ties"; Crenson, "Social Networks and Political Processes in Urban Neighborhoods."

8. Residents who reported attending worship services inside their neighborhoods were only somewhat more likely to contact city officials directly than those who attended outside the neighborhood or not at all (gamma = .15). Doing one's grocery shopping inside the neighborhood rather than outside was unrelated to the occurence of personal contacts with city officials (-.03). Whether the respondents worked inside the neighborhood, less than five miles away, or more than five miles away made almost no difference for the likelihood that they would speak for themselves to municipal authorities (.08).

9. In fact, communities where a relatively high proportion of residents reported that most of their friends lived inside the neighborhood tended to produce more individual contacts with City Hall than communities where medium or low proportions of residents reported a predominance of neighborhood friendship ties. Here again, however, the relationship between neighborhood solidarity and direct contacts with city government was not strong (gamma = .26).

10. Verba and Nie find that socioeconomic status is virtually unrelated to "particularized contacting," a form of political participation that seems roughly comparable to the kind of activity discussed here. The inconsistency between their findings and the present ones is probably explained by the fact that contacting City Hall about neighborhood problems may not be so "particularized" as the kind of participation that they have defined. See Sidney Verba and Norman Nie, *Participation in America: Political Democracy and Social Equality* (New York: Harper & Row, 1972), pp. 66, 132.

11. See n. 14 in Chapter 5, above. After controlling for individual status, the relationship between informal direct action and membership in community groups remained (partial gamma = .31), but it was substantially weaker than the one between informal direct action and contacts with city government.

12. Controlling for the problem perceptions of respondents weakened but did not eliminate the association between annoyance at neighbors and complaints to City Hall (partial gamma = .41). The same is true of the association between arguing with neighbors and contacting city officials (.25).

13. Peter Eisinger, "The Pattern of Citizen Contacts with Urban Officials," in Harlan Hahn, ed., *People and Politics in Urban Society* (Beverly Hills, Cal.: Sage, 1972), pp. 55-56.

14. It should be remembered that a gamma coefficient of − .44 in this case measures the strength of a relationship between two neighborhood characteristics, not between the attributes of individual residents. Since there are only twenty-one sample neighborhoods, the size of the coefficient is much less impressive than it would be if found in a sample of two thousand individual residents.

A further consideration substantiates the contention that the relationship between neighborhood factionalism and City Hall contacts is not merely a by-product of the neighborhood's socioeconomic status. If it were true that status explained away this relationship, then it would follow that complaints to City Hall officials would *increase* as neighborhood status declined. The evidence shows just the opposite.

15. The gamma coefficient for the relationship between neighborhood status and the extensiveness of neighborhood discourse is only .25.

16. Davidson, *Political Partnerships*, pp. 107-110.

17. Fights with City Hall were more closely related to the organizational mobilization of high- and medium-status residents than of low-status residents. For the high-status respondents, reports of neighborhood conflict with city government were related in a substantial way to membership in community organizations (gamma = .37). The relationship was only slightly less strong for medium-status residents (.31), but it became quite weak among low-status respondents (.08).

18. Differences in the extensiveness of informal direct action among the three categories of neighborhoods were not pronounced. One-half of the "isolationist" neighborhoods scored high in informal action. The proportion was one-third for neighborhoods that had achieved organizational unity and

carried on extensive diplomatic relations with city government. Among the diplomatically active neighborhoods that had not achieved organizational unity, four out of seven scored high on informal direct action.

Conclusion

1. Baltimore *Evening Sun*, November 2, 1981.

2. Ibid.

3. Robert A. Dahl, *Who Governs?* (New Haven, Conn.: Yale University Press, 1961), pp. 200-214; Robert Salisbury, "Urban Politics: The New Convergence of Power," *Journal of Politics*, 26 (1964), 775-797.

4. See Douglas Yates, *The Ungovernable City: The Politics of Urban Problems and Policy Making* (Cambridge, Mass.: MIT Press, 1977); New York City's fiscal crisis of the mid-1970s seems to have occasioned a significant loss of confidence in the political efficacy of city government. See, for example, Charles R. Morris, *The Cost of Good Intentions: New York and the Liberal Experiment, 1960-1975* (New York: W. W. Norton, 1980).

5. See Fred Durr, "The Corporate Branch of Baltimore's City Government," paper presented to the Policy and Planning Committee, City Council of Baltimore, October 19, 1981.

6. Baltimore *Evening Sun*, November 3, 1981.

7. Ibid.

8. Ibid., November 2, 1981.

9. Walter Bagehot, *Physics and Politics* (New York: Knopf, 1948), p. 40.

10. Jeffrey Pressman, "The Conditions for Mayoral Leadership," *American Political Science Review*, 66 (1972), 311-324.

11. Norman and Susan Fainstein, *Urban Political Movements* (Englewood Cliffs, N.J.: Prentice-Hall, 1974), pp. xii, 53-54.

12. Ibid., p. 211.

13. See J. David Greenstone and Paul Peterson, *Race and Authority in Urban Politics* (New York: Russell Sage, 1973), pp. 195-196.

14. See Matthew A. Crenson, "Urban Bureaucracy in Urban Politics: Notes toward a Developmental Theory," in J. David Greenstone, ed., *Public Values and Private Power in American Politics* (Chicago: University of Chicago Press, 1982), pp. 209-245.

15. Yates, *The Ungovernable City*, p. 85.

16. Jane Mansbridge, *Beyond Adversary Democracy* (New York: Basic Books, 1980), pp. 30-31; Claude S. Fischer, *The Urban Experience* (New York: Harcourt Brace Jovanovich, 1976), pp. 122-123.

17. Lyn H. Lofland, *A World of Strangers: Order and Action in Urban Public Space* (New York: Basic Books, 1973), p. 177.

18. Locke, *Second Treatise*, pp. 57, 63.

19. Douglas Yates, *Neighborhood Democracy* (Lexington, Mass.: D. C. Heath, 1973).

20. Some decentralization proposals have attempted to address the ine-

qualities that might result from the delegation of political authority to neighborhood groups and institutions. Attention has been concentrated, however, on arrangements that will help to equalize revenue among neighborhoods so public services may also be equalized. Less attention has been paid to the problem of overcoming the significant inequalities in organizational capabilities between rich and poor neighborhoods. See Richard Rich, "Equity and Institutional Design in Urban Service Delivery," *Urban Affairs Quarterly*, 12 (1977), 383-410; Howard Hallman, *Neighborhood Government in a Metropolitan Setting* (Beverly Hills, Cal.: Sage, 1974).

21. Previous research has suggested that residents' social ties to neighbors and neighborhood institutions help to create positive attitudes and commitments to the neighborhood itself. The research results reported here do not necessarily contradict those findings, but they indicate that favorable attitudes toward neighbors and neighborhood are not always accompanied by actual efforts to preserve or enhance the quality of the neighborhood environment. In fact, there are cases in which the contrary seems to be true. Moreover, social ties among residents need not be friendly ones in order to foster efforts at informal neighborhood action. Concerning the role of residents' relationships with neighborhood institutions, see Roger S. Ahlbrandt, Jr., and James V. Cunningham, *A New Public Policy for Neighborhood Preservation* (New York: Praeger, 1979); Rachelle and Donald Warren, *The Neighborhood Organizer's Handbook* (Notre Dame, Ind.: University of Notre Dame Press, 1977); Abraham Wandersman, "A Framework of Participation in Community Organizations," *Journal of Applied Behavioral Science*, 17 (1981), pp. 27-58.

22. Hunter, "The Loss of Community;" Scott Greer, "Urbanism Reconsidered: A Comparative Study of Local Areas in a Metropolis," *American Sociological Review*, 21 (1956), 19-25; Morris Axelrod, "Urban Structure and Social Participation," *American Sociological Review*, 21 (1956), 13-18.

23. Jacobs, *The Death and Life of Great American Cities;* Janowitz, *The Community Press in an Urban Setting.*

24. Eugene J. Meehan, *The Quality of Federal Policymaking* (Columbia: University of Missouri Press, 1979), pp. 133-134; Rainwater, *Behind Ghetto Walls.*

25. See Anthony Downs, *Neighborhoods and Urban Development* (Washington, D.C.: Brookings Institution, 1981); Rolf Goetze, *Building Neighborhood Confidence* (Cambridge, Mass.: Ballinger, 1976); Philip L. Clay, *Neighborhood Renewal: Middle-Class Resettlement and Incumbent Upgrading in American Neighborhoods* (Lexington, Mass.: Lexington Books, 1979).

26. Arnold, "The History of Urban Development in Baltimore."

Index

Costello, Delores, 92
Crooks, James, 32
Curry, Marie, 239–243, 247, 255
Curry's Crusaders, 240–242, 255, 289

Dahl, Robert, 291
Daley, Richard J., 290–291
Dalton, Robert, 94–97
Darby. See U.S.N.S. *William O. Darby*
Davidson, Jeffrey, 274
Davies, Marion, 92
Davis, Willie Mae, 6, 8, 202–205, 289–290
Decentralization, 14, 299–300
Department of Housing and Community Development, 21, 40, 96, 118, 140–141, 198
Detroit, Michigan, 110

Eastside Democratic Organization, 94–96
Economic Opportunity Program, 14
External relations, 44, 258, 271–272; and sense of neighborhood identity, 39–40, 53; and political integration, 236, 242, 255–257, 273–277; and neighborhood power, 280–285. *See also* Contacts with city government

Factionalism, 201; in neighborhood organization, 218, 226, 230; and external relations of neighborhoods, 266–267, 274–276, 286. *See also* Neighborhood organizations; Political integration
Factorial ecology, 57
Fainstein, Norman, 295
Fainstein, Susan, 295
Federal Maritime Administration, 252, 254
Fells Point, 244, 253
Fischer, Claude, 297–298
Fortune 500, 33

Gorsuch family, 91–92
Greater Baltimore Committee, 291
Greer, Scott, 90
Gruenberg, Barry, 58, 66, 68

Hays, Samuel P., 33
Holliday, Billie, 27

Homeownership, 108, 173, 211–212
Homestead-Montebello Churches and Community Organizations, 95, 97–98
Homestead-Montebello Community Council, 95
Housing. *See* Department of Housing and Community Development
Hull, Stephanie, 6, 195–200, 205–206
Hunter, Albert, 29, 53, 100

Informal direct action, 171, 180; defined, 156, 158–159; as production of public goods, 160–161; and perceptions of neighborhood problems, 164–167; and political integration, 216–218; and contacts with city government, 263–265, 279
Informants, interviews with, 23–25, 219–220

Jacobs, Jane, 168–174, 186, 192, 300
Janowitz, Morris, 300
Johnson, Doris, 96–99, 117, 204

Kelch, Bill, 248–254, 289
Keller, Suzanne, 27, 38–39
King, Martin Luther, Jr., 93
Kotler, Milton, 9

Lawlor, Nancy, 5–6
Locke, John, 17–20, 123, 127, 167, 235, 297–299. *See also* Political society

Mandel, Marvin, 249, 254
Mansbridge, Jane, 297
Marshall, Thurgood, 27
Maryland State Board of Movie Censors, 137
Maryland State Penitentiary, 250
Mencken, Henry L., 35, 134–135, 138
Messiah Lutheran Church, 239
Mikulski, Barbara, 244, 246, 251–254
Model Cities Program, 14
Moore, Kenneth, 246
Morrison, Mertha, 7

Nagle, Conrad, 92
Nasdor, Albert, 49
Neighborhood culture: conceptions of, 50–54, 72–73; identification of, 55–59, 78–79; importance of, 66–67, 79,

293; political character of, 69–72, 81–82, 84; and neighborhood organization, 70, 80, 83; and neighborhood social composition, 51–54, 66, 72–85. *See also* Neighborhood identity

Neighborhood discourse, 142–155, 158, 209, 302–303; and neighborhood identity, 144–146; and perception of neighborhood problems, 145–146, 148–150; compared with discussion of personal problems, 146–147, 150–153; and antagonism toward neighbors, 148–154, 159–160, 163, 190; and informal direct action, 156, 158; in political society, 143; and socioeconomic status, 146, 183–184; as lateral integration, 267–268, 283–285

Neighborhood foreign relations. *See* Contacts with city government; External relations

Neighborhood identity, 29, 43–44, 89–91, 209; role in neighborhood polity, 90–91, 123–124, 127–128; and friendship with neighbors, 99–102, 104–105, 127, 154, 190; and use of local facilities, 102–105, 127; as framework for perceiving neighborhood problems, 116–124, 127; and neighborhood discourse, 144–146

Neighborhood organizations, 33, 37, 41, 44, 110; as pressure groups, 14, 294–295; and neighborhood culture, 70, 80, 83; and political integration, 192, 207–208, 213–219, 229–234, 280; participation in, 207–236; and socioeconomic status, 211–218, 235–236, 299–300; friendship in, 221–222, 227; effectiveness of, 223–224, 227; financial support of, 224–225; and neighborhood representation, 230–234; and external relations of neighborhood, 265, 280–281; cooptation of, 295–296. *See also* Neighborhood polity; Political integration

Neighborhood polity, 9, 11, 13, 15, 23, 44; defined, 10, 16; and political society, 17–19, 20, 299; as parapolitical system, 13–14, 17; and sense of neighborhood identity, 90, 123–124, 127–128; external relations of, 255, 278, 280; and inequality, 301–302

Neighborhoods: sampling of, 21–22, 26; strength of, 27–29, 167, 257, 300; definition of, 37–39; as communities, 39, 106; methods for identifying, 40–43; names of, 40–41, 49–50, 71, 79, 100; boundaries of, 40–43, 82, 105, 112–113; external relations of, 39–40, 44, 53, 255

New Era Democratic Club, 95
New Haven, Connecticut, 95, 291

Oakland, California, 294
O'Donnell, John, 239, 248
O'Donnell Square, 239, 243, 247–248
Olson, Sherry, 30

Patterson family, 92
Patterson, Elizabeth, 92
Payne, Bernice, 5–6
Philadelphia, Pennsylvania, 28, 31
Political integration: as political connectedness, 187, 234; and unofficial public service, 187–189, 202; and neighborhood organization, 192, 207–208, 213–219, 229–236, 274, 277; and informal direct action, 216–217; and neighborhood representation, 230–234; and external relations of neighborhoods, 236, 242, 265, 267–270, 273–277, 282–286. *See also* Neighborhood organizations; Neighborhood polity

Political parties: functions of, 11; in Baltimore, 33, 37; in Canton, 245, 257–258

Political society, 17–20, 44, 126, 298–299; and sense of neighborhood identity, 91; and neighborhood discourse, 143; equality in, 192, 235–236, 297

Powell, G. Bingham, 13
Powell, Dick, 92
Pressman, Jeffrey, 294
Pressure groups, 10, 294. *See also* Neighborhood organizations
Public goods, 16, 19; and neighborhood polity, 10, 12; economic theory of, 161–162; as products of informal direct action, 157, 160–161, 163

Representation: through neighborhood organizations, 230–234; index of, 231

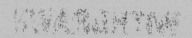